Constitutional Law and Federations

Constitutional Law and Federations

Iacovos Kareklas

LEXINGTON BOOKS
Lanham • Boulder • New York • London

Published by Lexington Books
An imprint of The Rowman & Littlefield Publishing Group, Inc.
4501 Forbes Boulevard, Suite 200, Lanham, Maryland 20706
www.rowman.com

86-90 Paul Street, London EC2A 4NE, United Kingdom

W.P. Kirkman's interview with Lord Caradon. Oxford, Bodleian Libraries, MSS. Brit. Emp. s. 395.
Lord Radcliffe's Report for a new constitution in the Republic of Cyprus (Constitutional proposals for Cyprus, Report submitted to the Secretary of State for the Colonies Cmnd. 42). Reprinted courtesy of The National Archives

British Library Cataloguing in Publication Information Available

Library of Congress Cataloging-in-Publication Data

Names: Kareklas, Iakōvos, 1976- author.
Title: Constitutional law and federations / Iacovos Kareklas.
Description: Lanham : Lexington Books, 2021. | Includes bibliographical references and index. | Summary: "This monograph analyzes classical Greek federal constitutions and modern federal government. Its central thesis is the proposition that a federation, modelled on the United States Federal Constitution, an ideal constitution of federalism, should provide the basis on which the Cyprus problem should be settled"—Provided by publisher.
Identifiers: LCCN 2021033570 (print) | LCCN 2021033571 (ebook) | ISBN 9781793642738 (cloth) | ISBN 9781793642745 (epub)
Subjects: LCSH: Federal government—Cyprus. | Cyprus—Politics and government. | Constitutional law—Cyprus—American influences.
Classification: LCC KJN237.3 . K37 2021 (print) | LCC KJN237.3 (ebook) | DDC 342.5693/04—dc23
LC record available at https://lccn.loc.gov/2021033570
LC ebook record available at https://lccn.loc.gov/2021033571

Contents

Introduction

This book, *Constitutional Law and Federations*, has as its central thesis the proposition that a federation, modeled on the United States Federal Constitution, should provide the basis on which the Cyprus problem could be settled. The monograph, in its first part, will seek to present the proposals which the British government had submitted in the context of its foreign policy before the grant of independence to the Republic of Cyprus in 1959. It will initially comprise a concise overview of some basic questions arising out of the British occupation of the island (1878–1959), and the efforts of the Greek Cypriots for independence before the UN institutions. Then it will move on to examine the gist of the ideas embodied in the constitutional plans for Cyprus as these were elaborated in the course of negotiations. Further, it will provide an analysis of the structure and peculiarities of the current Cyprus Constitution, and will most likely end up with the conclusion that, despite its drawbacks, this very political Constitution, with some fundamental amendments, could form the basis for a viable settlement of the pending international Cyprus Question.

The second part serves as an introductory analysis of federal states and the concept of federalism. Federations are historically analyzed, both in the context of the classical Greek world, where they allegedly originate from, and in the sphere of modern federal government. The purpose of this part of the monograph is to indicate that federations worldwide and in every era have come into being because of important political and security reasons dictating or necessitating the creation of such governmental organizations, and that the bi-zonal federation envisaged for Cyprus, according to the Accords of 1977 and 1979 respectively, is not in compliance with these prerequisites. On the contrary, as it will be shown in subsequent parts (see III, IV and V), a federation modeled on the United States of America federal Constitution could, indeed, provide an ideal framework for settling the Cyprus problem and safeguarding the protection of basic human rights and constitutional freedoms for all sections of the population on the island.

The third part is intended to explore the question whether a bi-zonal Federal Constitution, agreed in the first instance between the Republic of Cyprus and the Turkish Cypriot community respectively in 1977, may form the basis for a just and viable settlement to the Cyprus problem; particularly whether this kind of constitutional government may properly safeguard International Human Rights Law on Cyprus. After reference to very important statements made by Turkish politicians revealing the real intentions of Turkey as against the island, as well as fleshing out the concept of federalism, five or six main arguments at least are employed to prove that the bi-zonal federal system cannot, in the opinion of the author, be an appropriate framework to the solution of the aforesaid affair. It needs be added, though, that this is not only a subjective proposition. First, I support the view that, historically, federations worldwide have been established as a result of common foreign and defense policy needs, and other considerations dictating such governmental schemes. Constitutional law and history, is, indeed, by far the most important and decisive argument upon which the rest of argumentation is pretty much based. Modern federal governments are briefly analyzed in this chapter, and finally contrasted to the framework designed for Cyprus, so that the central thesis may be strengthened.

Second, the political and legal principle of self-determination, the cornerstone of international human rights, namely the unfettered right of peoples to decide about their own fate in the international sphere and simultaneously choose their mode of government internally, is thoroughly explored. Its repeated violation on the island provides evidence that *bi-zonal* federalism cannot most probably—all public polls considered—function successfully on Cyprus, and that it cannot generally be implemented or enforced upon peoples unwilling to endorse it.

Third, a series of human rights are thus violated precisely because of the non-implementation of self-determination.

Fourth, democracy, itself also regarded as a human right by a certain group of scholars and international conventions, cannot be adequately materialized in the context of a *bi-zonal* federal constitution.

At this stage, the role of the European Union in reaching a peaceful settlement to the issue is also put under scrutiny and various scenarios are examined. It is to be emphasized that the European Union, on its own initiative, cannot improve the possible deficiencies of a bi-zonal federal constitution, if this were to be imposed upon the people of Cyprus.

Fifth, there is ample evidence to suggest that at the High Level Agreements of 1977, pressure was exerted upon the president in signing the treaty on part of the Cyprus Republic. This is per se a valid ground for rendering the agreements void *ab initio* or certainly voidable at any subsequent stage.

Sixth, an argument of crucial importance shall be stressed to strengthen the case against *bi-zonal* federation, namely the *fundamental change of circumstances* since the aforesaid agreements. This principle is reflected in the Latin legal maxim *rebus sic stantibus*. The pronouncement of the so-called Turkish Republic of Northern Cyprus in 1983 on part of the Turkish Cypriots (nine years after the Turkish invasion in the Republic of Cyprus), gives sufficient legal and political ground for abrogation of the treaties envisaging bi-zonal federation. There follows well-documented and originally presented instances of political practice whereby treaties have been terminated on grounds of fundamental change of circumstances. So, the present work, among other things, will provide quite substantial guidelines on practical political arguments to be put forward and mechanisms to be used, so that the central government of the Republic may get disentangled from what has undoubtedly been an onerous obligation upon past and current executives consecutively.

Let me expressly say that I am not favoring *bi-communal bi-zonal* federation in the Cyprus case. According to objective legal norms, bi-communal and bi-zonal federation flagrantly violates international law and is incompatible with the notion of human rights with regard to Cyprus. It must be stressed, however, that the United States Constitution, a model constitution of federalism, could, in my opinion, potentially be enforced in Cyprus mutatis mutandis. The US Constitution does not contain, for example, the vices of bi-communalism and the bi-zonal character. Such an effort would not be a solution without difficulties, but could provide the framework for a viable settlement if every other lawful and peaceful alternative cannot materialize. Therefore, parts IV and V of the monograph analyze the basic provisions of the American federal Constitution (federal executive, federal legislature, federal judiciary, and federal protection of fundamental freedoms). It should be added that, the axioms of international law, especially those comprising human rights, should certainly act as guidelines to a settlement.

Part VI analyzes the security policy that should be pursued in settling the international problem of Cyprus. Initially, it proves that the international community through the United Nations has not been successful in providing security for Cyprus over the last several decades; it proves that the system of Guarantor States does not comply with rules of international legal and political morality. Then, it explores ways in which security can be achieved in cooperation with the United Kingdom government and the British Sovereign Base Areas. Also it extensively examines how NATO, and, in particular, the United States, Greece, and Israel could fruitfully contribute to security arrangements on the island. Furthermore, gas politics is pointed out as being a factor which could ensure security in the Mediterranean region in the context of the current negotiations for a solution of the Cyprus issue.

Part VII publicizes the papers of Sir Hugh Foot, last governor of Cyprus prior to the granting of independence in 1959, and provides useful information on the constitutional life of the country in years preceding the establishment of the Cyprus Republic Constitution. The papers will be published with permission granted to the author by Rhodes House in the University of Oxford, where important papers and documents of the British Commonwealth are kept.

Finally, it remains an axiom that any solution must safeguard fundamental human rights in their entirety for all the sections of the Cyprus people, without any derogation from the whole body of international human rights and fundamental freedoms. This need is not at all, and ought not to be looked at, as excessive. It is a basic human one, befitting the race of human beings.

I am hopeful that this book will be useful to specialists in the field, postgraduate students in Constitutional law, international law, and international relations as well as diplomats, who deal not only with the Cyprus issue but also with related regional and international issues. It may further be of use to undergraduates and postgraduates in law or political science whochoose to write a BA, MA, or doctoral dissertation on Cyprus or on topics such as federalism, international law, Constitutional law, or international politics. Finally, it could be a timely contribution to the diplomatic efforts for settlement of the Cyprus problem.

I would like to express my deepest thanks to the preeminent publisher Rowman and Littlefield: Lexington Books for the excellent collaboration, in order that this book may see the light of day. Special thanks go to Lexington Books director, Julie Kirsch, and to Becca Beurer for splendidly editing and producing this academic work, which will be a great contribution to scholarship.

PART I

British Constitutional Policy and the Cyprus Republic Constitution

Chapter 1

Legal Questions Arising from the British Occupation

There is no unanimity as to the legal position of Great Britain with respect to Cyprus during the period from its occupation in 1878 till the annexation in 1914. A view was expressed that Great Britain acquired a de facto though not a de jure sovereignty over Cyprus under the Convention. The concept of sovereignty, as supreme authority which is independent of another authority, coincides with that of the political power and has different aspects. Insofar as it excludes the dependence upon any other form of authority of another state, sovereignty is independence. It is external independence with regard to the liberty of action outside the borders of a state in its intercourse with other states and internal independence with regard to the liberty of action inside the borders. As regards the power of a state to exercise authority over all persons and things within its territory, sovereignty is territorial supremacy (dominion, territorial sovereignty).[1] With respect to the territorial sovereignty, three theories were expounded especially in international law.

One theory supports that the territory is the object of state power. According to the writers supporting this theory (Oppenheim and Lauterpacht in the U.K.) the territory is an object over which the state exercises a true right. According to the second theory, which is extensively accepted in Germany (by Jellinec) and was introduced in Greece by the late Professor Saripolos, the territory is a constituent element of the concept of the state. The territory is not a part of the possessions of the state but a prerequisite of its existence. A third theory inspired by the Austrian school (Kelsen, Verdross) maintains that the territory should be immune from any juristic or geographical element and should be approached from the angle of the exercise of the competence of the state *ratione loci*. Under this theory the relations of the colonial territories to the metropolitan state territory could be better explained.

The supreme authority which the state exercises over its territory would seem to suggest that on one and the same territory there can exist only one full sovereign state and that two or more sovereign states on one and the same territory are an impossibility. But the controversy over the non-divisibility of sovereignty, prevalent in the sixteenth, seventeenth, and eighteenth centuries, was dying out in the nineteenth century especially with the appearance of colonialism.

Among the examples of the divisibility of sovereignty is the case where one state actually exercises sovereignty which in law is vested elsewhere, as where a piece of territory is administered by a foreign power with the consent of the state to which the territory belongs. In this respect reference is made to the position of Cyprus from 1878 to 1914 under British administration and that of Bosnia and Herzegovina from 1878 to 1908 under the administration of Austria-Hungary[2] where a cession of territory has for all practical purposes taken place although in law the territory belonged to the former owner state.

This is borne out by the provisions of the Convention itself under which Turkey assigned the administration of the island of Cyprus to Great Britain, an expression which denotes transfer of title, while at the same time provision is made in the annex for the eventual return of Cyprus on the fulfillment of certain conditions.[3] That sovereignty remained in Turkey was never disputed by Great Britain on taking up the administration of the island.[4] The occupation of Cyprus lacked juristic precision but it was analogous to protectorate in the sense that it fell within the designation of a country under the protection of Great Britain.[5]

Great Britain immediately after the outbreak of war with Turkey in 1914, annexed Cyprus by Order in Council of 5 November 1914[6] and as from that date Cyprus formed part of the Her Majesty's dominions.[7]

Cyprus, when annexed, had been under British administration since 1878. Such annexation in time of peace without the consent of the state which in law owns the territory is unlawful and it is of doubtful legality in war.[8] In any event the annexation was recognized by Turkey by article 20 of the Treaty of Lausanne 1923. It was particularly important that Turkey furthermore, by Article 16 of the same treaty, renounced all rights and titles whatsoever over or respecting inter alia the islands other than those over which the sovereignty is recognized by the present treaty (and therefore over Cyprus as well) and by Article 27 Turkey was precluded from exercising any jurisdiction in any political, administrative, or legislative matter outside the territory of Turkey, on any national of a territory put under the sovereignty of the other signatory Powers (as in the case of Ottoman subjects in Cyprus).

NOTES

1. Oppenheim-Lauterpacht, *International Law* (London, 1948), p. 286; Starke, *An Introduction to International Law* (London, 1972), p.106; Hall, *A Treatise in International Law* (Oxford, 1924), pp. 56–58.

2. See Oppenheim-Lauterpacht, *International Law, ante*, p. 455, where it is observed that "such nominal sovereignty is not totally devoid of practical consequences." See also the observations of Phillimore, *Commentaries upon the International Law* vol. I (London, 1879), pp.131–132.

In the case concerning the Light House in Crete and Samos, the Permanent Court of International Justice held in October 1937 that notwithstanding the very wide autonomy conceded by Turkey to the islands of Crete and Samos, these territories must be regarded as having been under Turkish sovereignty in 1913 with the result that Turkey could properly grant or renew concessions with regard to these islands. In a dissenting opinion Judge Hudson, regarding this point, said that "a juristic conception must not be stretched to the breaking point, and a ghost of hollow sovereignty cannot be permitted to obscure the realities of the situation" (P.C.I.J. Series A/B No.71).

3. See Roberts-Wray, *Commonwealth and Colonial Law* (London, 1966), p. 28. A very wide jurisdiction was granted to Britain to administer Cyprus, during the period it had the administration of the island.

4. The British government did not wish to ask the sultan to alienate territory from his sovereignty. It has been asserted that until the annexation, Great Britain refused to extend the protection of her consuls to Cypriots resident outside the island (see Hill, *A History of Cyprus,* Cambridge University Press, 1948, Vol. IV, p. 285); O'Connell, *International Law* Vol. I (London, 1965), 354: "the British government in fact acknowledged that it had no intention of alienating territory from the Sultan's sovereignty." The British foreign secretary was also of the opinion that the transfer of the island to the Great Britain had all the incidents of cession for so long as the British occupation lasted (O'Connell, Legal Aspects of the peace treaty with Japan, *British YB.I.L.,* 1952 vol. XIX, 423, p. 426).

5. See Oppenheim-Lauterpacht, *International Law supra*, p. 455, note 2; O'Connell, *International Law, supra*; Roberts-Wray, *op.cit.* (considers as doubtful whether, in English Law, Cyprus could accurately be regarded as a territory under the Sovereign's protection and points out the difficulty of grouping Cyprus with other territories by referring to pre-1915 Acts of Parliament).

6. The Cyprus Annexation Order in Council 1914, Statutory Rules and Orders Revised 1924, No. 1629, vol. II pp. 577–578. During World War II Great Britain offered to transfer Cyprus to Greece in exchange for Greek support for Serbia, an offer which was later withdrawn.

7. It is an indication that the United Kingdom did not subsequently deny the Enosis to the Greeks of Cyprus because of any strategic agreement with Turkey, but on other grounds which will be discussed later in this chapter.

8. Oppenheim-Lauterpacht, *International Law*, *ante,* p. 567, note 3.

Chapter 2

The British Position against Cyprus U.N. Applications for Self-Determination

The British colonial policy (i) exacerbated existing linguistic, religious, and ethnic differences; (ii) destroyed, by its vertical separation of the two communities, the horizontal bonds that had developed across the communities, whose task became the promotion of their respective national interests; (iv) gave rise to separate political alliances to the people of the two Cypriot communities; and (v) gave rise to the demands by both groups to control the various aspects of their communities' fate, and their claims to a separate political autonomy.[1]

Therefore the roots of political partition were set during the period of the British administration. Subsequently in the aftermath of the 1931 rebellion in Cyprus, Britain introduced legislation in order to eliminate the demands of the Greek Cypriots for *Enosis*.

On the assumption of the government by the Labour party in 1945, the secretary of state for the colonies stated that it was proposed to seek opportunities to establish a more liberal progressive regime in the internal affairs of the island. For this purpose a Consultative Assembly was convened in 1947 but the response was discouraging.[2] These constitutional proposals, though constituting a step toward self-government, were inspired by an imperial spirit and were inconsistent with the ideals for which World War II had been fought and the declared promises during and after the war by the British government. The limitations imposed by the constitutional proposals and the powers reserved to the governor with respect to defense and external affairs had not left any room for their acceptance. The Greek Cypriots under the leadership of the Archbishop Leontios had decided that their future aim should be *Enosis and only Enosis* (Union with Greece). An aim followed by Leontios's successors Makarios II and Makarios III. The demand for Enosis was becoming more persistent and on 15 January, 1950, a plebiscite was held, under the aegis of the Ethnarchy Council, among Greek Cypriots, at which 96 percent of those taking part voted for Enosis of Cyprus with Greece.

In 1953, before the beginning of the E.O.K.A. riot, the visit of the British foreign minister in Greece was the pretext of a would-be controversy between Greece and Great Britain. The refusal of Anthony Eden to meet with the Greek prime minister, Papagos, to discuss the Cyprus issue outraged the latter, who then decided (with the subsequent exhortation of Archbishop Makarios) to place the Cyprus problem before the political organs of the United Nations. The consequences of this act, though, were not foreseen at the time. Both the United Kingdom and the United States were firmly opposed to such an action. Only before the first attempt of the Greek government at the United Nations, 1954, Foster Dulles, sent a personal message to Papagos, advising him not to place the Cyprus problem before the General Assembly of the United Nations, and expressing the willingness of the U.S. government to mediate in order that the dispute might be settled. Dulles stressed that the unity of the North Atlantic Treaty Organization should not run the risk of breakdown by a possible conflict between Greece and the Allied Powers, that is, the United Kingdom and Turkey.

Despite the U.S. piece of advice, the Greek government proceeded with five successive applications to the General Assembly of the U.N.[3]

On 20 August 1954, the permanent representative of Greece to the United Nations puts down to the secretariat of the organisation an application, claiming the implementation, under the auspices of the United Nations, of the principle of equality and self-determination of peoples in the case of Cyprus. The Assembly resolved not to deal further with the issue of self-determination for the people of Cyprus. Fifty votes were cast for the adoption of this resolution (including that of Greece), and eight states abstained (including the Soviet Union, as it then was).

On 21 September 1955, the Political Affairs Committee of the General Assembly discussed the issue of whether a renewed claim of the Greek government should be put on the Agenda (although the Greek foreign minister had received a clear warning by Dulles that the U.S. would vote against this). Greece did not even achieve the inclusion of the problem in the agenda. The decision of the Political Affairs Committee was approved by the Assembly (including NATO member states, except Greece and Iceland).

In 1956, Greece, in a third attempt before the organs of the U.N., was accused by Britain of instigating acts of terrorism. On 22 February, the General Assembly issued a vague resolution by which the settlement of the Cyprus issue should be democratic and just, according to the purpose of the United Nations and expressed the wish that negotiations would commence for this purpose.[4] However, the General Assembly resolution did not mention that the basis of negotiations should be the principle of self-determination, as prescribed by the U.N. Charter.

On 14 January 1957, a draft resolution submitted by the Political Committee Affairs to the General Assembly, explicit stating, for the first time, that negotiations should start, so that the principle of self-determination may be implemented in the case of Cyprus. As a result of strong opposition, mainly coming from the U.S., the majority did not vote for the adoption of the draft resolution.[5] By the time the fifth application was submitted (1958), the policy of Cyprus had changed. Archbishop Makarios, in an historic interview to Barbara Castle, stated that the claim for self-determination and possible Union of Cyprus with Greece had been abandoned. From then on, the claim for independence was put forward.

The general applications of Greece to the General Assembly failed, because the Western powers, much like today, had a predominant position in the international community, especially in the international organization. Also, the grounds for failure are to be traced in the side of the applicant state, too. The Greek State pursued conflicting policies, which eventually were proved to be fruitless. On the one hand, it was (as always has been) attached to the Western Alliance, which was, according to experts, in the security interest of the country. On the other hand, it would wish to see Cyprus becoming part of the mainland, thus making the national ideal of *Enosis* come true.

Further, the United States, close ally of the U.K., played a decisive role in turning down the applications of Greece seeking for self-determination in the case of Cyprus. It should be noted, albeit in brief, that the United Kingdom, being the Imperial Power, reacted intensely against the internationalization of the Cyprus issue.

Certain measures were employed to render unsuccessful the action at the U.N. One such measure was the 1955 Tripartite Conference in London, which, though ending up in failure, achieved an important diplomatic goal for the Foreign Office. The Cyprus dispute was dealt with in the context of the Anglo-Greco-Turkish relations. More importantly, it brought Turkey to the forefront of political developments. Turkey was thus presented as a directly interested party in the settlement of the Cyprus issue, and as having equal status at the negotiating table to that of the Greek government. It is noteworthy the British ambassador in Athens, in a letter to the Greek government, says that the Cyprus issue is not a matter of self-determination, but one of defense of the West in the Eastern Mediterranean.[6] The government as well as the opposition were agreed. Sophocles Venizelos, leader of the Center, stated that a possible denial on part of Athens to come to negotiations would present the government as intransigent.[7] At the same time, though, Ankara urged the Turkish Cypriots to take up arms and engage in inter-communal fighting in order that coexistence between the two communities might be proved to be impossible.[8]

Another of these measures taken by Great Britain was the London Conference leading to the London Treaties of February 1959, establishing an independent Cyprus Republic. What is relevant from the Agreements is that no provision was made by which possible disputes could be submitted to an international body, like the International Court of Justice (ICJ) or the European Court of Human Rights (given that a case of human rights violations arose). Any controversy over the implementation of the Agreements was to be settled by the parties to the treaty. The parties to the Cyprus Treaties were thus moving away from the internationalization of the Cyprus issue.

NOTES

1. See Coufoudakis, *Essays on the Cyprus Conflict* (New York: Pella Publishing Company, 1976), p. 34.
2. For details of the Plan, see Kyriakides, *Cyprus, Constitutionalism and Crisis Government* (University of Pennsylvania Press, Philadelphia, 1968), pp. 30–32.
3. For a detailed account, see Stephen G. Xydis, *Conflict and Conciliation, 1954–1958* (The Ohio State University Press, 1967). This work could be seen as the standard textbook, the most exhaustive on this period of the Cyprus issue.
4. *Review of the United Nations*, December 1957, p. 48–57.
5. *Ibid*, p. 48–57 (31–32–24).
6. See Linardatos, *From Civil War to the Junta*, 1952–1955 (in Greek, Athens, 1978), p. 309.
7. Indeed, negation of this argument was put forward by the Greek government and the Republic of Cyprus as justification for taking part in the inter-communal talks which followed, but was, in my view, the cause of a policy of constant concessions to Turkey.
8. The 1955 anti-Greek actions (massacres, vandalisms, and other criminal acts) in Constantinople and Smyrna were committed based on the same methodology of the Turkish State, namely to make the Greek State assume that the Greek populations of Constantinople, Imbros and Tenedos were held *hostages* as it were and could suffer enormously, if that state was to continue the policy of internationalization of the Cyprus issue, clearly against the interests of Turkey.

Chapter 3

British Constitutional Proposals for Cyprus

In the meantime, the British government announced that it intended to introduce a constitution as a first step toward self-government, an announcement which was met by an immediate reaction by the Greek Cypriots. For overcoming such reaction and winning their cooperation, the British government thought that the best way was to carry with it some good will from Greece and Turkey, and for this purpose the British government decided to invite Greece and Turkey to send representatives to a conference to be held in London and collaborate for an agreement there. The theme of the conference was to cover all the common interest of the three powers in the eastern Mediterranean. [1]

The proposed conference was held without the approval of the archbishop who publicly declared that the convening of such a conference was a trap and a means of undermining Greece's appeal to the United Nations. It is significant that at the conference, Macmillan, the British foreign secretary, frankly admitted that: "It is an undoubted anomaly and it is in our view wrong that while so many other parts of the world have made steady progress in the art and practice of self-government there has been no comparable advance in Cyprus. We must put this right. Internal self-government has to be the first aim."[2] The Greek Foreign Minister Stephanopoulos supported the application of self-determination to Cyprus,[3] while Zorlu, the Turkish foreign minister, maintained that it was not right to consider the Cyprus question from the angle of the present day composition of the people and the guiding principles should not be the consideration of majorities and minorities but rather the granting of full equality to the two groups. Furthermore, he added that the status quo should be maintained in Cyprus. If this were to be upset then the island should revert to Turkey.[4]

In broad lines it was proposed that a Constitution be established providing for an assembly with an elected majority, a proportionate quota being left for to the Turkish Cypriot community and for the progressive transfer of the departments to Cypriot ministers responsible to the assembly with the exception of foreign affairs, defense and security which would be left for the governor. A proportion of the ministerial posts would be reserved for the Turkish Cypriots.

There was no agreement regarding the future international status of Cyprus and confronted with this deadlock the Conference came to an end.[5]

The Greek Cypriots then undertook an armed struggle for the satisfaction of their demands. The governor was replaced by Field Marshall Sir John Harding, chief of the imperial general staff, who on arriving at Cyprus in 1955 started protracted negotiations with the Ethnarch, Archbishop Makarios, in an attempt to find a solution to the problem. The proposals put forward by the British government during the talks, as far as the constitutional problem was concerned, were as follows:

a. Though the British government admitted that the principle of self-determination may be applicable to Cyprus, nevertheless its position was that it was not a practical proposition on account of the situation then prevailing in the eastern Mediterranean.[6]
b. The details of the constitution would be a matter for a discussion between the representatives of all section of the population. Nevertheless the following points were clarified by the British government:
   i. That it offers a wide measure of democratic self-government and to this end it proposed the drawing up of a new and liberal constitution in consultation with all sections of the community.
   ii. The constitution would enable the people of Cyprus, through responsible Cypriot ministers, to assume, by suitably phased process, control over the departments of government except those relating to foreign affairs and defense which would be reserved to the governor, and public security which would be also be reserved to the governor for as long as he deemed necessary.
   iii. The constitution would provide for an assembly with an elected majority.
   iv. A Cypriot premier would head the new administration who would be chosen by the assembly with the approval of the governor. Ministerial portfolios would be allocated by the premier subject to a constitutional provision relating to participation of Turkish ministers in the Council of Ministers.
   v. There would be proper safeguards for the rights of the individual citizens.[7]

Eventually no agreement could be reached, not only on the constitutional question but also on other matters.[8]

The British government concentrated on the action necessary to prepare a working plan for self-government of Cyprus and for this purpose entrusted Lord Radcliffe to prepare and submit constitutional proposals for Cyprus in 1956.[9]

By his constitutional proposals Lord Radcliffe recommended a diarchy for Cyprus, consisting of the section of matters reserved for the governor, comprising foreign affairs, defense and internal security, and the self-governing section consisting of the legislative assembly, the cabinet, and the judiciary and comprising all matters other than the reserved ones.

The legislative assembly would consist of a Speaker, a Deputy Speaker appointed by the legislative assembly, and 36 other members of whom 6 would be nominated from among members of the minority communities and 30 members would be elected (6 voters on the Turkish communal roll and 24 elected voters on the general roll). The legislative assembly would pass all the bills dealing with self-government matters which would become laws on being assented to by the governor.

The executive power of the self-governing section would be exercised by a cabinet consisting of the chief minister, appointed by the governor from among the members of the legislative assembly and enjoying the largest measure of general support in the assembly and five other ministers appointed by the governor on the recommendation of the Chief Minister from among members of the legislative assembly. There would be also a minister of Turkish Cypriot Affairs, appointed by the governor at his discretion from among the members of the legislative assembly elected by the voters on the Turkish Cypriot communal roll, who would be responsible for the office dealing with Turkish Cypriot affairs.

Regarding the judicature there would be a Supreme Court consisting of the chief justice who would be appointed by the governor after consultation with the chief minister and two other judges, or such increased number of members as might be provided by law, being uneven, appointed by the governor after consultation with the chief justice.

The attorney-general would be appointed by the governor on the recommendation of the chief minister and his appointment could be revoked accordingly.

A tribunal of guarantees would be established, the members of which would be appointed by the governor in consultation with the chief justice and the chief minister. The membership of tribunal would include an equal number of Greek Cypriots and Turkish Cypriots under the chairmanship of a person who would not be either Greek Cypriot or Turkish Cypriot. The tribunal would deal with individual complaints against acts of the administration.

The conclusions of Lord Radcliffe are pertinent, even today. For this reason the relevant paragraphs of this report are quoted in full:

1. I have given my best consideration to the claim, put before me on behalf of the Turkish Cypriot community, that they should be accorded political representation equal to the of the Greek Cypriot community. If I do not accept it I do not think that it is out of any lack of respect for the misgivings that lie behind it. But this is a claim by 18 percent of a population to share the political power equally with 80 percent and, if it is to be given effect to, I think that it must be made on one of the two possible grounds. Either it is consistent with the principles of a constitution based on liberal and democratic conceptions that political power should be balanced in this way, or no other means than the creation of such political equilibrium will be effective to protect the essential interests of the community from oppression by the weight of the majority. I do not feel that I can stand firmly on either of these propositions.
2. The first of embodies the idea of a federation rather than unitary state. It would be enough to accord to members of a federation equality of representation in the federal body, regardless of the numerical proportions of the populations of the territories they represent. *But can Cyprus be organized in this way? I do not think so. There is no pattern territorial separation between the two communities, and apart from other objections, federation of communities seems to be a very difficult constitutional form.*[10] If it is said that what is proposed is in reality nothing more than a system of functional representation, the function of in this case being the community life and organization and nothing else. I find myself baffled in the attempt to visualize how an effective executive government for Cyprus is to be thrown up by a system in which political power is to remain permanently divided in equal shares between the two opposed communities. Either there is stagnation in political life, with the resulting frustration which accompanies it, or some small minority group acquires an artificial weight by being able to hold the balance between the two main parties. My conclusion is that it cannot be in the interest of Cyprus as a whole that the constitution should be formed on the basis of equal political representation for the Greek Cypriots and Turkish Cypriot communities.
3. Does the second ground lead to a different result? I do not think so. To give an equal political strength in a unitary state to two communities which have such a marked inequality in numbers—an inequality which, so far as signs go, is as likely to increase as decrease—is to deny to the majority of the population over the whole of the field of self-government the power to have its will reflected in effective action. Yet it might be well right to insist on this denial if the constitution could not be equipped with any other means effective of securing the smaller communities in the possession of their essential special interests. Not

only do I think that it can be equipped with such means by placing those interests under the protection independent tribunals with appropriate powers and relying only to a limited extent on direct political devices, but I also think that the legalist solution which this depends on is in fact better suited to provide the protection that is required, and it does not have the effect of denying the validity of the majority principle over a field much wider than that with which special community interests are truly concerned.

The Radcliffe constitution was not accepted either by Archbishop Makarios or by the Greek government.[11] The armed struggle in Cyprus continued.

Sir John Harding was succeeded as governor by Sir Hugh Foot whose links with the island dated back to 1943 when he was colonial secretary. It was the governor's ideas that mainly inspired the Macmillan Plan, which was announced on 19 June 1958.[12] Sir Hugh Foot summarized its aims in a broadcast to the troops in Cyprus:[13] "It may be summarized in three sentences. First, we want to give the best possible deal to all the people of the island. Second we want to bring the three Governments of Great Britain, Greece and Turkey together in a joint effort to make sure that they get it. Third, we believe that this can only be achieved by Great Britain giving a definite and determined lead to break the vicious circle from Cyprus which has suffered so long."

Under the Macmillan Plan a partnership scheme was proposed for Cyprus-partnership between the two communities in the island and also between the governments of the United Kingdom, Greece, and Turkey. For this purpose:

a. The Greek and Turkish governments would each be invited to appoint a representative to cooperate with the governor in carrying out the plan.
b. The island would have a system of representative government with each community exercising autonomy in its own communal affairs. To this end there would be a separate House of Representatives for each of the two communities, which would have the final legislative authority in communal matters.
c. Authority for internal administration other than communal matters and internal security will be undertaken by a council presided over by the governor and including representatives of the Greek and the Turkish governments and six elected members drawn from the Houses of Representatives, four being Greek Cypriots and two Turkish Cypriots.
d. The governor, acting after consultation with the representatives of the two governments, would have the reserve powers to ensure that the interests of both communities were protected.

e. External affairs, defense, and internal security would be matters specifically reserved for the governor, acting after consultation with representatives of the two governments;
f. Such representatives would have the right to require legislation which they consider discriminatory to be reserved for consideration by an impartial tribunal.[14]

It is to be noted that the proposed constitutional arrangements not only did not satisfy the national aspirations of the Greek Cypriots, but also brought Turkey to share the administration of Cyprus. It should be recalled that by the aforementioned provisions of the Treaty of Lausanne Turkey renounced any rights of sovereignty over Cyprus.[15]

Early in 1959 negotiations were held in Zurich between the Greek and Turkish governments for the purpose of finding a solution.[16] On 11 February 1959 an agreement was reached at Zurich between the Greek and Turkish ministers for the establishment of an independent state, the Republic of Cyprus. At a conference held in London in February 1959 attended by the prime ministers of Great Britain and Greece, the Turkish foreign minister, the foreign ministers of Great Britain and Greece, and the representatives of the Greek Cypriot communities, a memorandum with documents annexed to it setting out the foundations of the final settlement of the problem of Cyprus was signed and adopted on 19 February 1959.[17] A joint constitutional commission prepared the Constitution of the Republic of Cyprus and London joint committees prepared the draft treaties giving effect to the conclusions of the London Conference. Agreement was reached on all points 1 July 1960.[18] The Constitution of the Republic of Cyprus was signed at Nicosia on 16 August 1960[19] by the then governor on behalf of the British government, by representatives of the governments of Greece and Turkey, by Archbishop Makarios, on behalf of the Greek Cypriot community, and Dr. Fazil Kutch on behalf of the Turkish Cypriot community and was put into force on that date.[20]

NOTES

1. Eden, *Memoirs,* 1960, p. 197; See also debates in the House of Commons in *Parliamentary Debates (Hansard), H.C. Debates* 1947–1948, vol. 451 col. 2159–2162.

2. Cmd 9594 (Miscellaneous No. 18 1955). *The Tripartite Conference on Eastern Mediterranean and Cyprus*, p. 13.

3. Cmd, pp. 17–18.

4. Cmd 9594 p. 25.

5., *Memoirs, ante* p. 4101; Cmd. 9594 supra p. 42; comments on the *Conference* by Kyriakides, *Cyprus, Constitutionalism and crisis Government, ante*, pp. 39–41.

6. The British government would be prepared to discuss the future of the island with representatives of the people of Cyprus when self-government has proved itself capable of safeguarding the interests of all sections of the community (correspondence exchanged between the governor and Archbishop Makarios, Cmd. 9708, p. 3); for these talks see S. G. Xydis, *Cyprus, Reluctant Republic* (The Hague 1973), pp. 44, 95, 206 note.

7. *Cyprus:* Correspondence exchanged between the Governor and Archbishop Makarios, Cmd. 9708 p. 8; Kyriakides, *Cyprus, Constitutionalism and crisis Government, supra*, pp. 42–44.

8. As a result, the archbishop, together with the Bishop of Kyrenia and other churchmen, was deported to the Seychelles. The armed struggle, however, continued. See the prophetic speech of Earl Attlee when he said, "I hold no brief for the Archbishop, but I remember that the rebels of the past generally tend, sooner or later, to be Prime Ministers in the British Commonwealth" (*Parliamentary Debates-Hansard, House of Lords Debates,* vol. 196 col. 462).

9. See *Constitutional proposals for Cyprus, Report submitted to the Secretary of State for the Colonies* Cmnd. 42.

10. Emphasis my own.

11. For the details of the *Radcliffe Constitutional Plan*, see Kyriakides, *Cyprus, Constitutionalism and Crisis Government, ante*, pp. 45–48.

12. Sir Hugh Foot, *A Start in Freedom* (London, 1964), pp. 159–163.

13. *Ibid,* p. 168

14. *Cyprus: Statement of policy Cmnd.* 455 pp. 2–3. Details as to the surrounding circumstances of the preparation of the Macmillan Plan and its contents see Xydis, *Cyprus, Reluctant Republic, op.* cit., pp. 130–143.

15. See further Eden, *Memoirs, op. cit.* p. 413. There exist instances of administration of a territory. Usually the condominium of the Anglo-Egyptian Sudan is referred to under the agreement of Great Britain and Sudan of 19 January 1899 signed at Cairo (see Oppenheim-Lauterpacht, *International Law, ante*, p. 453, note 4). For other instances see Oppenheim-Lauterpacht, *International Law, supra*, pp. 453–455. For instances of common control of territory see Roberts-Wray, *Commonwealth and Colonial Law, ante*, pp. 53–54, O'Connell, *International Law, ante*, pp. 352–353.

16. For details of the circumstances which led to the Zurich Agreement see Sir Hugh Foot, *A Start in* Freedom, ante, pp. 176–179; Xydis, *Cyprus, Reluctant Republic, ante*, pp. 359–419.

17. See Conference on Cyprus signed at Lancaster House on 19 February 1959, Cmnd 79 p. 4. The documents annexed to the memorandum were: (a) Basic structure of the Republic of Cyprus pp. 5–10, (b) the Treaty of Cyprus pp. 10–11, (c) additional article to be inserted inn the Treaty of Alliance between the Republic of Cyprus and Greece and Turkey p. 11, (d) declaration made by the government of the United Kingdom of February 127, 1959, pp. 11–123, (e) additional article to be inserted in the Treaty of Guarantee p.13, (f) declaration made by the Greek and Turkish government foreign ministers of 11 February 1959 p. 13, (g) declaration made by the

Representative of the Greek Cypriot community on February 19, 1959 p. 14, (h) declaration made by the representative of the Turkish Cypriot community p. 174, (h) declaration made by the Representatives to prepare for the new arrangements in Cyprus pp. 14–15. For details of the conference see Xydis Cyprus, *Reluctant Republic op. cit.* 00. 420–460; Ehrlich, *International Crises and the Role of Law* (Oxford: Oxford University Press, 1974), pp. 20–35.

18. The Treaty of Establishment between the United Kingdom, Greece, and Turkey and the Republic of Cyprus with its annexes.

19. Cyprus Act 1960 section 1, Republic of Cyprus Order in Council 1960 SI. 1368/1960 appointing on 16 August, as the day of the coming into operation of the Constitution.

20. Why the British denied Enosis? From 1951 onward, the Greek government made it clear that in return for Enosis it was quite willing to grant Britain whatever bases she required either in Cyprus itself, or on the Greek mainland. This made the connection between Western defense and the necessity for continued British sovereignty problematical. One British official summed it up as follows: "If we link Cyprus with NATO and implicitly admit its value lies in its usefulness for NATO purposes we destroy the case for the retention of the sovereignty by the U.K. on strategic grounds. As a NATO base Cyprus could just as well belong to Greece as to us. Our whole case depends upon our need for Cyprus as an extra-NATO base for our own purposes in the Middle East (PRO, *Foreign Office*, FO 371/117653). In defining the core NATO area in 1949 special care had been taken to exclude Cyprus, although this fact was not communicated at the time to Greece or Turkey. Such an exclusion was not affected by the entry of the latter two countries into NATO during 1952 (PRO, FO 0371/1117631). In the British mind it was because Cyprus was a crown colony and that the United Kingdom therefore possessed tenure in the island, that they were adamant as to the legitimacy and continuance of their sovereignty. The most signal proof of this came in July 1954 when British Middle East Headquarters covering both Land and Air Forces was formally transferred from Suez to Cyprus. See Public Record Office, *British Cabinet Minutes* C 54 245, 21.7.54: "In a top secret briefing in 1950, British military chiefs of staff spelled out the importance of Cyprus." See also Robert Holland, *Britain and the Revolt in Cyprus* (Oxford: Oxford University Press, 1998).

Chapter 4

The Structure and Legal Peculiarities of the Constitution

The structure provided by the agreement was based on the recognition of the existence of two communities, the Greek and the Turkish—which, in spite of their numerical disparity, were in certain cases given equal treatment. The aim was to ensure that each community participated in the exercise of the functions of government.[1] The official languages of the Republic are the Greek and Turkish.[2] For each community a communal chamber is established exercising legislative and administrative power on certain restricted subjects relating to religious matters, educational, cultural, and teaching matters, and instances of courts dealing with civil disputes relating to religious matters and personal status and on matters relating to institutions of purely communal character and having a right to oppose taxes and fees on members of their respective communities in order to provide for the needs of bodies and institutions under the control of the communal chamber.[3]

The president of the Republic shall be a Greek Cypriot and the vice president of the Republic a Turkish Cypriot elected separately by universal and secret ballot.

The president and the vice president of the Republic jointly exercise executive power in respect of subjects exclusively laid down in the Constitution except on certain occasions, addressing messages to the House of Representatives, and the exercise of the prerogative of mercy in respect of members belonging to their own community.

The president and vice president of the Republic either jointly or separately have a right of return of any law or decision of the House of Representatives or of the Council of Ministers, respectively, for consideration and of final veto against any law or decision of the House of Representatives or any decision of the Council of Ministers relating to foreign affairs, defense, or security as defined in Article 50 of the Constitution.

The main executive organ is the Council of Ministers. There shall be seven Greek Cypriot ministers and Turkish Cypriot ministers nominated by the president and the vice president of the republic respectively but appointed by them jointly. The Council of Ministers is the highest organ in the Republic for formulating policy and exercising executive power in all respects except for the specific subjects allotted to the president and the vice president of the Republic, to ministers and the communal chambers respectively.

The president and the vice president jointly promulgate the laws or decisions of the House of Representatives and the decisions of the Council of Ministers and each one of them separately does the same in respect of the laws or decisions of the communal chamber of his own community. Before such promulgation the president and the vice president in respect of any law or decision of the communal chamber to his own community may refer to the Supreme Constitutional Court for its opinion any law or decision or any part thereof which appears to be inconsistent with constitutional provisions.

The president of the House of Representatives shall be a Greek Cypriot and the vice president a Turkish Cypriot, and they shall be elected separately by the representatives of the Greek community and the Turkish Community respectively. In case of vacancy in either office, an election shall take place and the functions performed by the eldest representative of the respective community.

The House cannot be dissolved either by the president or the vice president but only by its own decision. The laws and decisions of the House of Representatives shall be passed by a simple majority of the representatives present and voting. Any modification of the electoral law and the adoption of law relating to the municipalities and imposing taxes shall be require a simple majority of the Representatives elected by the Greek and the Turkish community respectively taking part in the vote.[4]

The judicial power of the Republic is exercised by the Supreme Constitutional Court and by the high court and its subordinate courts.

The Supreme Court shall consist of a president and a Greek and a Turkish judge, citizens of the Republic, all of them appointed by the president and vice president of the Republic.[5] The main jurisdiction of the Supreme Court relates to whether a law or decision of the House of Representatives is either totally or partly contrary to constitutional provisions. If a law or decision is declared by the Supreme Constitutional Court as unconstitutional, the law or decision is annulled. In the case of any law before promulgation such law or decision is not promulgated and in case of a reference by a trial court on a point raised by a party to judicial proceedings the law becomes inapplicable to such proceedings only.[6] The Supreme Constitutional Court has exclusive jurisdiction to adjudicate finally on a recourse made to it on a complaint that a decision or omission of any organ, authority, or person exercising any executive or administrative power is contrary to the Constitution or any law or is made in abuse of power, in which case the court may annul or confirm such act.[7] Any decision of the Supreme Constitutional Court on any matter within its competence shall be binding on all courts, organs, authorities, and persons.[8]

The high court, on the other hand, is the highest appellate court and has also power to issue writs of habeas corpus, mandamus, prohibition, and certiorari.[9]

The independent officers of the Republic are the attorney-general assisted by his deputy, the auditor-general assisted by his deputy and the governor of the issuing bank assisted by his deputy, all of whom are appointed by the president of the Republic. The first two are not removable from office except on the same grounds and through the same procedure as a judge of the high court.[10]

The public service shall be composed as to 70 percent of Greeks and as to 30 percent of Turks. There shall be a Public Service Commission consisting of a chairman and nine other members appointed for a term of six years by the president and the vice president seven of whom shall be Greeks and three shall be Turks. It shall be the duty of the commission to make the allocation of public offices between the two communities and to appoint, promote, transfer, and exercise disciplinary control over, including dismissal or removal from office, public officers.[11]

Under the Treaty of Guarantee the Republic of Cyprus undertakes to ensure the maintenance of its independence, territorial integrity, and security as well as respect for its constitution and it undertakes not to participate in whole or in part in any political or economic union with any state whatsoever or to promote the partition of the island (Article 1).[12] Part II of the Constitution deals with human rights and mainly based on the European Convention.[13]

It is made clear that the Constitution of Cyprus was imposed upon its people by the Zurich Agreement. It is therefore, of the character of a granted constitution, which the monarch, in past centuries, consented to grant to his people, but is rather inconsistent with the prevailing principles of democracy, by which the power is exercised by the people.[14] But it is not only the manner in which the Constitution was granted that is against the principles of public law, but also the contents of the Constitution as such which rather go against established principles of international law. The right of self-determination of peoples as developed from World War I and adopted by the Charter of the United Nations[15] and the International Covenants[16] consists in the liberty of peoples[17] to determine their own government without any foreign intervention—internal self-determination—and in the external field their future—external self-determination. The right to self-determination is denied to the people of Cyprus by the constitutional provisions whereby the constitutional structure created by the Zurich Agreement was to remain unalterable by any means and that the basic Articles of the Constitution could not be amended by way of variation, addition, or repeal.[18] These provisions are contrary not only to the principles of public law[19] and constitutional practice,[20] but go against the purposes of the U.N. Charter.

A lot of debate has erupted on the issue whether Article IV of the Treaty of Guarantee is in accordance with international law principles. This matter stands beyond the scope of the present article.[21]

The constitutional provision relating to the decision-making competence of the Public Services Commission in case of appointment, promotion, transfer, and discipline of public officers belonging to one of the communities by an absolute majority of the members of the commission including a fixed number of votes of its members belonging to such community, amounts to the exercise of a right of veto by the latter, and the communal criteria contravene universal criteria.

As regards the constitutional provision relating to the proportion of the participation of the Greeks and Turks in the composition of the Public Service, the implementation of such a provision creates situations leading to a deadlock. The Public Service Commission, in considering appointments and promotions, is obliged not to use criteria such as the qualifications and suitability of the candidate, because it has to take into account the community to which the candidate belongs.[22]

The final veto accorded to the president and vice president against any law or decision of the House of Representatives or decision of the Council of Ministers relating to foreign affairs or certain matters of defense is against the principle of the separation of powers and could bring the president and vice president in direct conflict with the legislature.[23]

The constitutional provision regarding the replacement of the president of the Republic in case of his temporary absence or incapacity, not by the vice president, but by the president of the House of Representatives not only bypasses the vice president, but also hinders the continuity of the smooth functioning of the executive power. The election, on the other hand, of the president of the Republic by the Greek community and of the vice president by the Turkish community and of the president of the House of Representatives by its members belonging to the Greek community and of the vice president of the House by its members belonging to the Turkish community, instead of uniting the people of Cyprus and allowing the Greeks and Turks to cooperate in a friendly manner, draws them apart.

But what is unprecedented is the division of justice in the sense that a court trying a case the parties to which belong to one community shall consist only of judges belonging to that community.[24]

The complicated character of the Constitution of Cyprus has been stressed by various authors. Professor Stanley de Smith wrote: "The Constitution of

Cyprus is probably the most rigid in the world. It is certainly the most detailed and (with the possible exception of that of Kenya's new constitution) the most complicated. It is weighed down by checks and balances, procedural and substantive safeguards, guarantees and prohibitions. Constitutionalism has run riot in harness with Communalism. The Government of the Republic must be carried on, but never have the chosen representatives of a political majority set so daunting an obstacle course by the constitution makers."[25]

In the face of this situation, whereby Articles of the Constitution prevented government from functioning smoothly, Archbishop Makarios, by a letter on 30 November 1963 to the vice president, submitted a thirteen-point memorandum. By this he suggested measures to remove some causes of inter-communal strife.[26]

NOTES

1. Such principles permeated through the whole constitution structure. It is obvious that these separatist elements were inspired by the Macmillan Plan. An equal status is given to the Greek community, representing the 80 percent of the population with the Turkish community, representing the 18 percent in many respects.

2. *Cyprus Constitution*, Article. 3.7.

3. Ibid. Articles 86–90. The communities are given the right of special relationship with Greece and Turkey respectively including the right to receive subsidies for educational, cultural, athletic, and charitable institutions belonging to the community and of obtaining and employing if necessary schoolmasters, professors, or clergymen provided by the Greek or Turkish government, as the case may be. (*Ibid*, Article 108).

4. *Ibid,* Article 78.

5. Unlike other countries where there exists a Constitutional Court, the Cyprus Constitutional Court consists (or used to consist before 1964) of only three judges, out of whom its president is not a citizen of the Republic. In the German Federal Republic the Federal Constitutional Court consists of federal judges and other members as regulated by law (Art. 94 of the German Constitution, Peasley: *The Constitutions of the Nations vol.* III Europe Part I, The Hague, 1968, p. 69). In Italy the Constitutional Court is composed of fifteen judges nominated in the manner provided by article 135 of the Constitution (Peasley: *The Constitutions of the Nations, supra*, p. 523). In Turkey the Constitution court consists of fifteen judges regular and five alternate members elected in the manner provided by Article 145 of the constitution (*Ibid.* vol. II Asia Part 2 p. 1118).

6. The law is not annulled *erga omnes*, the U.S. system being adopted (see Schwartz, *Constitutional Law*, Cambridge: Cambridge University Press, 1955, p. 9; Southerland, How and Brown, *Constitutional Law*, vol. I, Boston, 1961, p. 112). Therefore, the principle of the separation of powers adopted by the Constitution is maintained, as the decision of the Supreme Constitutional Court *declaring* a law or a provision as contrary to the Constitution is of *judicial* and not of a *legislative*

character. On the contrary, in Italy the declaration of a law as unconstitutional operates *erga omnes* (Article 136 of the Constitution). The same applies in Turkey (Article 152 of the Constitution) and in Austria (Article 140 of the Constitution).

7. *Cyprus Constitution*, Article 146.

8. *Ante*, Article 148.

9. The High Court constitutes also the Supreme Council of Judicature for the appointment, transfer, removal, and disciplinary control over the judges of the subordinate courts (*Ibid,* Article 157).

10. *Ibid.,* Articles 112, 121.

11. *Ibid.,* Articles 122–125.

12. By the Draft Treaty of Alliance the three parties undertake to cooperate for their common defense and resist any attack or aggression directed against the independence and territorial integrity of the Republic of Cyprus. For this purpose a Tripartite Headquarters shall be established on the territory in which Greece and Turkey shall participate by a military contingent of 950 Greeks and 650 Turks officers and men. In the Treaty of Alliance provision is made for the operation of the Tripartite Headquarters.

13. See Tornaritis, *The European Convention of Human Rights in the Legal Order of the Republic of Cyprus* (Nicosia 1976), pp. 10–15; *Idem,* "The Human Rights as Recognized and Protected by Law with Special Reference to the Law of the Cyprus," *Cyprus Law Tribune*, parts 4–6, p.3; *Idem*, "The Right to Freedom of Movement and Residence Specially Under the Law of the Republic of Cyprus," *Cyprus Law Tribune*, Nicosia, 1974, parts 1–3.

14. See the judgment of Chief Justice Marshall in the case *Marbury v. Madison,* U.S. Constitutional Supreme Court. Reference may be made to the constitutions of the nineteenth century as the constitutions of *Belgium* 1831, Article 25, 31, *Greece* 1864, Articles 21 and 1and *France* 1848 Article 1. In the twentieth century most of the constitutions adopted the principle of sovereignty of the people. See, *inter alia*, the constitutions of *Austria,* Art. 1; *Bulgaria*, Art. 1 and 2; *Finland*, Art. 2; *France* 1958, Art. 1 and 2; Basic Law of the *Federal Republic of Germany*, preamble; *German Democratic Republic*, preamble; *Greece* (1975) Art. 1.3; *Ireland*, preamble and Art. 1; *Italy*, Art. 1; *Burma*, preamble; *India,* preamble; *Turkey*, preamble where reference is made to the Turkish nation; *Libya*, preamble.

15. *U.N. Charter* Articles 1, 2 and 55; See also Bassiouni, "Self-Determination as a General Principle of International Law," *American J.I.L.* (1971) 61, pp. 31–35.

16. International Covenant on Civil and Political Rights, 1966.

17. The concept of "people" presupposes a *territory* and *permanence* of a group of persons linked together by certain bonds on such territory.

18. *Cyprus Constitution*, Article 182.1.

19. Since the time of the French Revolution the right of the people to revise and alter their constitution has not been challenged. See Article 1 of Title VII of the French Constitution of 1791 (Peasley, *The Constitutions of the Nations*, *ante* p. 31). The special provision for revision is hereby provided as a guarantee that the alteration is proceeded after mature consideration, but such restriction may be considered as of a *political* rather than *legal* character.

20. According to constitutional practice a constitution may be revised either unrestrictively (as the constitution of Switzerland [Art. 118] and of certain Latin American states) or subject to certain conditions relating either to the revisional organ and the procedures to be followed or the imposition of a time limit before the expiration of which no revision can take place (as the constitutions of Greece of 1964, 1911, and 1927 and the constitution of the United States [Art. V], which could not be revised before 1808) or to certain provisions which could not be revised in any event (such as the provisions of the form of government or specifically provided articles as under the constitutions of Italy [Art. 139], and of France [1958] [Art. 89]).

21. Article IV of the Treaty provides, inter alia: Insofar as common or concerted action may not prove possible, each of the guaranteeing powers reserves the right to take action with the sole aim of reestablishing the state of affairs created by the present treaty. For representative, but by no means exhaustive, bibliography on the matter by authors of the two communities, see respectively Tornaritis, Whether the resort to force or armed intervention would be justified either under the Charter or customary international law, *Cyprus Today*, vol. III. 3 Supplement, 1964, p. 2; Zotiades, The Treaty of Guarantee and the principle of non-intervention, *Cyprus Today* vol. III (1965) pp. 5–8; Necatigil, *The Turkish Position in International Law* (Oxford: Oxford University Press, 1993), p. 109 seq.

22. The rigid provision about the ratio of participation in the public service is against the internationally accepted principle of the right of every one of equal access to the public service of his country (Universal Declaration of Human Rights Article 21[2]; International Covenant on Civil and Political Rights, 1966, Article 25 [c]).

23. In the U.S. the president has only qualified negative prerogative commonly called a "suspensory veto" but actually it is a right of return for the bill for reconsideration (*Constitution of the U.S.A.*; Schwartz, *Constitutional Law, ante*, p. 99; for instances of its use, see Binkley, *The Man in the White House* /Baltimore, 1959], pp. 175–176).

24. Such a division is not only detrimental to the course of justice, but also tends to render the judges communally minded and suspicious of one another. Further, it tends to shake the confidence of the public in the administration of justice.

25. S. A. de Smith, *The Commonwealth and its Constitutions* (Stevens, 1964), p. 295. Reference may also be made to the Constitution of India with 395 Articles.

26. The proposals were also communicated to the governments of the three Guaranteeing Powers. For the letter together with the memorandum containing the proposed amendments, see *The Cyprus Question: A Broad Analysis*, Press and Information Office, Nicosia, 1969, pp. 9–20. Makarios was encouraged to take this course by the then British High Commissioner Sir Arthur Clark, who went so far as to make suggestions on the proposed letter (Glafkos Clerides, *My Deposition, ante*). On the proposals see also Kyriakides, *Cyprus, Constitutionalism and Crisis Government, ante*, pp. 104–109; Ehrlich, *International Crises and the Role of Law, ante*, pp. 57, 118–119.

Chapter 5

Initial Thoughts on a Settlement of the Cyprus International Dispute

The president put forward the following points:

1. The right of veto of the pPresident and vice president to be abandoned;
2. The vice president of the Republic to deputize for the president in case of his temporary absence or incapacity to perform his duties;
3. The Greek president of the House of Representatives and its Turkish vice president to be elected by the House as a whole and not, as under the Constitution, the president by the Greek members of the House and the vice president by the Turkish members of the House;
4. The vice president of the House of Representatives to deputize for the president of the House in case of his temporary absence or incapacity to perform his duties;
5. The constitutional provisions regarding separate majorities for enactment of certain laws by the House of Representatives to be abolished;
6. Unified municipalities to be established;
7. The administration of justice to be unified;
8. The division of the security forces into police and gendarmery to be abolished;
9. The numerical strength of the security forces and of the defense forces to be determined by a law;
10. The proportion of the participation of Greek and Turkish Cypriots in the composition of the public service and the forces of the Republic to be modified in proportion to the population of Greek and Turkish Cypriots;
11. The number of members of the Public Service Commission to be reduced from ten to five;
12. All decisions of the Public Service Commission to be taken by majority;
13. The Greek communal chamber to be abolished.

It is here submitted that these very constitutional proposals can potentially provide the framework for a viable settlement of the pending Cyprus question,[1] following the Turkish intervention of 1974 and ongoing occupation of 37 percent of the Cyprus Republic territory. I believe that these proposals are valid today in spite of the subsequent Turkish positions regarding federation.

The Turkish side, by its proposals submitted at the Geneva Conference, supports the adoption of the partition of the one and indivisible territory of the Republic of Cyprus into many states, zones, or cantons for the purpose of changing the unitary Republic of Cyprus into a federal state. The prerequisites for the federal state of the type it propounds do not exist. The prerequisite for the establishment of a federal state is the prior coexistence of two or more independent states or other territorial units exercising regional government which desire, for one reason or another such as common defense, economic advantages, geographical factors, to be independent of foreign powers, to be under a single government for some purposes at any rate, while at the same time they like to maintain their independent status for some other matters. A comparative constitutional law analysis would attest to the validity of this assertion.[2] On Cyprus there have not been separate geographical units, which could form the composite parts of the proposed federal state. Such a course would be against not only the principles of public law, but also contrary to the prevailing constitutional practice. Federation aims at uniting already existing separate territorial units and not at artificially creating separate territorial areas within an existing unified territory for the aim of achieving the establishment of a federal state.

The ostensible reason put forward by Turkish officials is that a bi-communal, bi-zonal federation is required for the physical protection of the Turkish Cypriots, and to prevent the Greek Cypriots from destroying or enslaving them. But in view of such an allegation (though it is clear that federation is proposed in order to promote strategic interests), one fails to see how the proposed extensive Turkish region could afford any such protection. The majority of the population in the region will be Greek Cypriots. Unless not all of the Greek Cypriot refugees are to return (which would virtually amount to violation of human rights) or / and Turkish settlers from mainland Turkey, illegally brought after the invasion, are to be accepted as Cypriot citizens (which would mean legalizing a war crime), so that separate majorities can be effected in the areas administered by the communities respectively (which is what bi-zonality means in the Turkish vocabulary).[3]

Further, it is submitted that bi-communal bi-zonal federation in the case of Cyprus cannot properly provide for adequate implementation of human rights. The first and foremost human right which would be violated is that of self-determination.[4]

The concept of self-determination consists in the liberty of peoples to determine on the internal plane their own government without any foreign intervention—internal self-determination—and on the external field their fate and international status—external self-determination.[5] It has to be noted that the right is seen by a large number of writers in international law as a rule of *ius cogens* (peremptory rule of international law).

It is worth noting that self-determination was openly violated when in 1977 and 1979 the people of Cyprus did not decide the island's own fate. It is submitted that a referendum regarding acceptance or rejection of federation as constitutional framework for settlement of the Cyprus issue should have been held before or immediately after the High Level Agreements of 1977 and 1979 respectively (where bi-communal federation was agreed by President Makarios and Denktash, and President Kyprianou and Denktash as the future resolution of the Cyprus problem). Deliberate delay of this process, unfortunately on part of successive Cyprus governments, aims at exerting pressure upon the people to cast vote in favor of federalism upon agreement of final settlement, at a stage when it would be rather difficult to decline this governmental system.[6]

It goes without saying that the Cyprus Constitution, which has operated continuously since the birth of the Republic of Cyprus, in case such amendments based on the Makarios proposals are pursued, will comply with fundamental principles of Constitutional theory, especially as these are safeguarded in British and Western Constitutional law and theory.[7]

NOTES

1. Most of the points had been accepted by Denktash and Orhan Aldicacti on 13 July 1974. The Constitutional Law expert Justice Dekleris gives details in his book *Κυπριακό 1972–1974: Η Τελευταία Ευκαιρία* (in Greek, Athens: Sideris)

2. See Kareklas, *International Law and Politics on Salamis* (Research Centre of Kykkos Monastery: Nicosia, 2007), pp. 180–206.

3. Kareklas, *International Law and Politics on Salamis, ante*, p. 207.

4. The Charter of the United Nations in Article 1, paragraph 2, indicates as one of the purposes of the United Nations "to develop friendly relations among nations based on respect for the principle of equal rights and self-determination of peoples."

5. See Emerson, Self-Determination, *American J.I.L.* (1971) vol. 65, p. 465.

6. For a full analysis of federalism and human rights in the case of Cyprus, see Kareklas, *Federal Constitution and Human Rights on Cyprus* (Harvard University Printing and Publications, 2005), *Idem*, *International Law and Politics on Salamis*, op. cit., pp. 208–212.

7. For a thorough exposition of the constitutional principles of parliamentary sovereignty, the separation of powers, and the rule of law, see among others the classic

works of Jennings, *The Law and the Constitution* (London University Press 1933), Dicey, *An Introduction to the Study of the Law of the Constitution* (London, 1889), Marshall, *Constitutional Theory* (Oxford: Oxford University Press, 1971), Wade, *Constitutional Fundamentals* (London: Stevens, 1980).

PART II

Classical Greek Federal Constitutions and Modern Federal Government

Chapter 6

Classical Greek Federal Constitutions

THE NATURE OF A GREEK FEDERAL STATE[1]

It is hardly necessary to say that the reason for the shortage of information concerning the federal states is the extent to which ancient political thought was dominated by the city-state. There is reason to believe that Aristotle or his pupils wrote descriptions of the governments of a number of federal states and understood the nature of such states.[2] If one of these descriptions had been preserved, we should probably have had for one Greek federal state something corresponding to Aristotle's Constitution of the Athenians, though it is unlikely that other constitutions were described at as great length as that of Athens. Lacking this, the best description we have of the government of the Greek federal state is the short description of the government of the Boeotian Confederacy given in the Hellenica Oxyrhynchia.

Moreover, if Aristotle studied and described the governments of federal states, this has scarcely left any mark on his politics. Yet Aristotle's indifference to giving adequate attention to the federal state is much less surprising than the failure of Polybius to do so. If there was any Greek writer from whom an account of federalism could be expected, it was precisely Polybius. His father, Lycortas, was a prominent Achaean statesman who served as general or president of the Confederacy more than once. In addition, he was the right hand man of Philopoemen, who, after the death of Aratus in 213 B.C., became the leading man of the Confederacy. Polybius was early associated with his father in Achaean politics. The relation of the two to Philopoemen is indicated by the fact that, when the latter was killed in Messenia in 182, Lycortas arranged to have his ashes brought home in state, Polybius carried the urn. For the early period of the history of the Confederacy after its revival in 280, Polybius relied on the recollections of older Achaeans and above all on the memoirs of Aratus. At the time, Polybius was elected ambassador as his father's son, but Polybius later became prominent in his own right and in 170–169 served as hipparch or vice president of the Confederacy. Nor did the fact that he later developed a great admiration for Rome prevent him from remaining an Achaean first, last, and all the time. He was first a citizen of Megalopolis and by descent an Arcadian. To him, however, the Arcadians were citizens of the new Achaean Confederacy.

Polybius, while aware that the Achaean Confederacy was a federal state, tends to apply to it terms that could equally be applied to city-states and to characterize the unification of the Peloponnesus by the Achaeans—undoubtedly inaccurately—as being almost as complete as that of a city-state. Yet he recognizes that what resulted from the adoption of the Achaean government and name by Arcadians, Laconians, and others was not a city-state but a nation (ethnos), which practically means that it was a federal state. Otherwise he too, like all ancient political theorists, was dominated by the idea of the city-state. He gives no analysis of federalism, gives very little information about the differences between the governments of various confederacies, and does not mention federalism in his account of the forms of government in his sixth book. He does give considerable information about the government of the Achaean Confederacy and a small amount about that of the Aetolians, but this comes in incidental remarks and has often proved difficult to interpret. He does not seem to have written any general description of the Achaean government aside from what little is contained in his account of the early history of the Confederacy. This is probably because he wrote primarily for those who did not need such information. This in turn means that our knowledge of Greek federalism is built up of odds and ends in literary sources and inscriptions.

Before proceeding to the description of Greek federal states, it may be useful to say a word about terminology.[3] The reader may have noticed that the term "Achaean Confederacy or Federation has been used instead of the more common "Achaean League." This form has been adopted in order to have a term which will distinguish a true federal state from a looser organization. The most important of the latter are the symmachies, the permanent alliances of the type of the Peloponnesian and Delian Leagues, much like the contemporary organizations of regional security (e.g., NATO, EU). Then there are also the amphictionies, in which the emphasis is more on religion and the maintenance of cults. In Greek any of these organizations could be called a koinon, a word which could be used about almost any kind of association. It goes without saying that it is sometimes difficult to know just how to classify an organization and, therefore, whether to call it a league or a confederacy. When applied to a federal state, koinon means the Commonwealth, or the federal state or government, often in opposition to the local community or government. Another word frequently used is ethnos, but close reading will reveal that the word has different connotations. It indicates the nation or people. A further word applied to a federal state is sympoliteia, which refers to the sharing of citizenship and thus is the most technical of the three terms. It can be applied also to the unification of two cities into one with a single citizenship. However, when applied to an organization in which there are several cities and a joint central government, it is enough to indicate that we are dealing with a federal state.[4]

In defining a federal state it is scarcely necessary to go further than say that it is a state, in which there is a local citizenship in the smaller communities, as well as a joint or federal citizen ship in which the citizens are under the jurisdiction both of federal and local authorities. The clearest proof to be found for the existence of a sympolity consists of records of citizenship granted simultaneously by local and federal authorities. Almost equally convincing is the application of the word sympoliteia to an organization embracing a number of cities.

The local units of federal states could be either cities or tribes, but cities were the more common for the simple reason that the city-state was the most widely prevalent political unit among the ancient Greeks. These city-states were so small that only a few of the largest, such as Athens and later Rhodes, could hope to have an independent foreign policy, and there tended to impose their leadership on lesser states. The stories of Corcyra and Corinth just before and during the early part of the Peloponnesian War as told by Thucydides illustrate the situation. Corinth tried to exercise leadership over a group of allies mainly consisting of colonies she had founded, but she was wise enough to retain membership in the Peloponnesian League. Within the league she was not always the subservient ally, but at times adopted a balance of power policy to prevent Sparta from becoming too strong. Thus she claimed to have opposed intervention by the Peloponnesian League against Athens at the time of the revolt of Samos. How she later practically threatened Sparta with secession from the league if the latter would not intervene against Athens at a time when Corinth desired the military intervention is known to all readers of Thucydides. Small cities, while knowing that they must have connections with others, also wished to retain their own independence. For that reason it seems they preferred to join symmachies, alliances which were formed for cooperation in war and foreign policy. Such organizations were not, but might have developed into, federal states.

Thus the tendency toward union did not necessarily produce federal states. Federal states, as noted above, also developed from tribal units or groups, such as the Boeotians, Achaeans, Aetolians, and Arcadians. Where there was a feeling of tribal kinship, some tradition of cooperation in war, or a special religious cult kept by the group, it was natural, when cities grew up, for a federal state to develop. Such states usually did not go beyond the boundary of a tribal unit. On the other hand, Ionians and Dorians, were never all united in a single federal state. The Ionian League, which was probably a federal state,[5] included only cities on the coast of Asia Minor and adjoining islands. Thus prerequisites, for the formation of federal States were both a feeling of kinship and geographical contiguity. States might make alliances with more distant cities of another tribe but did not readily combine with them in the closer bonds of federalism. To create federal states of some considerable size and stature, it was necessary to overstep the ethnic boundary and admit members of other tribes. Thus it can be said that Greek federalism proved reasonably successful on a small scale.

To bring out more clearly the nature of federal institutions, it may be useful to sketch briefly the institutions of the quasi-federal alliances, and see to what extent the federal states went beyond the institutions of these symmachies. In the symmachies, the executive department was at first in the hands of the state having the hegemony or leadership of the league, for instance Sparta in the Peloponnesian League and Athens in the Delian League. Any administrative officials needed were supplied by this city. This was true of the Hellenotamiae, the treasurers of the Delian League (change came with the Hellenic League of Philip II and his successors). In the Hellenic League a committee of five presiding officers called proedroi served as chairmen of the assembly, and had a part in determining when and where extraordinary meetings were to be called. The proedroi also had the task of preparing the material to be presented to the assembly (exercised the probouleutic function). It was the duty of the proedroi to see that the secretaries correctly recorded the measures adopted.[6]

To return to the federal states, the great question is whether they went so far beyond the symmachies as to really deserve the name. Did the cities actually cooperate much except in war or did they go their own way? Did the citizens in one community of the confederacy possess civil rights within the others or did the cities treat each other as foreign countries? In general it can be said that institutions were not uniform in all Greek federal states, but that they were unified and centralized far more than the symmachies. Thus, while in the normal city-state outsiders could not acquire land unless they had been given the special right to do so known as enktesis, in a normal federal state citizens possessed this right in all the cities of the confederacy. Thus there was an economic advantage in belonging to a federal state which there was not in a symmachy. In a symmachy, the members might receive protection and possibly some preferential treatment from other members. On the whole, there were no greater privileges for citizens of a member state than for other foreigners, and any special privileges had to be arranged by negotiations and treaties. In a federal state, on the other hand, citizens of one city could own land in any state within the confederacy and conduct business, there on the same terms as its own citizens. With this went also the right of intermarriage.

The political rights of local citizenship, voting, and holding office naturally could be exercised by a citizen only in one of the cities of a federal state, normally his native city. Thus a citizen of a federal state could vote for representatives of his home community in the federal council. If he attended a federal council or assembly, he did so as a representative or citizen of a particular community. In the second century of the Christian era it was common for prominent citizens to be honored for having performed public services in all the cities of Lycia. They were frequently honored by the granting of citizenship by cities belonging to the Confederacy. Nevertheless, they exercised active local citizenship only in the ancestral city (patris).

When we turn to the machinery of government, it is seen that the federal states possessed a more highly developed executive and offered more opportunities for quick action than the symmachies. There was, in the first place, a federal council executive department which could be approached at any time of the year. The head of the state was usually a single official, though sometimes a larger group of officials filled the place. Thus, the Achaean Confederacy from 280 to 255 B.C. had two generals at its head, but thereafter one. The most common title for the head was strategos or general, but here, too, there are exceptions. The Thessalians in the fourth century adopted a title with less warlike implications, namely, archon. In the Boeotian Confederacy the real leadership certainly belonged to the board of Boeolarchs. Nevertheless, in the fourth century a single archon is mentioned in the documents. Yet the most common form of leadership was by a single official with the title of strategos. Alongside him there was some kind of group or board of magistrates which he could consult on decisions which could be made or had to be made without referring the question to the assembly. In the Achaean Confederacy the group contained the general himself, the hipparch or vice president or cavalry commander, and the ten damiorgoi; in Boeotia the Boeotarchs served the purpose.[7] For Lycia we have evidence for the functioning of a cabinet.

Cabinet actually seems to be the best name to apply to such bodies or committees. This institution is one of the chief contributions of Greek federalism to the development of government.

In federal states, the federal assembly met only a few times a year—two regular meetings a year in the Aetolian Confederacy, four in the Achaean—and extraordinary meetings were serious and not to be thoughtlessly called. Even meetings of the council (boule, synedrion) were ponderous. In c. 200 B.C. the Achaeans even ruled that the ekklesia was not to be summoned to the four regular meetings of the year but only to extraordinary meetings for major decisions on questions of foreign policy. The Lycians retained both boule and ekklesia. Therefore, it became necessary to have some organ which could make decisions on actions that had to be taken without waiting for a meeting of one of these bodies. The earliest cabinet of the kind known to us is that of the Boeotarchs of the period 447–386 B.C. who, at the same time, were also the chief magistrates and the commanders of the army. Thus here was less specialization than, for instance, in the later Achaean Confederacy, in which the damiourgoi were distinct from the generals.

Most federal states possessed a board or boards of officials charged with the drafting of laws and responsible for having them recorded correctly. It is even possible that such officials were charged with bringing to trial magistrates who violated or disregarded the laws, much as the Areopagus did at Athens before 462. Little is known about the nomothetai of Athens but very little about the nomographoi and nomophylakes mentioned for several Greek states.[8] Probably the one single best piece of evidence concerning them is a statement by Cicero in De legibus (iv. 46–47) in which he laments that in Rome there was no authority responsible for seeing that the texts of laws were preserved correctly. Instead, the Greeks, he adds, did better. They had nomophylakes who not only kept watch on the text of the laws but also took action against individuals who disregarded the laws. This seems to imply that nomophylakes exercised a certain guardianship of the laws. Also, not nomophylakes but nomographoi and periodic revisions of the laws are known for the Achaean, Aetolian, and Acarnanian confederacies. This suggests that it was common in federal states to have such a board which functioned in connection with the drawing up and revising of laws. The relatively great size of the Achaean board indicates that it was an important body. The laws proposed by it probably were submitted to the federal council or assembly or both.[9]

With regard to the army, the method followed was for the federal government to assess contributions by the members in proportion to their representation in the federal council. For Achea there is abundant evidence that the cities collected and sent in their contributions. The army was composed of contingents from the various cities under the command of local officers with the central command in the hands of federal officials. At Delium in 424, though, the commander-in-chief of the Boeotians did not even decide how the troops were to be drawn up. The local authorities had a threefold task, to provide contingents to the federal army, to maintain permanent guard of the walls and gates of the city, and to defend the territory outside the walls against raids by robbers and pirates and sudden attacks by more official enemies. The quality of an army made up of contingents from various cities naturally would depend partly on the training and military system and partly on the morale and the confidence or lack of confidence of the local authorities in the federal commanders. The army of the Achaean Confederacy was often inefficient and lost many battles. The Achaeans proper, however, were efficient, light-armed troops, and particularly produced excellent slingers. They could hit not only the head of an enemy but also any part of the face they wished. They lacked, nevertheless, heavy armed troops suitable for pitched battles. This was all changed with the military reform of Philopoemen in 209 and 208. In 207 the Achaeans were able to defeat the Spartans in a pitched battle at Mantinea. Foreign affairs and diplomacy were primarily the province of federal government. Local authorities could at times send embassies abroad after securing permission from the federal government. Otherwise, when cities seem to take independent action in foreign affairs, this action usually turns out to be connected with some such matters as the recognition of a religious festival or of the inviolability of a sanctuary.

THE AETOLIAN CONFEDERACY

Aetolia of the fifth century B.C. is the best example known of a Greek tribal state. Later it developed into a very efficient federal tate on sympolitical lines, though, even then, it retained its primary assembly. The transformation cannot be traced in detail, but it is clear that though the tribal organization was retained at the time, the Aetolians had developed an efficient control of foreign policy and of the army already by the time of the Peloponnesian War. Soon afterward—again it is impossible to date the change precisely—Aetolia was reorganized on sympolitical lines with the local government in the hands of cities. The development was largely determined by geography. There was some fertile land in the country, but much of it was mountainous and pretty cut off from the outside world. Most of the passes communicating with the outside world were difficult. There was a coastline on the Gulf of Corinth, but conditions were not such that any great commercial port developed in Actolian territory. Eastern Aetolia was separated from the coast by mountains, south of which lay Western Locris. Here there were several ports, among them Naupactus, which later was to become one of the chief cities of the Aetolian Confederacy. Farther west the harbors tended to be obstructed by silting, and even here the most important port, Oeniadae, was considered Acarnanian. Into this country invaders brought a northwest Greek dialect at the time of the Doric migration. The organization remained tribal probably as late as the early fourth century.

The development of Aetolia before the King's Peace can be treated very briefly. In connection with the Athenian expedition into Aetolia in 426, Thucydides gives a description of the Aetiolians which shows them to have constituted a typical tribal state. He mentions three main tribes, the Apodoti, the Ophiones, and the Eurytanes, and refers to sub-tribes. They lived scattered in unfortified villages. Yet the account of the campaign shows that their opponents were surprised by the efficient conduct of war by the Aetolians. Both this and the subsequent management of their foreign policy show that there existed a central government of some sort for the conduct of war and foreign relations, though the organization on tribal lines still was retained.[10] Otherwise Thucydides tells nothing about their government; nothing about the chief magistrates or assemblies. The leaders who conducted the successful campaign against the Athenians remain nameless. The only Aetolians mentioned by name are the three ambassadors, one from each of the three tribes, sent to Corinth and Sparta later in the year.[11] Thus it is not known then, whether as later, a single general was head of the central government or what other officials there were. The assembly, if one existed, was almost certainly a primary assembly. Even in Hellenistic times the Aetolian Confederacy had a primary assembly in which all adult male citizens appear to have had the right to vote, and in which it seems that the votes, as in the ekklesia of Athens, were counted by heads and not by voting units.

This assembly held two regular meetings a year, in the spring before the campaigning season began and in the autumn after it was over. The members of the assembly and the men under arms seem to have been approximately identical. This, of course, hardly means that the older men who no longer went campaigning were deprived of their vote. Since the Aetolians of this period fought as light-armed troops (*peltastai*),[12] the assembly would be rather democratic, much more so than that of the Boeotians, who confined the vote to the cavalry and hoplites and excluded the lower classes. This Aetolian assembly must go back to early times and must have assumed prominence as soon as the Aetolians began to be involved in wars with their neighbors.

It is not clear whether they at this time possessed a federal boule or council, or whether the conduct of joint business, except for the meetings of the assembly, was left to a few magistrates or a smaller committee. In all likelihood a boule did exist. The discovery a few years ago of an inscription mentioning the federal boule of the early Achaean Confederacy[13] supplies one more piece of evidence indicating that federal states at an early date, like city-states, commonly possessed a boule. However, the organization with cities represented in proportion to their population, which existed in Hellenistic times, cannot antedate the organization of the Confederacy on the basis of cities, but a boule with a somewhat different organization may well have existed. The adoption by the Confederacy of an organization by cities seems to have come early in the fourth century. It was completed by 367 B.C. and probably had been adopted somewhat earlier in connection with the struggles centering around Acarnania and the development of other confederacies at the time. Some of the cities may have been country districts grouped round some village or hill fort.23 The earliest proof for the existence of an Aetolian boule is a reference in an Athenian inscription of 333–332 B.C. or thereabouts to an Aetolian boularch, a presiding officer of the boule.[14]

THE ACHAEAN CONFEDERACY

Let us now examine the institutions of the Achaean Federation, as this was developed after the King's Peace. The head of the Confederacy was a general (*strategos*) elected annually. The hipparch was the second highest official of the Confederacy. Less is heard about the *nauarch* or admiral, but he seems to have been a regular member of the government. Another high military official, a *hypostrategos*, a commander of the troops of a district (*synteleia*) is mentioned occasionally. The one such district known is that of Patrae, Dyme, Pharae, and Tritaea. This is known from the Social War. Since this is the only *synteleia* adequately attested, it is possible that it was unique. The four cities mentioned were the ones which revived the Confederacy in 281–280, and it is possible that the *synteleia* is a survival from this original union.

From the manner in which Polybius, in his brief statement about the government of the period 280–255, lists the secretary ahead of the two generals, it has been concluded that at the time the secretary was an official of great importance.

The Achaean organ of government which seems to have ranked next to the general in importance was the board of ten *damiourgoi*. This is mentioned in the fourth century fragment of a treaty, which also attests the existence of a federal boule at the time, but this document does not help to determine the number of members. Thus it is not certain that the number was always ten. The connection of the *damiorgoi* with foreign affairs was particularly extensive. The incidents in connection with which *damiorgoi* are mentioned how them to have been so prominent that it is virtually certain that they were included in the body of officials called the *synarchiai*. This body, acting as a sort of cabinet, met secretly and at times made decisions of great importance.[15] It is not certain that the *synarchiai* always comprised the ten *damiorgoi* and the general.

With regard to the Achaean assemblies, certain things must he said in connection with the meetings. The term *synodos* occurs frequently. *Synkletos*, seeming to mean a specially summoned or extraordinary meeting, appear once in Polybius and once in an inscription referring to events of about 155. In both cases a *synodos* was followed by a *synkletos*, and in Polybius xxix. 24.6 this is described as a meeting attended not only by the boule but also by all citizens over thirty. This, supported by other evidence, led to the conclusion that *synodoi* were regular meetings attended only by the federal boule, while *synkletoi* were extraordinary meetings of the primary assembly. This meant that most of the work of the government was performed by the representative body. The use of the *synkletoi* was much like submitting important questions to the voters by means of a referendum. Later, beginning at least as early as 200 and probably in 217, they began to rely chiefly on the representative boule and to summon the *ekklesia*, the primary assembly, only from time to time for extraordinary meetings.

The key to the solution of the composition of the assemblies was the conclusion that, when Polybius used the words *boule* and *ekklesia* in his statements concerning Achaean affairs, the words had their normal meaning, boule meaning a council and ekklesia a primary assembly in which all male citizens of the proper age were allowed to take part.

The difference in procedure before and after this change can be seen in the descriptions of meetings. In 229, for example, when Aratus and the other officials felt that Spartan aggression had gone too far, they convoked the Achaeans and in conjunction with the boule decided to go to war with the Lacedaemonians. This must have been an extraordinary meeting attended by both the boule and the *ekklesia* and one in which the boule acted as a probouleutic body.[16] The decision made at this meeting would later have been reserved for a *synkletos* of the *ekklesia*.

With the change eliminating the use of the primary assembly except for a few extraordinary meetings, the importance of the boule naturally increased. The Achaean boule was a body of considerable size. This is implied in the reports of meetings and is suggested also by the examples of other federal councils. That of the Aetolians numbered over 550. These large councils were made up of delegations from cities varying in size according to the population of the city. Boule also suggests that boularchs and *proedroi* presided over the council, but there seems to be no record of such officials. Instead, the accounts of meetings give the impression that the same federal officials who presided over the *synkletoi* of the primary assembly also took charge of the meetings of the boule.

The chief aid in differentiating between the two types of meetings in the second century is the account of a *synodos* at Corinth and a *synkletos* at Sicyon, both in 168. Ambassadors from the Ptolemies appeared before the *synodos* requesting that the Achaeans send them 1,000 infantry and 200 cavalry under the command of Lycortas and Polybius. This plan was opposed by Callicrates, who managed to hold up action on the ground that it was contrary to law to consider a question of military aid at the meeting. The result was the summoning to Sicyon of a *synkletos*, which was open not only to members of the boule but also to all citizens over thirty. This is the only passage in the preserved parts of the history of Polybius in which he applies the term *synkletos* to an Achaean assembly or meeting.

The council of *gerousia* must be mentioned in passing for the sake of completeness. The *gerousia* is mentioned only once. At Corinth in 146, after the general Critolaus already had opposed the other magistrates, he became so abusive to the Roman ambassadors that the members of the *gerousia* sought to lay hands on him and restrain him.[17] Though they failed, the story implies action by a body which felt that it had a right to control the behavior of any speaker, even the general. This can hardly have been anyone but the *damiorgoi*. Hence, of the various theories concerning the *gerousia*, the most plausible is that the word designates the college of *damiorgoi*.

It is noteworthy that the *boule* and *ekklesia* of the Achaeans suggest democracy. In addition there is the boast of the Achaean democracy on the part of Polybius. But this does not mean that the Achaeans had a government as democratic as that of Athens in the fifth century. It should no longer be necessary to argue that the meaning of *demokratia* had changed, so that in Hellenistic times states which once would have been considered oligarchic could be called democratic. In the Achaean Confederacy the right to vote was limited to men over thirty. This limitation combined with the absence of pay for magistrates might be enough to place control of the state in the hands of men of property.

The federal finances at the other end is a subject of special importance for the functioning of government, but it is also a difficult problem. There was a federal treasurer (*tamias*), but he is seldom mentioned and seems to have been relatively unimportant. There must normally have been little money in the treasury to provide for minor current expenses—a sort of petty cash fund made up of sums sent to the treasury by the constituent cities. There is no proof that there existed any tax which was collected directly by the federal government. The federal government, however, had the right to compel the cities to send their contributions.

Extraordinary payments (*eisphorai*) on part of the cities were occasionally demanded.

The systems of taxation and coinage and most of the details of administration were handled by local authorities. Hence it need hardly be demonstrated that the cities had laws and law-making machinery of their own. There were cities as well as federal *nomographoi*. This must mean that there were differences in details between the laws of the cities. Hence, when Polybius (ii.37.10) states that the Achacans used the same laws or had uniform laws, this, strictly speaking, is not true about local laws but only about federal laws. The latter largely concerned constitutional law, such as the law frequently mentioned which regulated the meetings of the *ekklesia*. The latter is an example of a piece of legislation altering the Constitution of the Confederacy. This need not mean that constitutional law was clearly distinguished from other law, but law and decree were distinguished. Concerning law making, it may be noted, once again, that the Achaean Confederacy was one of the federal states for which there is evidence for a board of *nomographoi* which staged periodic revisions of the laws. Mention of the *nomographoi* is found in a decree of Megalopolis (capital of the Arcadian League) of the late third century preserved at Magnesia.[18]

The federal courts had jurisdiction in cases of treason and were competent not only to impose fines but also to inflict the death penalty.

The analysis of the sphere of power of federal government and the federated states respectively aims at showing that federation is a union of preexisting entities and that the bonds of religion, language, and common descent are of fundamental importance in the smooth functioning of it. Many conclusions may be drawn. This will be left for the individual reader.[19]

NOTES

1. The best account of Classical Greek federal states may be found in Freeman, *History of Federal Government in Greece and Italy*, 2nd ed. by J. B. Bury, 1893. Good general introductions include Mann, *Ancient and Mediaeval Republics* (New York, 1879), Hart, *Introduction to the Study of Federal Government* (1891), Howard, *Comparative Federal Institutions* (University of Nebraska, 1907), Larsen, *Greek Federal States: Their Institutions and History* (Oxford: Oxford University Press, 1968), and Beck and Peter, eds., *Federalism in Greek Antiquity* (Cambridge: Cambridge University Press, 2015).

2. *Classical Philology*, XL (1945), 74 and n. 55; Walker, *The Hellenica Oxyrhynchia* (Oxford, 1913).

3. For a discussion see Larsen, *Representative Government in Greek and Roman History* (1955), pp. 23–25.

4. One of the best sources for a study of the use of the aforementioned terms is an inscription from Lydia (*Supplementum Epigraphicum Graecum* xviii. 570).

5. See Larsen, *Ionian Trade and Colonization* (1959), pp. 28–31.

6. Information about the proedroi is derived mainly from *Inscriptiones Graecae*, iv. An inscription found at Epidaurus which gives the constitution of the Hellenic League as re-founded in 302 B.C. by Demetrius Poliorcetes. At the time the proedroi were delegates of the king and were to continue to be so as long as the current war lasted. What is given above is a description of their position in time of peace. This is based on the theory that this was the original system of Philip II later modified by Demetrius for the duration of the war in which he was engaged. Of course, under Demetrius the permanent or peace-time system was never used.

7. Polybius, when he describes the government of the Achaeans after the revival of their

Confederacy in 280, states that they elected for a fixed term a federal secretary.

8. The most important evidence that has come to light after its publication is probably Supplementum Epigraphicwn Graecum ix. I, which shows that in the late fourth century, Cyrene had nine nomophylakes and five or more—probably more—nomographoi.

9. The nomothetai, as it were, drew up the probouleuma, which afterward was submitted to the people. Note also that in a letter of Antigonus Monophthalmus concerning a proposed synoecism of Teos and Lebedus, it is suggested that six nomographoi be selected to draw up laws which afterward arc to be submitted to the united demos of the synoecized community (*Sylloge Inscriptionum Graecarum* 344).

10. Thucydides, *History of the Peloponnesian War*, Book III, paragraphs 94–98 (Harvard University Press, Loeb Classical Library).

11. Thucydides, *History of the Peloponnesian War*, Book Ill, *supra,* paragraph 100.

12. *Ibid.* Book Ill, paragraphs 94, 97.

13. *Supplementum Epigraphicum Graecum*, xiv. 375. This dates from the fourth century 23 Tarn-Griffith, Hellenistic Civilization, p. 71.

14. *Inscriptiones Graecae*, ii. 358.

15. On the secrecy of meetings of *synarchiai* see Polybius xxx viii. 13. 4–5.

16. Polybius, ii. 46.6

17. Polybius, xxxviii. 12. 7, 13. I.

18. *Sylloge Inscriptionum Graecarum* 559.

Chapter 7

Modern Federal Government

In the United States of America, the federal state was established in 1787, by the thirteen then British colonies, which constituted separate states in the federation. The independence of the states of New Hampshire, Massachusetts Bay, Rhode Island and Providence Plantations, Connecticut, New York, New Jersey, Pennsylvania, Delaware, Maryland, Virginia, North Carolina, and Georgia was acknowledged by his Britannic majesty in a definitive treaty of peace concluded 3 September 1783, and proclaimed 14 January 1784. A confederation of these states had been formed under Articles of Confederation adopted 1 March 1781. A federal union of the same states, established by a Constitution which became effective in 1789, was extended during the next sixty years to include the entire area form the Atlantic to the Pacific Ocean between Canada and Mexico. The territory from Alaska, to the northwest of Canada, was acquired by purchase from Russia in 1867; the Territory of Hawaii was annexed, at the request of the Queen of Hawaii, 1898; and several island possessions, including the Philippines and Puerto Rico, were ceded by Spain in 1899. The independence of the Philippines was recognized by the United States on 4 July 1946.[1]

However it should be noted toward the end of the Convention, even George Mason became critical of some of its decisions, especially the compromises concerning the navigation acts and the international slave trade. His views are still pertinent nowadays, as seen in the fast-growing complexities posed by the clash of cultures within the United States and elsewhere. Mason drafted his objections as the Convention neared adjournment, refused to sign, and permitted the following critique to be published in various newspapers during November 1787: "*There is no declaration of Rights; and the laws of the general Government being paramount to the laws of the several States, the Declaration of Rights in the separate States are no security. Nor are the people secured even in the Enjoyment of the Benefits of the common law: which stands here upon no other Foundation than its having been adopted by the respective Acts forming the Constitutions of the several States.*

In the House of Representatives there is not the Substance, but the Shadow only of Representation; which can never produce proper information in the Legislature, or inspire Confidence in the People: the Laws will therefore be generally made by Men concern'd in, and unacquainted with their Effects and Consequences.

The Senate have the Power of altering all Money-Bills, and of originating Appropriations of Money and the Galleys of the Officers of their own Appointment in Conjunction with the President of the United States; altho' they are not the Representatives of the People, or amenable to them. These with their other great Powers (viz. Making Treaties, and in trying all Impeachments) their Influence upon and Connection with the supreme Executive from these Causes, their Duration of Office, and their being a constant existing Body almost continually sitting, joined with their being one compleat Branch of the Legislature, will destroy any Balance in the Government, and enable them to accomplish what Usurpations they please upon the Rights and Libertys of the People.[. . .] Hence also sprung that unnecessary and dangerous Officer, the Vice; who for want of other Employment, is made President of the Senate; thereby dangerously blending the executive and legislative Powers; besides always giving to some of the States an unnecessary and unjust Pre-eminence over the others."

The American holocaust, however, was and remains unparalleled in terms of magnitude, and will here be elaborated in depth. The ideological matrix of its denial is also among the most well developed of any genocide, for which a considerable amount of information is available, including official primary records. The director of the National Endowment for the Humanities, Lynne Cheney, in collaboration with the United States Senate, prepared for the 1992 Columbus quincentenniary by refusing to fund any film production, which proposed to use the word "genocide" even in passing, to explain the subsequent liquidation of America's indigenous population. They were joined by the then Secretary of Education William Bennett, who stated that "popularization of such distortions of history would signify an undermining of the Western cultural tradition which has made this great nation what it is today." Such sentiments, which have been ascendant in the United States and Canada since 1980, have been represented in the mass media. Charles Krauthammer, for instance, one of *Time* magazine's columnists, used an entire column [May 27, 1991] to label as "politically correct" opportunists anyone who dared express regret over the killing of millions of innocent people and the destruction of entire ancient cultures in the Americas. What happened in the wake of European invasion was only what has always characterized human history, Krauthammer claimed, citing the Norman conquest of Britain as an apt (though inaccurate, to say the least) comparison. "The real question is," he noted, "what eventually grew on this bloodied soil. For regardless of the level of destruction and mass murder that was visited upon the indigenous peoples of Western Hemisphere, it was, in retrospect, entirely justified because in the process it wiped out such alleged barbarisms as the communally based Inca society (which really was only a beehive and gave the world a culture of liberty that endowed the individual human being with dignity and sovereignty."[2] To Christopher Hitchens, the "eminent" British journalist, anyone refusing to join him in celebrating with great vim the annihilation of the native peoples of the Americas was self-hating, ridiculous, ignorant, and sinister. "People who regard critically the genocide that was carried out in America's past," Hitchens continued, "*are simply reactionary, since such grossly inhuman atrocities happen to be the way history is made. And thus to complain about them is as empty as complaint about climatic, geological or tectonic shift. Moreover, such violence is worth glorifying since it more often than not has been for the long-term betterment of mankind-as in the United States today, where the extermination of American Indians has brought about a nearly boundless epoch of opportunity and innovation.*"[3]

There have certainly been exceptions to this "rationale." The American Indian Movement (AIM), following the legal definition of the crime which was adopted by the United Nations in 1948, began to apply the concept of genocide with accuracy to American history. The AIM was soon joined by various other groups as well as members of the academic community. Sherburne F. Cook, Henry F. Dobyns, and Russell Thornton are some of the scholars who laboriously excavated the data necessary to reveal the true size of the native population of 1492, and entered into the process of honestly describing the means by which it was reduced to almost nothing.

GENOCIDE IN LATIN AMERICA FROM 1492 TO NOWADAYS

On 12 October 1492, the day Christopher Columbus first landed in the so-called New World, the Western Hemisphere was inhabited by a population of well over 100 million people. Two centuries later, it is estimated that the indigenous population of the Americas had been diminished by some 90 percent and was continuing to fall steadily.[4]

Into this sheepfold there came some Spaniards who immediately behaved like ravening beasts. And Spaniards have behaved in no other way during the past forty years down to the present time, for they are still acting like ravening beasts, killing, terrorizing, afflicting, torturing, and destroying the native peoples, doing all this with the strangest and most varied new methods of cruelty, never seen or heard of before.[5]

In 1519, when the Spanish conqueror, Hernan Cortes, captured the Mexico (Aztec) capital—a huge metropolis constructed in the midst of a volcanic lake—he first laid siege and allowed a smallpox epidemic to run its course, weakening the city's defenses.[6] Then, after a series of assaults resulting in the Indians being reduced to the point of almost complete defenselessness—they no longer had nor could find any arrows, javelins, or stones with which to respond, his letters recount—he initiated the wholesale slaughter of those who surrendered, were captured, or were simply trapped by his troops. Twelve thousand people, many of them non-combatants, were butchered in a single afternoon, another 40,000 the following day, before Cortes withdrew because his men could no longer endure the stench of the dead bodies.[7]

When the Spaniards returned the next day, their commander surveyed his starving and disease-wracked opponents, and announced his intent to attack and slay them all. By the time it was over, about 350,000 were dead.

The people of the city had to walk upon their dead while others swam or drowned in the waters of that wide lake where they had their canoes; indeed, so great was their suffering that it was beyond our understanding how they came to endure it. Countless numbers of men, women and children came out towards us, and in their eagerness to escape many were pushed into the water where they drowned amidst that multitude of corpses; and it seemed that more than fifty thousand of them had perished from the salt water they had drunk, their hunger and the vile stench. . . And so in the streets, where they were, we came across such piles of the dead that we were forced to walk on them.[8]

By 1525, with the conquest of the Mexicas complete, one of Cortes's lieutenants, Alvarado, mounted a campaign to the south, against the Mayans and other peoples of what are now the southern part of Mexico, as well as Guatemala, Honduras, Nicaragua, and Panama. They advanced killing, ravaging, robbing, and destroying all the country as they went.

By massacres and murders . . . they have destroyed and devastated a kingdom more than a hundred leagues square, one of the happiest in the way of fertility and population in the world. This same tyrant [Alvarado] wrote that it was more populous than the kingdom of Mexico; and he told the truth. He and his brothers, together with the others, have killed more than four or five million people in fifteen or sixteen years, from the year 1525 until 1540, and they continue to kill and destroy those who are still left; and so they will kill the remainder.[9]

The Conquest of the Incas, on the other hand, in what are now Chile and Peru, evidenced less direct killing. This was because the conquerors in this region captured much of the Incan leadership very early on in their enterprise, and developed certain methods of forcing them to betray their people.

One ingenious European technique of getting what they wanted involved burying Indian leaders in earth up to their waists . . . In that helpless position, they were beaten with whips and given instructions . . . When they did not comply more earth was piled about them and the whippings continued. Then more earth. And more beating. At last, says the Spanish informant on this particular matter, "they covered them to the shoulders and finally to the mouths." He then adds as an afterthought, "I even believe that a great number of natives were burned to death."[10]

Generally, numerous reports, from numerous reporters, tell of Indians being led to the mines in columns, chained together at the neck, and decapitated if they faltered. Of children trapped and burned alive in their houses, or stabbed to death because they walked too slowly. Of the routine cutting off of women's breasts, and the tying of heavy gourds to their feet before tossing them to drown in lakes and lagoons. Of babies taken from their mothers' breasts, killed and left roadside markers. Of Indians dismembered and sent back to their villages with their chopped off hands and nosed strung round their necks. Of pregnant and confined women, children, old men, as many as they could capture, thrown into pits which stakes had been embedded and left stuck on the stakes. And much, much more.[11]

The numbers of those perished are really terrible. Within the area of the former Mexico kingdom, the people, who numbered more than 25 million at the time of the conquerors' arrival, were literally put to death, mainly in mining and plantation enterprises. According to the Spanish census of the time hardly 1.3 million indios remained alive in the entire region by 1595. By 1542 Nicaragua alone had seen the export of as many as half a million of its people for slave labor (effectively a death sentence) in distant areas whose populations had been destroyed. In Panama, between the years 1514 and 1530 up to 2,000,000 Indians were murdered. In Guatemala, the population fell by 82 percent within the first half-century following European arrival, and by 94 percent—from 260,000 to 16,000—in less than a century and a half. In western Nicaragua, 99 percent of the people were dead (falling from more than 1,000,000 to less than 10,000) before sixty years had elapsed from the time of the Spaniards' initial presence.[12] Further south, in the Andes, the population dropped from as many as 14 millions before the invasion to a million by the end of the sixteenth century. The manner of their killing was pretty much the same as that of their compatriots in Mexico and Central America by and large.[13] Less than 10 percent of Brazil's population of 2.5 million prior to the invasion survived into the seventeenth century. It is noteworthy that over a third of a million of these Indians were held in forced labor.

For the Indians brought to the slave markets of the coast, life was frightful. Families were broken up during the raids, and a large proportion of the men killed. The women and children were taken down [Amazon] river in chains and sold. On the sugar plantations, they were forced to work seven days a week. The work was punishing. It required clearing and irrigating huge tracts of land, building mills, houses and roads, and cutting and pressing cane. Like the Indians who were subjected to the Spanish, the Indians of Brazil, by virtue of enforced labor and on the onslaught of disease, suffered greatly. Not many survived.[14]

Genocide even became a mode of recreation. An innovation, "dogging," made its appearance. A properly fleshed dog could pursue a "savage" as zealously as a deer a boar. . . To many of the conquerors, the Indian was merely another savage animal, and the dogs were trained to rip apart their human quarry with the same zest as they felt when hunting wild beasts.[15]

GENOCIDE OF THE NORTH AMERICAN INDIANS

From the early sixteenth to the eve of the twentieth century, up to 99 percent of the continent's indigenous population was eradicated. As of 1900, the U.S. Bureau of the Census reported barely over 237,000 native people surviving within the country's borders, and the Smithsonian Institution reported less than a third of a million for all North America, including Greenland.[16]

Although the literature of the day confidently predicted that North American Indians would be completely extinguished within a couple of generations at most,[17] the magnitude of the demographic catastrophe has always been officially denied in both the United States and Canada.

The primary means by which this outcome was achieved has been through a systematic and deliberate falsification or suppression of information concerning the size of the pre-invasion aboriginal population. By minimizing estimates as to how many people there were to begin with, the extent of native population reduction was made to seem far less severe than it had actually been. Such demographic manipulations fostered the impression that North American territory was, in public international law terminology, a terra nullius, vacant land, unoccupied, more accurately land of no one,[18] and thus open for settling by any "pioneer."

Historians and their equivalents in the cinema and literature of the populace have been able to present the process of Euro-American nation building as a noble achievement, not always devoid of conflict situations, but predominantly well intended and finally in the best of interests of everyone involved. In such a version of the events, the relatively few aboriginal people who were at the outset living in what was to become the United States of America, died because of unintended, unfortunate, inadvertent, and eventually inevitable circumstances.[19]

Virtually all of this is very far from true. A glance at the numbers will be illuminating.

Throughout most of the present century, the federally established and maintained Smithsonian Institution in Washington, D.C., America's official repository of truth in such affairs, has categorically asserted that the size of the indigenous population everywhere north of Mexico added up to not more than a million in 1492.[20] As Francis Jennings and others have demonstrated, the Smithsonian supposedly scientific estimates have not only been fundamentally low, but also have always depended on a combination of manipulated data and no data at all. The estimate originated from the anthropologist James M. Mooney, first published in 1928.[21] A hint of Mooney's method appears in a remark about the estimates for New England. Mooney wrote that the "original Indian population of New England was probably about 25.000 or about one half what the historian John Graham Palfrey makes it." Apparently Mooney had followed the tradition of Palfrey's own acceptance; that is, he took the estimate of a predecessor and discounted it. The same sort of process had been pursued by every generation of scholars since the original data was recorded in the seventeenth century, and by Mooney's time discount upon discount had reduced the figures to a small portion of what was mentioned in the sources. Jennings attributes such bias on part of Mooney, Palfrey, and others to doctrines of racist pseudoscience with which the American academy was being filled.[22] False classification was furthered by Alfred Kroeber, a leading anthropologist of the day, who deduced a final estimate in North America of slightly under a million.

Kroeber emphatically rejected the notion that the nations of North America could be considered capable of so ordering their societies and technologies as to increase their populations beyond a static and sparsely distributed token representation. Kroeber's allotment of one million persons divides into the total area of Canada and the United States (including Alaska) in the ratio of one person per seven square miles. His explanation for this sparsity virtually blamed the condition of savagery, though he must be credited with avoidance of the term itself. He reasoned that Indian societies were characterized by insane, unending, continuously attritional warfare and by the absence of all effective political organization, of the idea of the State."[23]

Fortunately, a different kind of research was going on among less establishment-oriented scholars at the University of California at Berkeley, by Sherburne F. Cook, Woodrow W. Borah, and a handful of others. Working directly from archives in the midlands of America, they assembled a demographic image of the people that the Spanish recorded in the first instance. This process brought about estimates several times those reported by the Smithsonian Institution. The followers of Kroeber insisted, of course, that most anthropologists will view Kroeber as a more accurate authority than Cortes, or registers of baptisms by priests and deaths, and did all they could to prevent their work from being published.[24]

Dobyns, meanwhile, had begun compiling data and in 1966 was prepared to present an estimate of the aboriginal population above the Rio Grande as having been as least 12.5 million. By this estimate, the Great Lakes region was inhabited by 3.8 million people in 1492. Another 5.25 million lived in the Great Mississippi River Valley, Ohio, and Kentucky. The Atlantic coastal plain from Florida to Massachusetts afforded about 2,211,000 Native Americans. After further research, Dobyns concluded that there may have been as many as 18.5 million people inhabiting pre-invasion North America. In any case, the demographic reality of autochthonous North American population was about fifteen times the one reported by the Smithsonian Institution.

What is more, after minimization, the most common mode of denying that genocide was perpetrated against the indigenous peoples of North America as well as the rest of the hemisphere is what is referred to as the disease factor. The standard histories to which students are exposed are along the lines that the populace kept dying off from contact with European diseases—not from contact with Europeans themselves—like smallpox, and various plagues and fevers. As a consequence the indigenous population of Mexico, for example, declined dramatically—by about 90 percent during the fifty years lapsing after the invasion of Cortes's regiments.[25] The army itself, it appears, had nothing to do with it.

Even those who are willing to admit that the size of the pre-invasion North America population have put forward arguments of this sort. Professor Steven Katz of Cornell University cites Dobyns in the relevant portion of his book on genocide, and then states:

Very probably the greatest demographic disaster in history, the depopulation of the New World, for all its death and terror, was largely an unintended tragedy, a tragedy that occurred despite the sincere and indisputable desire of the Europeans to keep the Indian population alive. The native people died primarily because of pandemics against which there was no protection.

Nature, not malice, was the cause of the massive, incomprehensible devastation.[26]

There are, of course, elements of truth to this. There can be no question that Christopher Columbus and his crew—and undoubtedly others of the early Spanish invaders as well—were unaware since the beginning that they were carrying with them pathogens to which America's native peoples had never been exposed and therefore possessed no panacea. By 1550 this was surely common knowledge in Europe, and it was "piously" attributed to the "hand of God." Even the Dean of the Cathedral of Guatemala put it thus: "the secret judgments of God were responsible for demolishing the Mayan population of this area, thus allowing the easy pacification and colonization by the Spaniards, an inherently superior group selected by heaven to perform this."[27]

Such propositions were not restricted to the Spanish. Oliver Cromwell—the Lord Protector of England—himself proclaimed God an Englishman at about the same time, albeit not in identical context. In describing the consequences of indigenous peoples' quarrelsome attitude about being pushed out of their land around the Massachusetts Bay in 1631, the Puritan leader Cotton Mather rejoiced that God ended the controversy by sending the smallpox among the Indians who were before that time exceedingly numerous.[28]

Again, even if one does not neglect taking into account the negative part played by diseases in the extermination of the Indians of North America, it remains the case nevertheless that nowhere does the record reveal anyone, at least in a position of public authority, suggesting that, in view of all this death, contact should be drastically eliminated, until some remedy could be discovered and employed.

To sum up, in reality, the motives underpinning resistance to a presentation of a revised demographic version have to do with crude policy considerations; such an eventuality, would destroy—as it has to a large extent—the "virgin land" myth,[29] which is so central to the prevailing view of American history, thereby paving the way to a severe consideration of the question of genocide or genocidal murder in the United States of America, especially the northern part.

I could multiply the examples by referring to the other federal states such as Canada, the federal states of South America, Australia, Yugoslavia, Federal Republic of Germany, Burma, the new African federal states, and others, in all of which its constituent parts preexisted the federal state. This is precisely where the foregoing discussion aims. In the United States, it must be emphasized, the establishment of the federal state has clearly been the outcome or genocide committed against the autochthonous Indian population. Conversely genocide or ethnic cleansing of autochthonous Greek people is exactly what has also been going on for decades on Cyprus. An outrageously unlawful act of the kind should not and cannot be a ground for a foundation of a *bi-zonal* federal state.

NOTES

1. Peasley, *Constitutions of Nations, supra*, Volume Ill, pp. 577–578. Mason had played a major role in writing Virginia's Constitution and declaration of rights. Although he served as a delegate to the Philadelphia Convention, Mason refused to sign the Constitution because it lacked a bill of rights and seemed to place the agricultural South at a disadvantage. Here are some of his remarks in a letter addressed to Thomas Jefferson 26 May 1788: "These Objections of mine were first printed very incorrectly, without any Approbation, or Privity; which laid me under some kind of

Necessity of publishing them afterward, myself. I take the Liberty of enclosing you a Copy of them. You will find them conceived in general Terms; as I wished to confine them to a narrow Compass. There are many other things very objectionable in the proposed Constitution; particularly the almost unlimited Authority over the Militia of the several States; whereby, under Colour of regulating, they may disarm, or render useless the Militia, the more easily to govern by a standing Army; or they may harass the Militia, by such rigid Regulations, and intolerable Burdens, as to make the People themselves desire its Abolition. By their Power over the Elections, they may so order them, as to deprive the People at large of any Share in the Choice of their Representatives. By the Consent of Congress, Men in the highest Offices of Trust in the United States may receive Emolument, Place, or Pension from foreign Prince, or Potentate, which is selling themselves up to the highc,1 Bidder." The letter may be found in Kammen, *The Origins of the American Constitution: A Documentary History* (Penguin Books, 1984).

2. Stannard, *The Politics of Holocaust Scholarship: Uniqueness as Denial* (Westview Press, 1996), p. 165. Arthur Schlesinger Jr. not only repeats "Krauthammer's argument but surpasses it. Schlesinger was not content to build his case on the purported shortcomings of the ancient societies of America. He asserted that without the European conquests and slaughter as least some New World societies today would be sufficiently unpleasant places to live so as to make acceptable the centuries of genocide that were carried out against the native population of the entire Western Hemisphere. Ibid., pp. 165–166.

3. *Op. cit*., p. 166.

4. Borah, "Conquest and Population: A Demographic Approach to Mexican History," *Proceedings of the American Philosophical Society*, No. 113, 1968, pp. 177–183.

5. Churchill, *A Little Matter of Genocide: Holocaust and Denial in the Americans 1492 to the Present* (City Lights Books, San Francisco, 1997), p. 98.

6. See generally Miguel Leon, ed. *The Broken Spears: The Aztec Account of the Conquest of Mexico* (Boston: Beacon Press, 1962).

7. Hernan Cortes, *Letters From Mexico* (New York, Grossman, 1971), pp. 257–62.

8. Cortes, *Letters from Mexico, ante*, p. 263.

9. Churchill, *A Little Matter of Genocide, op. cit*. p. 99. To the north of the Mexico empire, things were much the same, or perhaps worse, at the conquest time. Beltran de Gunzman (a Spanish Jew) was one of those who led armies to the north, torturing or burning at the stake native leaders, while seizing or destroying enormous native stores of food. As elsewhere, disease, enslavement, and outright massacres combined to extinguish entire Indian cultures in Mexico's northwest (Stannard, *American Holocaust, ante*. 81, relying primarily on Donald E. Chipman, *de Guzman and the Province of Panuco in New Spain 1518 - 1610 [*Glendale, CA: 1967]).

10. Stannard, *American Holocaust, supra*, p. 87; the notes are taken from John Hemming, *The Conquest of the Incas* (New York: 1970), p. 359.

11. Stannard, *American Holocaust, op.cit*. pp. 82–83.

12. Ibid, pp. 82, 86, based on George Lovell, *Conquest and Survival in Colonial Guatemala: A Historical Geography of the Cuchumatan Highlands, 1500–1821* (Montreal: McGill-Queen's University Press, 1985), p. 145.

13. The Indians were being totally destroyed and lost. Tragically, some of them pleaded with a cross (!) to be given food for the love of God. The cross is originally an ancient Greek religious symbol, also found among the Indian Americans (quoted in Hemming, *Conquest of the Incas, op. cit.* p. 351). There is ample evidence to suggest that ancient Greeks came to contact with the native autochthonous population of the Western world and peacefully spread elements of the Hellenic culture, which is beyond the scope of the present analysis.

14. Churchill, *A Little Matter of Genocide, op. cit.*, p. 104.

15. John Grier Varner and Jeanette Johnston Varner, *Dogs of Conquest* (Norman University of Oklahoma Press, 1983).

16. U.S. Bureau of the Census, *Fifteenth Census of the United States, 1930: The Indian Population of the United States and Alaska* (Washington, D.C.: U.S. Government Printing Office, 1937), esp. Table II, "Indian Population by Divisions and States, 1890–1930."

17. See B. O. Flower, "An Interesting Representative of a Vanishing Race," *Arena*, July 1896; Simon Pokagon, "The Future of the Red Man," *Forum*, August 1897; William Draper, "The Last of the Red Race," *Cosmopolitan*, January 1902; Charles M. Harvey, "The Last Race Rally of Indians," *World's Work*, May 1904; E. S. Curtis, "Vanishing Indian Types: The Tribes of the Northwest Plains," *Scribner's*, June 1906; J. L. Hill, *The Passing of the Indian and the Buffalo* (California, 1917); John Collier, "The Vanishing American," *Nation,* January 11, 1928; *Proceedings of the Second Pan-American Scientific Congress, Section I: Anthropology* (Washington, D.C.: Smithsonian Institution, 1909–1910)

18. This notion and its application are articulated by Richardson in his *People of Terra Nullius: Betrayal and Rebirth in Canada* (Seattle/Vancouver: University of Washington Press, 1993); Green and Duncan, *The Law of Nations in the New World* (University of Alberta Press, 1989); Williams Jr., *The American Indian in Western Legal Thought: The Discourses of Conquest* (Oxford University Press, 1990).

19. This treatment appears for example in Kirby Martin, Steven Mintz, Linda O. McMurry, and James H. J. Jones, *America and Its People, Volume 1: To 1877* (New York: Harper Collins College, 2nd ed. 1993). This is a standard textbook used in undergraduate American history courses!

20. Similar view was put forward by Douglas Ubelaker in his "Prehistoric New World Population Size: Historical Review and Current Appraisal of North American Estimates," *American Journal of Physical Anthropology*, No. 45, 1976. The number he at last arrives at is exactly 2,171,125 (1,850,011 in the States area; 73,326 in Alaska; 237,798 in Canada; 10,000 in Greenland).

21. Mooney died in 1921. The publication posthumously was titled *The Aboriginal Population of America North of Mexico*, and the estimates included were not based on specific or adequate documentation.

22. Jennings, *The Invasion of America: Indians. Colonialism and the Cant of Conquest* (Chapel Hill: University of North Carolina Press, 1975), p. 20. The

emergence of actual "scientific racism" in the United States can probably be dated from Samuel George Morton's *Crania Americana, or, A Comparative View of Skulls of Various Aboriginal Nations of North and South America* (Philadelphia, 1839).

23. Jennings, *The Invasion of America, supra*, pp. 18–19.

24. The work of the Berkeley scholars was not sent to the press until after Kroeber's death, and then only through the press of their home institution. By the early 1950s, the "Berkeley School" had begun increasingly to integrate what might be called agricultural archaeology—extrapolating from the aggregate in regions known to have been under cultivation at the point of contact, in combination with soil type / richness, types of crops planted, and meteorological records to arrive at carrying capacity for local agricultural systems, and thus, population estimates—into their research methods. This allowed them not only a greater degree of precision in computing the numbers of Indians alive in the post-invasion selling, but in the immediate pre-invasion context as well. They were able to advance a hemispheric population estimate of up to 100 million (Woodrow W. Borah and Sherburne F. Cook, *The Aboriginal Population of Central Mexico on the Eve of the Spanish Conquest* /Berkeley: University of California, 1963]).

25. Kirby Martin et al., *America and Its People, op. cit.* pp. 17–19.

26. Steven Katz, *The Holocaust in Historical Context, Volume I: The Holocaust and Mass Death before the Modern Age* (Oxford University Press, 1992), p. 20.

27.Quoted as a title in Nobel David Cook and W. George Lovell, "*Secret Judgments of God*": *Old World Disease in Colonial Spanish America* (University of Oklahoma Press, 1992).

28. Quoted in Ashburn, *The Ranks of Death*, p. 19.

29. Jennings pointedly describes North America as a "widowed" rather than "virgin" land (*Invasion of America, ante*, p. 30).

PART III

Federal Constitutions and Human Rights Law

Chapter 8

Turkish Promotion of Federation

"The proposed creation of two separate states or zones in a small country of the size of Cyprus under the ostensible pretext of the security of the Turkish Cypriot community has no other purpose than under the guise of federation to achieve a partition of the of the island and eventually satisfy the expansionist aims of Turkey which has been the aspiring at such a solution since 1955."

This statement, made by Criton Tornaritis Q.C., formerly attorney-general of the Republic of Cyprus, biased though it may seem, remains to be confirmed in the context of statements made by Turkish politicians.

The Turkish foreign minister the late Zorlu, made no secret at the Tripartite Conference on the Eastern Mediterranean and Cyprus held in London in August–September, 1955 that Turkey had claims on Cyprus. He stated on 1 September 1955: "Turkey is not only in her rights in making such a claim, but it is also in duty to do so. For the importance of Cyprus to Turkey does not arise from a single cause; it is a necessity which emanates from the exigencies of history, geography, economy and military strategy, from the right to existence and security, which is the most sacred right of every State, in short, from the very nature of things."[1]

He supported that in case of self-government, the Greeks and Turks should be treated on a full equality basis without any consideration of numerical majorities and he concluded that, in case the then status quo was disturbed, Cyprus should revert to Turkey. The people of Turkey, he said, cannot conceive in any other way the fate of the island which is of vital importance for the defense of their own soil.

That Turkey raised claims over Cyprus for its own interests rather than the protection of the Turkish Cypriots appears from what the Turkish foreign minister, Mr. Erkin, said at the London Conference on 16 January 1964. After referring to the familiar argument, that of the strategic importance of Cyprus to Turkey, and the geographical position of Cyprus as being a continuation of the Anatolian peninsula he concluded that part of his address, remarking: "all these considerations clearly demonstrate that Cyprus has a vital importance for Turkey not merely because of the existence of a Turkish community on the island, but also on account of its geo-strategic bearing."

Mr. Erkin, furthermore in June 1964, in a newspaper interview in Athens, said that the radical solution would be to cede one part of Cyprus to Greece and the other, closest to the Asiatic coast, to Turkey.[2]

A clear indication of the tactical nature of the use of federation as an official camouflage of partition is contained in the statement of the then Turkish Prime Minister Ismet Inonu in his address to the Turkish National Assembly. On 8 September 1964: *"'officially' we promoted the federation concept, rather 'than the partition thesis so as to remain within the provisions of the Treaty.'"*[3]

It is significant that Mr. Gunes, the Turkish Foreign Minister, put the matter thus:

"Prior to the presumption of the enlarged local talks in Cyprus there were certain agreements referring to the principles on which a possible solution to the Cyprus problem should be based. The granting of local autonomy to the Turkish Cypriot community and the preservation of the fundamental principles, on which the 1960 international agreements are based, were among these agreements. As long as these agreements were respected, some progress was made in the course of the local talks. The difficulties arose when these agreements, which should be respected to the end, were affected by a tendency not to recognize any more the status of partner,[4] enjoyed by the Turkish Cypriot community on the basis of equality with the Greek Cypriot community regarding the participation in the independence, sovereignty and territorial integrity of the state. Consequently, if this tendency were to be abolished and the above agreements as well as the bi-communal character of the Cyprus state were to be respected, I think that it would not be difficult to solve the Cyprus problem in a way satisfying all the parties concerned. For this reason the parties concerned must examine the question sincerely, in a constructive way without insisting on matters of terminology. They must work to find a solution in accord with the island's realities.[5]

NOTES

1. Cmnd. 9595.
2. *Vema,* Greek Newspaper, 1964.
3. Emphasis supplied. The statement may be found in Criton Tornaritis, *Cyprus and its Constitutional and Other Legal Problems, ante* p. 1.
4. The Turkish side used to put forward the allegation that the Republic of Cyprus was run in partnership between the Greek and the Turkish communities, as if it were a joint business concern. From a strict legal point of view, that is not correct. The

1960 Constitution does not contemplate any notion of partnership. The concept was taken from the Macmillan Plan for the solution of the Cyprus problem under which a scheme of partnership was proposed for the government of Cyprus between the three Guarantor states of Great Britain, Greece, and Turkey (Foot, *A Start in Freedom,* London, 1964, pp. 168–170) solution of the problem. There could be a partnership between states in the administration of a certain territory (such as the condominium in international law as to which see Oppenheim-Lauterpacht, *International Law, vol. I*, London 1955, pp. 453–455), but not partnership between two communities.

5. Interview to the Greek Newspaper *Vema*, June 1974.

Chapter 9

The Concept of Federalism

Before embarking upon a detailed examination of the issue whether the federal system may be implemented in the case of Cyprus and particularly, whether it would be compatible with the notion of human rights, let us consider what is meant in public law by federalism and federal state.

The states from a constitutional law standpoint and according to the structure of the state power are classified in *simple* or *unitary* and *composite* states. In the unitary state the state power is one and indivisible comprising all the state functions and is vested in the legal person of the state, which through its organs exercises such power on all physical and legal persons within its territory. The composite state on the other hand consists of the linking together by legal bonds of two or more states, which constitute a union of states. When by the union a new state is created such state is a composite state in contrast to the unitary state.

While in the unitary state power is one and indivisible, in the composite state such power is distributed between the composite state and its constituent members, each of which within its own sphere is sovereign and exercises exclusively the state power conferred on it. In the composite state, the main form of which is the federal state,[1] the political power is divided between the federal state itself and its component parts which usually are states or other territorial areas under various names such as provinces, cantons, and regions having the status of states.

Federalism is a sociological phenomenon. The federal state is constituted by the permanent union of states of restricted competence under a common government and organs.[2]

In the federal state the federal government prevails, which, according to Professor Wheare, "is a system of government which embodied predominantly a division of powers between the general and regional authorities, each of which in its own sphere is co-ordinate with others and independent of them."[3]

Federal government is governed by the federal principle which, according to Professor Wheare, "is the method of dividing the powers so that the general and regional governments are each, within a sphere, co-ordinate and independent, the important point being whether the powers of government are divided between the co-ordinate independent authorities or not."[4] The powers granted to the federal state are of legislative, executive and judicial kind. These powers are exercised by the federal state through its own organs.

NOTES

1. Confederacy constitutes a more loose form of federation between two or more confederated states linked together by a recognized international treaty into a union, for the maintenance of their external and internal independence. History, however, proved that the confederation of states has not been satisfactory. Such confederations were those of the United States of America from 1778 to 1787, of Germany from 1815 to 1866, of Switzerland from 1291 to 1798 and from 1815 to 1848, and the Republic of Central America, which comprised the sovereign states of Nicaragua, Honduras, and San Salvador from 1895 to 1898.
2. Oppenheim-Lauterpacht, *International Law ante*, p. 175.
3. Wheare, *Federal Government*, London, 4th ed., 1963, p. 33.
4. *Ibid*, p. 10.

Chapter 10

Federal State for Cyprus: A Constitutional Law Perspective

Can a federal state be established in Cyprus? It is my submission that such a form of state and system of government would be a very difficult constitutional system. This proposition remains to be examined in the context of constitutional law and history. By the Turkish Cypriot proposals submitted at the Geneva Conference, the Republic of Cyprus shall be composed of two federated states with full control land autonomous within the boundaries of their respective geographical boundaries. The area of the Turkish-Cypriot Federated State shall cover 34 percent of the territory of the Republic falling north of the a general line starting from the Limnitis–Lefka area in the west and running toward the east, passing through the Turkish-controlled part of Nicosia, including the Turkish part of Famagusta and ending at the port of Famagusta. The area so claimed by the Turkish Cypriot side coincides with that of the Attila line. And it is of an extent of 1,075.20 sq. miles (out of 3,572 square miles of the whole area of Cyprus) with a total population of 183,859 inhabitants (out of 577,625 the whole population of Cyprus on the census of 1960). Out of the 183,859 inhabitants of the area, 128,563 are Greek Cypriots and 55,296 are Turkish Cypriots; the percentage of Greek Cypriots being thus 69,92 percent and of the Turkish Cypriots 30.8 percent. In that area there are 94 purely Greek villages with a population of 72,546 44 purely Turkish villages with a population of 15,170 and 444 mixed towns and villages (including the whole town of Kyrenia and part of the town of Famagusta) with a population of 56,017 Greek Cypriots and 40,126 Turkish Cypriots. The total number of the villages in Cyprus is 625 out of which 392 are Greek Cypriots, 120 Turkish Cypriots, and 113 mixed villages.

The prerequisite for the establishment of a federal state is the prior coexistence of two or more independent states or other independent territorial units exercising regional government which desire, for one reason or another such as common defense, economic advantages, geographical factors, to be independent of foreign powers, preexisting political association and the like, to be under the single independent government for some purposes at any rate while at the same time they like to maintain their independent status for some other matters.

Such was the case in Switzerland, which is due to a historical evolution. The Swiss cantons were not formed on the basis of a deliberate application of the principle of nationalities but they were political organizations, which were formed for a number of historical reasons. It is important to remember that the cantons preexisted the Swiss confederation, which for the first five hundred years of its existence was composed of entirely German cantons. From 1291 until the end of the thirteenth century the three forest cantons, Waldstatten Uri, Schwyz, and Nidwalden, forming a union by virtue of the Convention of Friendship of 1291 to which until the sixteenth century another ten civil German cantons have acceded by virtue of the Convention of Stans. The Swiss confederation was recognized by the Treaty of Westphalia of 1968. During the French Revolution and the Napoleonic wars in 1798, a new constitution was imposed under which Switzerland ceased to be a federation, the cantons lost their status as independent states, and the Swiss Republic was created as a unitary state and associated by alliance with France. It was only with the Act of Mediation of Napoleon of 1803, which was based on federal principles, that six French- and Italian-speaking cantons were added to the already existing thirteen, making a total of nineteen, a number increased with the addition of three more French-speaking cantons at the Conference of Vienna 1815, bringing the total number to the present twenty-two. On 12 September 1848 a new constitution of the Swiss state, which though called Confederation is a federal state, was introduced. This constitution was extensively revised in 1874 and finally in 1964.

Switzerland is a federal state consisting of sovereign cantons which exercise their sovereign state power insofar as such power is not restricted by the federal constitution. The federal state guarantees the constitutions of the cantons (article 13). The federal constitution describes in detail the subjects which fall within the competence of the central government and that of the cantons (articles 7–10, 20–41).

Also in the United States of America the federal state of the United States was established in 1787, by the thirteen then British colonies, which constituted separate states in the Federation.

I could multiply the examples by referring to the other federal states such as Canada, the federal states of South America, Australia, U.S.S.R, Austria, Yugoslavia, Federal Republic of Germany, India, Burma, the new African federal states, and others, in all of which its constituent parts preexisted the federal state.

The Turkish side by its proposals submitted at the Geneva Conference supports the adoption of the partition of the one and indivisible territory of the Republic of Cyprus into many states or zones or cantons for the purpose of changing the unitary Republic of Cyprus into a federal state. The prerequisites for the federal state of the type she propounds do not exist, as there were not separate geographical units, which could form the constituent parts of the proposed federal state.[1] Such a course would be against not only the principles of public law but also contrary to the prevailing constitutional practice. The federation aims at uniting already existing separate territorial units and not at artificially creating separate territorial areas within an existing unified territory for the aim of achieving the establishment of a federal state.

The ostensible reason put forward by Turkish officials is that such a region is required for the physical protection of the Turkish Cypriots and to prevent the Greek Cypriots from destroying or enslaving them. But even if such an allegation is correct, one fails to see how the proposed extensive Turkish region could afford any such protection. The majority of the population in the region will be Greek Cypriots. Unless not all of the Greek Cypriot refugees are to return (which would virtually mean violation of human rights) or/and Turkish settlers from mainland Turkey are to be accepted as Cypriot citizens (which would mean to legalize a war crime), so that separate majorities can be effected in the areas administered by the two communities respectively. Conversely, such a settlement would be problematic, as Turkish Cypriots might want to return to their properties in the state under Greek Cypriot administration.

It looks as though it would be necessary to have an exchange of populations so as to turn the predominantly Greek region into a Turkish one. The exchange of populations has been alluded already in 1965 to the United Nations Mediator Dr. Galo Plaza by the then leader of the Turkish Cypriot community, Dr. Kutchuk. But an exchange of populations, even on a voluntary basis,[2] is not an easily feasible matter. It entails many financial but mainly humanitarian repercussions leaving apart its remote consequences and is not looked upon favorably in public law.[3]

NOTES

1. Lord Radcliffe in paragraph twenty-eight of his report says: "But can Cyprus be organized as a federation in this way? I do not think so. There is no pattern of territorial separation between the two communities and, apart from other objections, federation of communities, which does not involve also federation of territories seems to me to be a very difficult constitutional form (Lord Radcliffe, *Constitutional Proposals for Cyprus*, London 1956, Cmnd. 42).

And Dr. Galo Palza in paragraphs 149 and 150, observes, on the other hand, the Turkish Cypriots envisage a federal system within which there would exist autonomous Turkish Cypriot and Greek Cypriot states, the conditions for whose existence would be created by the geographical separation, which they insistently demand of the two communities *(Galo Plaza Report op. cit).*

150. "It is essential to be clear what this proposal implies. To refer to it simply as federation is to oversimplify the matter. What is involved is not merely to establish a federal form of government but also to secure the geographical separation of the two communities. The establishment of a federal state regime requires a territorial basis, and this basis does not exist. In an earlier part of this report, I explained that the island-wide intermingling in normal times of the Greek Cypriot and Turkish Cypriot populations. The events since December, 1963, have not basically altered this characteristic; even the enclaves where numbers of Turkish Cypriots concentrated following the troubles are widely scattered over the island, while thousands of other Turkish Cypriots have remained in mixed villages."

2. It is noteworthy that the Republic of Cyprus government has repeatedly stated in public that what is sought for in the context of a settlement is to secure the *right* to return. But has stressed, nevertheless, that the conditions in the Turkish Cypriot administered state of the federation could be so burdensome for the Greek Cypriots that the refugees might not choose to return. It is here submitted that rights that cannot be implemented are not rights at all and that the aforementioned stance on part of the Cyprus government constitutes political hypocrisy.

3. After the disaster in Asia Minor in 1922 about one and a half million Greeks had to leave their homes. The Conference at Lausanne was faced with a fait accompli and by the Convention VI attached to the Treaty of Lausanne in 1923 a compulsory exchange of populations was provided (see Oppenheim-Lauterpacht, *International Law, op. cit.* p. 553, note 1). Such a course today would be against the accepted principle of self-determination of peoples (Article 1 of the International Covenant on Civil and Political Rights) and the individual right of residence and movement (Article 12 of the International Covenant on Civil and Political rights and relevant articles of the European Convention of Human Rights). Same considerations may be applicable to the voluntary exchange of populations of which we have two examples in diplomatic history; that under the Treaty of Trianon of 27 November 1919, between Greece and Bulgaria, concerning the Greek minority in Bulgaria and the Bulgarian minority in Greece respectively; and the Albanese declaration for the protection of minorities of 2 October 1920.

Chapter 11

Federation and Human Rights

In this section what is to be explored is whether federation for Cyprus could safeguard human rights of the people of Cyprus.

It is here submitted that bi-communal, bi-zonal federation in the case of Cyprus cannot properly provide for adequate implementation of human rights. The first and foremost human right which would be violated is that of self-determination.

The concept of self-determination of peoples was developed especially after World War I.[1] Under the U.N. Charter it became the cornerstone of the General Assembly's decolonization policy of the 1960s and 1970s.

The Charter of the United Nations, in Article 1, paragraph 2, indicates, as one of the purposes of the United Nations "to develop friendly relations among nations based on respect for the principle of equal rights and self-determination of peoples." Articles 55 and 56 of the U.N. Charter develop further this very purpose and have direct relevance to non-self-governing territories. "With a view to promoting the creation of conditions of stability and well-being which are necessary for peaceful and friendly relations among nations based on respect for the principle of equal rights and self-determination of peoples, the United Nations shall promote . . ."[2] In the Declaration on the Granting of Independence to Colonial Territories and Peoples, in paragraphs 1 and 2, the General Assembly declared that: "the subjection of peoples to alien subjugation, domination and exploitation constitutes a denial of fundamental human rights, is contrary to the Charter of the United Nations and is an impediment to the promotion of world peace and co-operation. All peoples have the right to self-determination; by virtue of that right they freely determine their political status and freely pursue their economic, social and cultural development."[3]

So, the concept of self-determination consists in the liberty of the peoples to determine on the internal plane their own government without any foreign intervention—internal self-determination—and on the external field their fate and international status—external self-determination.[4]

The latter has two aspects, a positive one and a negative one. Under the positive aspect peoples may secede from the state to which they belong either by joining another state or by establishing a state of their own while under the negative aspect the peoples cannot be exchanged or ceded against their will, enjoying in this respect a right of independence.

It has to be noted that the right is seen by a large number of writers as a rule of *ius cogens.*[5]

It is worth noting that self-determination was openly violated when in 1977 and 1979 the people of Cyprus, Greek Cypriots as well as Turkish Cypriots, did not decide about their own fate.

Referendum means the process by which the population of a state living in a specific territory decides on the future of that territory. The great number of referendums in history concerns cases of annexation of territories. A referendum can actually bring about three main alternative results: annexation, independence, or federal settlements.

It has to be stressed that the power to conduct the referendum is in the hands of the government, a joint committee or an international commission. It is here submitted that the referendum regarding acceptance or rejection of federation as constitutional framework for settlement of the Cyprus issue should have been held immediately after the High Level Agreements of 1977 and 1979 respectively. Deliberate delay of this process, unfortunately on part of successive Cyprus governments, aims at exerting pressure upon the people to cast a vote in favor of federalism upon agreement of a final settlement, at a stage when it would be rather difficult to decline this governmental system.

It is submitted that the violation of the principle of self-determination, by far the most important human right, brings with it the non-implementation of other basic human rights, namely the right of each Greek Cypriot citizen to settle, to establish himself, to acquire property, to work wherever he pleases. The bi-communalism and the bi-zonal character of the federal state would not allow for implementation of these and other equally important rights. Will the members of the Greek community who will be living in the Turkish zone (and will therefore be a minority) have guarantees for exercising the freedom of religion, of education or of language?[6] The reservation is worth taking into account. It has already been pleaded before the European Court of Human Rights that the obligation of non-discrimination gives way to regional homogeneity;[7] in its decision on the *Case related to certain aspects of the laws on the use of language in education in Belgium*, the European Court of Human Rights seems to have approved this thesis which—it must be recognized—ruins to a large extent the scope of the general principles that one had thought oneself able to deduce. Some elements of an answer appeared in Article 20 of the 1960 Constitution, which gave to each community the task of seeing to the education needs of the whole of the territory. Elements of an answer appear especially in the Greek proposals (list of regional powers) of April 1977 which give exclusive competence to the regions in matters of culture, teaching, and education but, in doing so, take equal account of the liberty given to the minority community to establish and to make its own schools function (which cannot be of an inferior quality the minimum requirements of the public schools of the region). This formula would allow, at least in the field of teaching and in matters annexed, an answer to the needs expressed by a minority community and would give it the opportunity not to disappear. It is noteworthy that article 27 of the pact of the United Nations related to civil and political states particularly that in states where ethnic, religious, or linguistic minorities exist, the individuals belonging to these minorities cannot be deprived of the right of having togetherness with other members of the group, their own cultural life, of exercising and practicing their own religion, or to use their own language. It must also be recalled that the Permanent Court of International Justice remarked, in its notice of 6 April 1935, on the minority schools of Albania (series A/B, no. 64 p. 17) that "the ideas, which form the basis of the treaties for the protection of minorities, is to ensure that the social groups incorporated in a state whose population is of different race, language, or religion from their own, have the possibility of peaceful co-existence and of cordial collaboration with this population, while at the same time maintaining the characteristics, which distinguish them fro m the majority." It is nevertheless, put forward, that the aforementioned rights could not be *effectively* exercised in the framework of a federation in the case of Cyprus. The effective exercise of rights is provided for in article 25, para. 1 of the European Convention of Human Rights. The right to settle, to movement, to acquire property (what are usually called the three basic freedoms) will not be effectively put in practice, simply because the Greek Cypriots would be reluctant to be ruled by the Turkish Cypriots in the land which has always been their own and run by themselves. It has already been stated above that federation is a sociological phenomenon and this aspect of it should not be ignored. There is no reason why the Greek Cypriots should live under the Turkish Cypriots. There are no needs dictating the establishment of a federation. More importantly, the right to education and religion, which are fundamental, the cornerstone of national identity, will not again be effectively implemented, as the meaning of religion, and especially education, in a region under Turkish Cypriot administration will fade away. What would be the point, for example, of teaching the values of Greek history, particularly that of freedom, if the Greeks, the original population of the territory are to be governed unwillingly, if not subjugated, to put the matter rather crudely, by the Turkish Cypriots. This clearly stems from the fact that they have not freely exercised the right of self-determination. Also, who, among young Greek Cypriot scholars and scientists, would go to the state administered by the Turkish Cypriots to practice his profession and, therefore, effectively exercise the right to work? I would certainly not, as I am sure a large percentage of the Greek Cypriot youth would not.

The question of political rights by the minority community in a region can no longer be evaded. Is it sufficient to give them the right to vote? In the best hypothesis, it would be useful to appoint to the assembly or the federal council a representative of the other community within a federated assembly. The constitutional proposals seem, in fact, to exclude the possibility of electing a representative of the minority to the assembly of the majority community: no Greek Cypriot in the Turkish federated assembly; no Turkish Cypriot in the Greek federated assembly. The question is important both on the level doctrine and on the level of politics. Are there two categories of citizens in the state, those who will have the power to exercise the political rights recognized to the citizens and who exercise them at all levels of power, and those who would have certain prerogatives withdrawn from them, because of their minority status, or who would not be able usefully to exercise them because of the general structure of the state? A positive answer would deprive the declarations of adherence to human rights—and in particular those to the political rights of the citizen—of sufficient credibility. A negative answer forces one to suggest techniques and procedures that would allow the minority members of a community to attach themselves *theoretically* and not *territorially* to their community, in order to exercise these rights more effectively. The Greek proposals of 6 April 1977 carry some elements of adherence an answer to this issue. They state in point 3.2 that each citizen must, at least in what concerns the federal state, be able to exercise political rights whatever their location on the territory of the Republic. This formula is particularly interesting. It arises from the idea that the federal authorities are called to exercise their powers, however reduced they be, over the whole of the territory of the state. Taking into account the criteria of balance of power fixed by elsewhere for the representation of the communities, it is justifiable to allow all citizens of the federation to compete directly for the appointment of these authorities. Nothing, for example, would prevent the nationals of the Greek community living in the north of the island from joining the votes with those of the south in electing their representatives to the federal assembly; the same solution would apply to the Turkish Cypriots living in the south of the island.

On the other hand, no suggestion is made for the exercise of political rights regarding the administration of the region in which the citizen resides; it is simply noted that this question should be the subject of constitutional arrangements. The problems of local administration, particularly that of towns, also remain in their entirety. The constitutional proposals formulated from both sides are discreet on this subject.

Furthermore, it should be noted that in the context of bi-zonal, bi-communal federation, the democratic principle is further violated, at the level of central government. It was obvious, since the Zurich Agreements and subsequent 1960 Constitution, that the ratio of participation of Turkish Cypriots in central government was not proportionate to their population percentage. Actually, it far exceeded this percentage. At points it even reached 40 percent. It is clear that at the executive, participation of the Turkish Cypriots to such an extent would be in violation of the accepted constitutional principle of democracy.[8] The one extreme of democratic theory says that peoples who should properly be treated as minorities cannot be granted privileges that are not proportionate to their numbers. At the other end, there are advocates of the opinion that they should be given governmental positions that do not necessarily equally correspond to their numeric capability.[9]

In my view, the proposed constitutional form will be worse than partition. The repercussions from such a solution would be catastrophic for both communities of Cyprus. I should like to make clear that, as a matter of principle I would never adhere to partition as possible settlement to the Cyprus issue. However, I must note that a bi-communal federal or confederate state, under the camouflage of federation, would bring about the end of the Cyprus Republic. It is essential that human rights are properly and fully safeguarded and expressly stipulated in any settlement plan. Deviations from human rights should not be acceptable by either community.

NOTES

1. See generally, Cassese, *Self-Determination* of Peoples (1995); Mullerson, *International Law, Rights and Politics* (1994), chapter 2; Shaw, *Title to Territory in Africa* (1986).

2. U.N. Charter Article 55. Article 56 of the Charter reads: "All members shall pledge themselves to take joint and separate action in co-operation with the organization for the achievement of the purposes set forth in Article 55."

3. G.A. Resolution 1514 (XV), 14 December 1960, *G.A.O.R. 15th Session, Supp.*16, p. 66. Also see International Covenant on Civil and Political Rights, 1966, Article 1, para 1: "All people have the right of self-determination." The issue of self-determination was further developed by the International Court of Justice in the Western Sahara Case (*Advisory Opinion, I.C.J. Reports* 1975, p. 12).

4. See Emerson, Self-Determination, *American.J.I.L.* (1971) vol. 65, p. 465. For the application of the right of self-determination to the Turkish Cypriot community, see the discussion in the context of the "TRNC," in chapter 5 above.

5. See for example Espiel, in Cassese, ed. *U.N Law / Fundamental Rights: Two Topics in International Law* (1979), p.167. See also Calogeropoulos-Stratis, *The Right of Peoples to Self-determination (in Greek) Athens, 1977 p. 335.*

6. Similar argument could be made for the Turkish Cypriot community; but one should be careful to see that the Turkish Cypriots, as already shown in chapter 5 above, cannot exercise the right to self-determination and establish a state of their own in a separate region, which has historically been predominantly Greek; it has also been indicated that Turks and Greeks lived peacefully together dispersed in various parts of the northern as well as the southern part of the island.

7. European Court of Human Rights, *A matter relative to certain aspects of the linguistic system of education in Belgium*, vol. 2 Strasburg 1968, p. 135. Similar the last paragraph of the proposals of the Turkish Cypriot community also provides that the rights will in principle be safeguarded and on condition that similar observances be submitted to the laws and regulations of the federated state and does not harm the territorial integrity and homogeneity of the population of the Turkish federated state of Cyprus.

8. See extensively, Ivor Jennings, *The Law and the Constitution* (Cambridge: Cambridge University Press, 1959).

9. See Vernon Bogdanor, *The Democratic Principle* (Oxford: Oxford University Press, 1990).

Chapter 12

European Union Involvement in the Settlement of the Cyprus Issue

Given the accession process of Cyprus into the European Union it is important to see if the Acquis Communautaire could bring about implementation of human rights in Cyprus. In an opinion, the European Commission concluded: "On the subject of respect for democracy and human rights, two points must be taken into account, namely that the island's forced partition alone represents a serious infringement of the fundamental freedoms of citizens of Cyprus and the rights of victims of the events of 1974 have not yet been restored owing to the lack of a political settlement. The presence of a considerable number of Turkish settlers and the demographic changes that result from this are also considered as an infringement of the political and economic rights of the people, including some sectors of the Turkish Cypriot public opinion. Apart from the direct and indirect consequences of the partition of the island, the human rights situation is as follows. The constitution of Cyprus protects the rights of people belonging to the three national minorities and establishes freedom of speech and the right to free assembly, equality of all before the law and bans all forms of discrimination. The independence of the judiciary is guaranteed. All these provisions are effectively respected. However, in the north of the island, opposition parties have mentioned certain constraints and restrictions in their activities, in particular as regards access to the media."[1] It goes on to say that "a settlement would open the way to the full restitution of human rights and fundamental freedoms throughout the island, and would encourage the development of a pluralist democracy."

Also the opinion says: "As result of the de facto division of the island into two strictly separated parts, the fundamental freedoms laid by the Treaty, and in particular freedom of movement of goods, people, services and capital, right of establishment and the universally recognized political, economic, social and cultural rights could not today be exercised over the entirety of the island's territory. These freedoms and rights would not have to be guaranteed as part of a comprehensive settlement restoring constitutional arrangements covering the whole of the Republic of Cyprus."[2]

The commission also refers to the political rights that should be safeguarded in the context of a settlement of the Cyprus issue. "This Opinion has also shown that Cyprus' integration with the Community implies a peaceful, balanced and lasting settlement to the Cyprus question—a settlement which will make it possible for the two communities to be reconciled, for confidence to be re-established and for their respective leaders to work together. While safeguarding the essential balance between the two communities and the right of each to preserve its fundamental interests, the institutional provisions contained in such a settlement should create the appropriate conditions for Cyprus to participate normally in the decision-making process of the European Union and in the correct application of Community law throughout the island."[3]

The possible scenarios, however, vary. One such scenario is that accession of Cyprus into the European Union can take place before a settlement of the Cyprus issue is found. Such a development would, according to one view, facilitate settlement, and European community law—especially the relevant corpus on human rights—would have to be implemented in any such settlement in the future. Another view, though says that such a possibility is rather distant, because the December 1999 Helsinki summit, noted that a political settlement was not a prerequisite to Cyprus' accession, but all factors should be considered in the decision on whether to proceed. The Turkish government has put forward legal arguments with regard to this, that Cyprus EU accession is illegal, basing their claim on the Cyprus Treaty of Guarantee. Professor Mendelson has given legal opinion to the government of Turkey maintaining that Article 1, paragraph 2 of the Treaty of Guarantee 1960, by which the Republic of Cyprus undertakes not to participate, in whole or in part, in any political or economic union with any state whatsoever and it accordingly declares prohibited any activity likely to promote, directly or indirectly, either union with any other state or partition of the island, runs contrary to Cyprus' accession to the European Union, because (a) it would amount to participation in whole in an economic union, (b) to the extent that the EU also constitutes a political union, this undertaking would also be infringed, (c) it would be likely to promote, directly or indirectly, union with Greece, the name of the European Union bears out the fact that it is about union between its members, (d) Cyprus had promised to refrain from any activity aimed at promoting, directly or indirectly, its union with any other state. In a footnote, he makes reference to the Austro-German Customs Union Case of the Permanent Court of International Justice, which held that Austria's entry into customs union with Germany would constitute an alienation of its economic independence, contrary to Protocol I of 4 October. The arguments of Mendelson have been repelled by Professors Crawford and Pellet, who refer to the *travaux preparatoires* of the Treaty of Guarantee. Specifically, they refer to point 22 of the Basic Structure of the Republic of Cyprus, signed at Zurich on 11 February 1959. According to this, "it shall be recognized that the total or partial union of Cyprus with any other State, or a separatist independence for Cyprus (i.e., the partition of the island into two independent states) shall be excluded. By referring to the Vienna Convention on the Law of Treaties they argue that the interpretation must be based on good faith and that the language must be seen in its context and in the light of its purpose. By reference to Articles 50 and 169 of the Cyprus Constitution which speak of international organizations and pacts of alliance or international agreements with a foreign state or any international organization relating to commercial matters, economic cooperation they point out that the treaty distinguishes between political and economic union with any other state and other forms of international cooperation. They say that what is prohibited is union with another state, not cooperation with a group of states in establishing a supranational organization of a political and / or economic union, and that a distinction has always been drawn between membership of multilateral organizations of states and the political or economic union with another state. The EU is not a state, it is a supranational organization or an independent legal order, a legal system of a trans-national character, although it aspires to more perfect union. Therefore membership of the EU does not involve political or economic union with any state. They further clearly distinguish the Austro-German Customs Union Case from the case of Cyprus, as the latter would be less independent on any single state such membership in contrast to the then eventual domination of Austria by Germany.

The Copenhagen summit meeting of 12 December 2002, however, has proved wrong the view above cited. At the summit, the Cyprus Republic has become member of the European Union without preconditions.

A second scenario has been put forward by two experts in international relations, namely Henri Barkey, Cohen Professor of International Relations at Lehigh University and a former member of the State Department's Policy Planning Staff, and Philip Gordon, senior fellow in Foreign Policy States at the Brookings Institution and former director for European Affairs at the National Security Council. According to this scenario, an option supported by many pro-European intellectuals and government officials in Turkey would be for the United States to encourage the EU to offer Turkey a date for the start of its own EU accession negotiations in exchange for a deal on Cyprus.[4] Turkey has long resented the fact that the EU offered Turkey candidacy status only reluctantly and under American pressure. This has led many Turks to conclude that the offer was not sincere, and that Turkey will never be allowed into the EU. A concrete date for starting accession negotiations—for example by 2004, when many of the other candidates are expected to join the EU would go far to change these perceptions.[5] There are problems with this approach, however. Most importantly, Washington would find it difficult to successfully persuade the EU to give Turkey the date it seeks. Brussels does not want to depart from its traditional process whereby accession negotiations begin when the Copenhagen Criteria are met, and not the other way around. The resurgence of the right in recent European elections this year, combined with growing European concerns about southern immigration waves, makes it even less likely that European leaders will want to make near-term overtures to Turkey.

Another scenario, enthusiastically endorsed by the American policy makers, is that if an early Cyprus settlement cannot be reached is to seek to link a Cyprus deal to Turkey's eventual EU accession. The biggest problem with the EU's regional accession process is the fact that the timetables for Cyprus and Turkey are so different. With Turkey's accession so distant, Ankara has little incentive to press for Turkish Cypriot concessions as a means of facilitating its own EU entry. Deferring a comprehensive Cyprus solution until the time when Turkey's accession is possible deals with this major problem. The United States should focus initially on minimizing the damage from a divided Cyprus' accession and keeping regional cooperation on track. Instead of denouncing the Turkish Cypriots and Turkey, Greece and the Greek Cypriots would explicitly state that the door to a Cyprus settlement and Turkey's EU accession remains open and that they look forward to working toward that goal.

If the Greek Cypriots refused to show such magnanimity, Washington would remind them that they would be writing off any prospect for a future settlement to the Cyprus deal, and buying themselves a tense relationship with Turkey that could not possibly be in their interest.[6] The United States and Europe would also need to persuade the Turkey not to carry out its threats to incorporate northern Cyprus into Turkey or take other provocative measures, which Washington would feel obliged to denounce in the UN Security Council and which could provoke even harsher measures from U.S. Congress or EU Parliament. Turkey would instead have to acknowledge the reality of the ultimate settlement of the Cyprus conflict will require the territorial concessions and acceptance of Cyprus as a loosely united entity. To bolster their cooperation while a long-term Cyprus solution is pursued, Greece and Turkey should commit to further progress in their ongoing economic and diplomatic rapprochement.[7]

Deferring a Cyprus settlement until Turkey can join the European Union would reassure the Turkish Cypriots, who understandably worry about their future within an EU that would not include Turkey as a counterweight to

Greece and the Greek Cypriots. It would not only give Turkey an added incentive to continue down the European path, but also it would give Greece and Turkey an added incentive to promote Turkey's EU membership with all the positive benefits for Turkish society, democracy, and relations with its neighbors that this would entail (even though such an eventuality seems to be rather difficult, because of influence of the Turkish military regime in the running of the state).

However, even if a settlement to the Cyprus issue along the lines of bi-communal federation is to be found after the accession of Cyprus to the EU (which is now the only prospect), it has to be noted that the federal system, given the particular circumstances of Cyprus, would be—according to the preceding analysis—*ab initio* in open violation to the acquis communautaire, especially that part of it dealing with human rights. In the *ex parte Brunner Case*, tried in the aftermath of the Maastricht Treaty before the Supreme Constitutional Court of Germany, it was held that the "member States are the masters of the Treaties." The clear implication of this important decision is that European community law is made by consent of the states members. Since, therefore, the communities of Cyprus have decided that the framework for a settlement is a bi-communal federation, which clearly stands in contradiction to human rights principles, then the European Union cannot rectify, so to speak, possible deficiencies of such a settlement. It can make sure, for instance, that no more settlers are brought from Turkey, that all refugees are granted the *right to return*, but the structure of the state, the governmental system as agreed at the High Level meetings between Makarios and Denktash in 1977 cannot be altered.

NOTES

1. Bulletin of the European Communities, 5/1997. *Ibid.* para. 17.
2. *Ibid.* para. 10.
3. *Ibid.* para. 47
4.See Henri Barkey and Philip Gordon, *Avoiding a Cyprus Crisis*, Policy Brief, July 2002, www.brook.edu/comm/policybriefs/pb102.htm.
5. *Ibid*, p. 4.
6. *Ibid.*, p. 5.
7. *Ibid.*, p. 5.

Chapter 13

The Legal Principles *Pacta Sunt Servanda* and *Rebus Sic Stantibus*

The aim of this chapter is to prove that the agreement concluded by Makarios and Denktash is not valid or has been void ab initio.

On the one hand, according to the international law principle pacta sunt servanda, as the name of the maxim goes, the parties to an Agreement have to comply with the agreement provisions. It is an axiom of international law, going back to the London Declaration of 1871, that international treaties concluded by consent of the parties are to be respected.

Following this principle, the High Level Agreements of 1977 and 1979 respectively are legally valid.

On the other hand, international agreements are not binding and therefore become ineffective if the consent given by a party is not genuine or has been extracted by coercion.

Writers on international law appear to be unanimous in the opinion that, with the possible exception of treaties of peace, which are often imposed by the victorious belligerent upon a state, which has been defeated in war, freedom of consent by the parties is an essential condition of the validity of a treaty. Grotius maintained that the law of nature required the observance of the principle of equality in the making of treaties, there ought to be freedom of choice by the parties and that their consent should not be induced by the fear.[1] To this principle he recognized one exception, which he said had been introduced with the consent of nations, namely that where a war has been publicly declared and waged on both sides, all promises made in the course of the war for the for the purpose of terminating it are valid to the extent that they cannot be made without the reason of fear unjustly inspired, except with the consent of the party to whom the promise has been made.[2]

Vattel also likewise recognized the treaties of peace constituted an exception to the general rule of freedom of consent. As to this he said:

"A sovereign cannot dispense himself from observing a treaty of peace by alleging that it was extorted to him by fear or by constraint. In the first place, if this plea were admitted, it would make it impossible for the any reliance upon to be put upon treaties of peace. For there are few such treaties against which that plea could not be brought as a cover for bad faith. To authorize such an evasion would amount to an attack upon the common safety and welfare of nations; the principle would be condemned as abhorrent by the same reasons, which make the faithful observance of treaties a universally sacred duty. Besides the plea would almost always be disgraceful and absurd. It hardly ever happens at the present day that a Nation waits until it is reduced to the last extremity before making peace; it may have been defeated in several battles, but it can still defend itself; and it is not without resources so long as it has men and arms. If a Nation finds it prudent to procure, by a disadvantageous treaty, a necessary peace; if it delivers itself from imminent danger, or from complete destruction, by making great sacrifices, whatever it thus saves is an advantage, which it owes to the treaty of peace; it freely chooses a loss that is present and certain, but limited in extent, in preference to a disaster, not yet arrived, but very probable, and terrible in character."[3]

Nonetheless, Vattel admitted that it was possible to conceive of treaties of peace so unjust and oppressive that the plea of constraint would be justified.

The Harvard Draft Convention on International Law states the position clearly: "As the term is used in this Convention, duress involves the employment of coercion directed against the persons signing a treaty on behalf of the a State or against the persons engaged in ratifying or acceding to a treaty on behalf of a state; provided that, if the coercion has been directed against a person signing a treaty on behalf of a state and if with the knowledge of this fact the treaty has later been ratified by that Sate without coercion."[4]

The High Level Agreements of 1977, according to the learned writers quoted above, have to be considered as legally invalid, as great pressure was exerted on Makarios upon signing the treaty. There is ample evidence to suggest that Clifford, the special representative of the U.S. president, exerted heavy pressure upon Makarios, so that he might persuade him to accept the Agreements. The treaty was not a treaty of peace, despite views to the opposite, that is the armed conflict between Turkey and Cyprus in 1974 could have been entirely catastrophic for the Republic of Cyprus; in other words, had the treaty not been signed, the whole territory of Cyprus would have been occupied by the Turkish troops. The Turkish intervention, furthermore, was an illegal act, and the occupation, a de facto situation created thereafter as a result, a manifest illegality in international law. *Debellatio,*[5] that is *total subjugation* of the Cyprus state, has never been the case.

Also, the 1977 Agreements ought to be considered invalid, because a principle of utmost importance so dictates, namely, *rebus sic stantibus*. This very principle, requires elaborate analysis.[6]

Some writers asserted that the doctrine originated in Roman Law, in the sense that every contract carried with it the implied condition of *rebus sic stantibus*.

Roman Law as it is laid down in the Corpus Juris Civilis of Justinian did not know the clause rebus sic stantibus, as a legal institution in the sense in which we understand it today. From the point of view of rebus sic stantibus, the most important institution of Roman law was the legis action per condictionem, one of the five actiones, through which the law recognized as a basis for claim the fact that one party had been unjustly enriched at the expense of the other.[7] A special case for the use of the condictio casus a date a causa non secuta[8] was one of the rules of Roman law from which the doctrine of rebus sic stantibus was subsequently derived. The particular rules which give the party concerned the right of rescission or withdrawal from the contract on account of the supervening changes in the circumstances are to be found in the various places as of the Corpus Juris Civilis of Justinian. It was the fact that as a result of the work of the glossators and commentators, extending over many centuries that a principle rebus sic stantibus was derived from unconnected individual cases scattered in various texts of Roman and Canon law and worked into a comprehensive theory.

On the assumption that legal relationships between states were not basically different from those between individuals, the early writers on international law transplanted the doctrine, together with an number of private law institutions, into the general corpus of international law.

The first writer to mention the doctrine in a work entirely devoted to a question of international law appears to have been Gentili, who conceives the doctrine as a general mental reservation implied in wills, and contracts.[9] His most significant contribution to the doctrine of rebus sic stantibus is its application to peace treaties. At the time of the general recognition of the doctrine, Grotius appears to have been the first to reject it, though his attitude toward rebus sic stantibus is not devoid of ambiguity. His innovation is to treat the whole question of changed circumstances as basically a problem of treaty, interpretation and so to give the rule of rebus sic stantibus a juridical foundation in the contractual intention of the parties. His overt rejection and at the same time covert admission of the clausula as a rule of treaty interpretation made it possible to both adherents and opponents of the doctrine of rebus sic stantibus to appeal to Grotius. He became, because of his great authority, the source of divergent, often contradictory views on the doctrine.

Vattel developed the Grotian interpretation and scrutinized the juridical foundation of the doctrine rebus sic stantibus. His theory derives the rule rebus sic stantibus from the intention of the parties at the time of the making of the treaty and thereby places the whole question of changed circumstances within the field of treaty interpretation.[10] He thus connected the doctrine with the notions of the motive of the promise Thus Vattel's contribution has decisively influenced successive generations of jurists and has become one of the main constructors of the doctrine.

It is the work of the International Law Commission and the resulting Vienna Convention on the Law of Treaties, 1969 that the doctrine of rebus sic stantibus has reached the last phase of its development and is now interpreted and an objective rule of law. The preponderance of the opinion of the commission has already had a decisive influence on the views of writers[11] and it is believed that it will determine the future position of the doctrine.

Already in the Harvard Draft Convention on International law 1934,[12] the principle was laid down explicitly. Article 28 stipulates: (a) A treaty entered into with reference to the existence of a set of facts the continued existence of which was envisaged by the parties as a determining factor moving them to take the obligations stipulated may be terminated, declared by a competent international tribunal or authority to have been ceased to be binding, in the sense of calling for further performance, when that state of facts has been essentially changed. (b) Pending agreement by the parties upon decision by a competent international tribunal or authority, the party, which seeks such a declaration, may provisionally suspend performance of its obligations under the treaty. (c) A provisional suspension of the performance by the party seeking such a declaration will not be justified definitely until a decision to this effect has been made rendered by the competent international tribunal or authority.

Paragraph (a) envisages a declaration by a competent international tribunal or authority that a treaty has ceased to be binding, in the sense of calling for further performance, provided: first, that the parties entered into the treaty with reference to the existence of a certain state of facts; second, that the continued existence of this state of facts was envisaged by the parties as a determining factor moving them to undertake the obligations stipulated; and third, that this state of facts has been essentially changed. The declaration is to be that the treaty has ceased to be binding in the sense of calling for further performance; it is to have no effect, therefore, upon stipulations of the treaty which have been performed prior to the occurrence of the change. The term international tribunal or authority would include such bodies as the International Court of Justice, arbitral tribunals, the U.N. Security Council, etc. The possibility will tend to discourage a provisional suspension of performance by a party unless it has substantial grounds to expect that a competent international tribunal or authority will render a decision declaring that the treaty is no longer binding and that the provisional suspension was definitely justified.[13]

Even though it has been subbed that justification if recourse to the doctrine of rebus sic stantibus could be derived from criteria, this is not to say that the opinion of the parties could be ignored altogether in this matter. In fact, when it can be established that at the time of the conclusion of a treaty the parties agreed that the presence of certain circumstances was a fundamental consideration, the treaty may be terminated, by applying the doctrine of rebus sic stantibus in the event of a supervening change of circumstances. But a state claiming that a change of circumstances has occurred which in its opinion justifies the application of the doctrine, has in general no right to terminate, suspend, or modify unilaterally the operation of the treaty.[14]

Once it is recognized that the doctrine rebus sic stantibus is a lawful ground for the termination of treaties, it is possible to explain its proper relationship to the rule *pacta sunt servanda*. This is necessary because in a number of cases an intended termination of a treaty by virtue of that rule was met with the objection that treaties were to be observed according to the rule pacta sunt servanda. This objection implies that this rule has a priority over, and therefore excludes, the operation of the rule rebus sic stantibus. This, however, is not the case. According to a widely accepted view, the particular rule rebus sic stantibus forms a special exception to the general norm pacta sunt servanda. This exception finds its juridical basis in the higher principles of good faith and justice, which, in certain recognized cases, set limits to the requirement of faithful performance of treaties.[15] Although this view is inadequate to reconcile the principle of rebus sic stantibus with that of pacta punt servanda, it fails to get to the root of the problem. In order to do so, one must start from the true meaning of both rules. Pacta sunt servanda means that every treaty in force is binding upon the parties to it and must be performed by them in good faith.[16] A treaty which is not in force either because it is invalid from origin (void) or because it has lost its force by virtue of its own terms or by operation of law is not governed by the rule pacta sunt servanda. The range of the application of the rule does not extend beyond two points; that is, where a legitimate ground for terminating, revising, or suspending the treaty, such as rebus sic stantibus, has begun to operate. Within this range pacta sunt servanda admits no exception. Pacta sunt servanda means that treaties are inviolable, but it does not mean that treaties cannot be terminated or modified. Where it is by law established that by lawful procedure a rule for the termination or revision of the treaty applies, the rule pacta sunt servanda ceases to operate. The sphere of its application ends where that of the doctrine rebus sic stantibus begins. The rule rebus sic stantibus is not in conflict with the rule pacta sunt servanda. It follows that objections to the doctrine of rebus sic stantibus on pacta sunt servanda grounds cannot be maintained, unless it is admitted that the purpose of such objections is merely to provide a procedural safeguard against the arbitrary application of the doctrine in the absence of compulsory international adjudication.

In the light of the above discussion, it may be inferred that the High Level Agreements 1977 and 1979 between Makarios and Denktash, and Kyprianou-Denktash respectively, are no longer legally valid. The fundamental change of circumstances in the intervening years leads to this conclusion; particularly the Unilateral Declaration of Independence of the Turkish Republic of Northern Cyprus in 1983 (as well as of the Turkish Federated State of Cyprus which preceded it) is a clear indication that the circumstances have severely changed, because of the Turkish insistence on the creation of two separate states in Cyprus. The Turkish plans to promote partition of the island have been pointed out at the beginning of this chapter.

Also the argument put forward by Turkey and the Turkish Cypriot Leadership (unfortunately adopted impliedly in the U.N. Secretary General's Statement 2000, "the equal status of the parties must expressly be recognized") namely that Confederation and not federation should be the constitutional framework for a settlement to the Cyprus issue, is indicative of the Turkish disregard of the High Level Agreements, and the real intentions behind the fig leaf of federalism.

NOTES

1. *De Jure Belli ac Pacis*, lib. II, Chapter XII, section. 10, Classics of International Law, Kelsey trans., p. 348.

2. *Ibid*., lib. II, Chapter XVII, section 19, and lib. III, Chapter XIX, section 11, Kelsey trans., pp. 445 and 798.

3. *Droit des Gens*, lib. IV, Chapter IV, section 37, Classics of International law, Fenwick trans., p. 356.

4. Harvard Law School, Harvard Draft Convention on International Law, *American J. I. L 1934, p. 1096–1097.*

5. On which, see generally Schwarzenberger, *A Manual of International Law, op. cit.*

6. See McNair, *The Law of Treaties, ante*, p. 68; *British YB.I.L.* 11 (1930), p. 109. But see Waldock, Second Report, p. 83. It would seem that both in Greece and Rome there were certain circumstances under which it was permissible to break a treaty. Thus the argument that a complete change of circumstances existing at the time of the conclusion of treaty an alliance gives release from the obligations of the treaty made by Lycius, the Acarnanian envoy at Sparta, with regard to the treaty between the Spartans and the Aetolians ("If the circumstances are the same now as at the time of the time when you made alliance with the Aetolians, then your policy ought to remain on the same lines. That was your first proposition. But if they have been

entirely changed, then it is fair that you should now deliberate on the demands made to you as on a matter entirely new and unprejudiced [Polybius, *Historiae,* IX, 37]).

7. Nicholas, *Roman Law* (London, 1975).

8. Institutes of Gaius, II, Commentary, p. 141, n. 3 (ed. F. de Zulueta, Oxford University Press, 1953).

9. *De Jure Belli Libri Tres* (q126212). The reservation is: provided affairs remain in the same condition.

10. If it is certain and evident that the consideration of the circumstances existing at the time of the treaty entered into the motive of the promise, that the promise was made in view and because of those circumstances, the promise is dependent upon the continued existence of the same circumstances. This is evident, since the promise was only made upon that supposition. When therefore the circumstances essential to the promise, and without which it certainly would not have been made, happen to change, the promise falls when its basis is destroyed; and in particular cases, when circumstances cease from tome to timer as be the same as those which brought about or helped to bring about the promise, an exception should be made to its enforcement *(Le Droit des Gens*, 1758, vol. III, p. 211).

11. See for example, Brownlie, *Principles of Public International Law, op. cit*, pp. 616–18; O'Connell, *International Law, ante*, p. 278, fn.

12. See Harvard Law School, Draft Convention on International Law, 1934 *American J.I.l.*

13. Instances of application of the doctrine include: the separation of Belgium from Holland in 1830/3–1839, the cession of Savoy and Nice to France in 1860, the unification of Italy in 1859–1861, the arrangement concerning the international status of Luxembourg in 1867, the abolition of the Anglo-French financial control of in Egypt in 1882–1883, the abrogation of the treaties relating to the international status of Belgium by Article 31 of the Versailles Treaty in 1919, the revision of the Lausanne Convention in 1936, especially the arguments of the Turkey, Greece, and the Soviet Union, and the revision of the Italian Peace Treaty in 1951 and 1954.

14. Such rule was expressed in the by the following states: The Netherlands in 1930–1931, Great Britain and France in 1846, Denmark, Great Britain, France, Russia, Sweden, and Norway in 1864, France in 1882, the United States in 1896, Great Britain in 1906, Austria, France, Germany, Great Britain, Italy, Russia, and the United States in 1914 and 1922–1923, France in 1928 and 1932, Great Britain, Italy, France, Belgium, Czechoslovakia, Spain, and the Council of the League of Nations in 1935–1936, Great Britain in 1947, Great Britain, the United States and France and the Federal Republic of Germany in 1958, Iraq in 1969, and Great Britain in 1973 (*U.S. Digest of International Law, op. cit*. pp. 184–185).

15.This view was developed by municipal courts in order to justify termination or modification of contracts on account of changes circumstances in the absence of a customary or statutory rule. This view is now generally accepted in municipal law, especially in English, German, Swiss, and French law.

16. Article 26 of the Vienna Convention on the Law of Treaties.

PART IV

American Federal Constitution: A Model for Cyprus

Chapter 14

Federal Judicial Power

The present chapter as well as the ones following are not designed to describe by way of summary the U.S. Constitution. It aims at analyzing some important features of the U.S. Constitution which might be implemented mutatis mutandis in the case of the Cyprus Republic.

OVERVIEW OF SEPARATION OF POWERS AND DIVISION OF POWERS PRINCIPLES

The separation of powers along with its vertical counterpart, sometimes called the "division of powers" that constitutes federalism commands and pervades American constitutional law. The separation of powers shapes not only topics that obviously implicate governmental structure or the allocation of power, such as the remedial powers of the federal courts or congressional delegations of authority to administrative agencies, but also issues that one might assume to be animated at least as much by substance as by structure, such as the values of fairness embodied in the law of due process. Separation of powers principles have this pervasive effect because they involve the very structure of government, and nothing lies closer to the core of constitutional law—law that constitutes (that, in its Latin roots, causes things to come together and stand up)—than the system of divided and interlocking powers embodied in the framework of government.

The separation of powers doctrine that has evolved over the last two hundred years is a product less of political philosophy than of practical experience. Modern notions of the separation of powers cannot easily be distilled from the philosophical inclinations of the Framers, whatever normative force those intentions might hold for constitutional interpretation today. Both the Framers and the men participating in the first administration under the new Constitution (often, of course, the same persons) were concerned more with improving the efficiency and capabilities of the national government than with creating a system of government based on the abstract maxims of political philosophers. Although separation of powers concepts played a role in shaping the views of those who forged the nascent government, the views expressed were not doctrinaire—in part because there was no clear doctrine. Although it may be something of an overstatement, it is roughly true that the historical evidence suggests that the Framers' idea of separation of powers was unformed and tentative, and that they had few fixed institutional arrangements in mind beyond the basic principle that there should be a separation. In many instances, separation of powers ideas were used as a rhetorical weapon with which to belabor political opponents or legitimize one's own constitutional preferences, rather than as a clear guide for the construction of a safe and effective government.

We must therefore seek an understanding of the Constitution's separation of powers not primarily in what the Framers thought, nor in what Enlightenment political philosophers wrote, but in what the Constitution itself says and does. What counts is not any abstract theory of separation of powers, but the actual separation powers operationally defined by the Constitution. Therefore, where constitutional text is informative with respect to a separation of powers issue, it is important not to leap over that text in favor of abstract principles that one might wish to see embodied in the United States regime of separated powers, but that might not in fact have found their way into the Constitution's structure.

Caution is called for as well when bringing abstract principles to bear in the interpretation of constitutional text. In *Morrison v. Olson*, a case in which the court upheld the judicial appointment of statutory independent prosecutors, Justice Scalia in dissent read into the vesting clauses of Articles I, II, and III a stark separation with respect to prosecutorial power—which he viewed as exclusively executive in nature—unsupported by any constitutional text and belied by history.

The same principle applies with equal force to interpretation of the Constitution's vertical structure. In order to grasp United States federalism, one must focus not primarily on abstract theories or examples from other national charters, but on the peculiar edifice of national and state governments erected by the Constitution—an edifice no less real by virtue of being implicit in the Constitution's plan rather than explicit in its text. Justice Scalia has emphasized the importance of this point in understating the concept of federalism. In *Printz v. United States,* a closely divided court struck down a federal law requiring county sheriffs and other local law enforcement officers to conduct background checks on prospective handgun purchasers as part of a federal gun control program. Under the Articles of Confederation, the national government, like some other current and former federations, had made laws addressed to the states as political bodies and used the states as instruments of federal governance. But the court held in *Printz* that the Framers of the Constitution rejected the concept of a central government that would act upon and through the states, and deliberately departed from these models to create a legal system unprecedented in form and design, establishing two orders of government, each with its own direct relationship, its own privity, its own set of mutual rights and obligations to the people who sustain it and are governed by it.

In response to Justice Breyer's urging in dissent that the majority consider the benefits that foreign nations and the European Union have derived from their versions of federal governance, Justice Scalia replied for the majority that such comparative analysis is inappropriate to the task of interpreting a constitution, though it was of course quite relevant to the task of writing one. The Framers were familiar with many federal systems, from classical antiquity down to their own time, but the fact is that US federalism is not Europe's. It is the unique contribution of the Framers to political science and political theory.

With respect to both federalism and separation of powers, the structure—as revealed by the explicit text and implicit plan or design of the Constitution—is paramount. At times, text will be sufficient, without necessarily developing an overarching vision of the structure, to decide major cases: thus, the Presentment Clause and the bicamerality requirement furnished the rule of decision in *INS v. Chadha*. The Presentment Clause alone furnished the rule in *Clinton v. City of New York*. The Appointments Clause did the same for *Buckley v. Valeo* and *Morrison v. Olson*. Sometimes, however, it will be necessary to extrapolate what amounts to a blueprint of organizational relationships from the fundamental structural postulates ones sees as informing the Constitution as a whole; such a method is appropriate, for example, to decide the kinds of federalism issues the court had to confront in cases like *National League of Cities v. Usery*, *New York v. United States*, and *Printz v. United States*. The sort of extrapolation appropriate in deciding such federalism issues is similarly appropriate where explicit constitutional text provides little help in deciding separation of powers issues, such as questions of presidential privilege or immunity, or questions of congressional standing.

The rise of the administrative state, and of independent agencies like the Securities and Exchange Commission and the Federal Reserve Board, presents a challenging case with respect to the Constitution's plan of government. Probably the fact that such agencies, despite their novelty in terms of anything imagined by the Framers, must operate within boundaries established by Congress and enforced by the federal judiciary prevents them from representing a true fourth branch of government and thus violating the Constitution, however great the supposed need for such agencies might be. It is useful to contrast the delegation of power to such agencies with attempts by Congress to delegate power to itself—or to one of its houses or a committee or other body within Congress or subject to Congress' control. Such inward-turning delegation, typically designed to attach a congressional leash to an agency to which Congress initially delegated broad power, might or might not make good practical sense in terms of the political dynamics of the situation, but certainly seems to change quite radically the design, or structure, of the Constitution's diagram of power, by entrusting to the national legislature a direct role in enforcing, applying, or implementing its own laws. The Supreme Court's decision in *INS v. Chadha*, which invalidated this so-called legislative veto on the theory that the congressional exercise of the veto necessarily represented legislative power and yet failed to comply with Article I, paragraph 7 procedures for enacting legislation, was not particularly persuasive, but any other result would have been extremely hard to square with the constitutional plan. Although it would be possible to support the Court's result by invoking the textual prohibition against members of Congress serving as officers of the United States, the deeper reason for the legislative veto's unconstitutionality is the fundamental difference between a constitutional design in which the national legislature is deliberately separated from the branch charged with executing the laws and an essentially parliamentary system in which the government is chosen from within the legislature and is in no sense separated from it. Again, the basis for the constitutional judgment becomes, at bottom, an organizing feature of policy. So too, if we return to the independent agencies. Whatever one's view of such agencies, and however much or little weight one should give to their entrenchment in the social and economic landscape through an enormous body of law and an equally vast array of practice, the point worth stressing at the end of the day is that their constitutional status must be measured in terms not of text alone but of the Constitution's history and structure, as well as considerations of constitutional doctrine and precedent.

JUDICIAL REVIEW AND DEBATE OVER THE NORMATIVE BREADTH, RETROACTIVE REACH, AND STARE DECISIS EFFECT OF A JUDGMENT OF UNCONSTITUTIONALITY

If, as a matter of constitutional law, the power of federal courts independently to interpret and apply the Constitution is an assumption and not a deduction, attention must be paid not only to the historical plausibility of that assumption but also to its internal structure. The concept of judicial review, as Marshall articulated in *Marbury v. Madison*, is by no means a simple one. Marshall first had to postulate that the Constitution was the fundamental and paramount law of the nation, and not merely the statement of an ideal political structure to which American government should aspire, or an initial distribution of rights and responsibilities which defined the starting point for bargaining among political institutions and individuals. Unless Marshall postulated that the Constitution was in some sense regulatory, he could not assume that an act of the legislature, repugnant to the constitution, is void. Second, Marshall had to assume that the Constitution is the sort of law which courts can recognize and apply. Unless Courts can determine whether Constitution and statute conflict with each other, unless courts can identify the rule to apply to particular cases, they cannot, regardless of their province and duty, say what the law is.

The twin assumptions that the Constitution is law and that the Constitution is law which courts can expound are quite easily and mistakenly collapsed into one. It is possible, for example, to equate the process of constitutional adjudication with the task of identifying the content of the Constitution, without any regard for the constraints which the institutional characteristics of courts put on the adjudicatory process. Alternatively, it is possible to identify the content of the Constitution with the results of the process of constitutional adjudication, ignoring any possibility that constitutional norms may be capable of statement in vocabularies other than that available to courts. A proper analysis of judicial review, therefore, must be careful to distinguish the dancer from the dance; otherwise put, the task is to avoid the extremes of both natural law and positivist analysis.

The practical implications of this distinction between the Constitution and judicial enforcement of its commands can be illuminated by considering a traditional issue associated with the exercise of judicial review: the effect of a judgment of unconstitutionality. Historically, the approach of the courts to this question has reflected the interaction of points of view. One position, perhaps the dominant view in the era between the Civil War and the Great Depression, holds that the term unconstitutional law, as employed in American jurisprudence, is a misnomer, and implies a contradiction; that enactment which is opposed to the constitution being in fact no law at all. Or, as stated in *Norton v. Shelby County*: "an unconstitutional act is not a law; it confers no rights; it imposes no duties; it affords no protection; it creates no office; it is, in legal contemplation, as inoperative as though it had never been passed."

The opposite position refuses to grant such import to a judicial pronouncement of unconstitutionality in a given case, and asserts that "the parties to that suit are concluded by the judgment, but no one else is bound." Adherents of this view argue that in future cases involving the allegedly unconstitutional act, "prima facie, and upon the face of the act itself, nothing will generally appear to show that the act is not valid; and it is only when some person attempts to resist its operation, and calls on the aid of the judicial power, to pronounce it void, as to him, his property, or his rights, that the objection of unconstitutionality can be presented and sustained." Thus, "the courts have no real power to repeal or abolish a statute, and . . . notwithstanding a decision holding it unconstitutional a statute continues to remain on the statute books."

Plainly, these two perspectives correlate with the twin assumptions underlying judicial review. The first approach emphasizes what is supposed to be a corollary of the fact of unconstitutionality itself: the Constitution operates of its own force; it is only judicial recognition of the fact which might be delayed. The second approach focuses on the fact that a finding of unconstitutionality comes in the context of adjudication; the result of a judgment of unconstitutionality is not the invalidation of a statute, but the resolution of a particular dispute between particular parties. Equally plainly, an appropriate resolution of the question of the effect of a judgment of unconstitutionality would be one which acknowledges both that such a judgment involves the statement of a constitutional norm and that the norm is, in the end, stated in an adjudicatory context.

Such a resolution can be achieved in part by recognizing that the two perspectives blur into one another with the passage of time. In handing down an opinion, it is true that "under Marbury the Court decides a case; it does not pass a statute calling for obedience by all within the purview of the rule that is declared." But although the decision immediately binds only the parties to the lawsuit, as word of it spreads—and assuming that it withstands attack to gain general acceptance—it eventually establishes a norm of broad applicability that cannot be ignored by future litigants. At that point in time, it may be said that "acceptance is demanded, without insisting on repeated litigation . . . both as the necessary implication of our constitutional tradition and to avoid the greater evils that will otherwise ensue."[1]

Of course, such acceptance is demanded only to the extent that the constitutional norm comes to bear in future situations in which its acceptability is sufficiently clear. The degree to which a constitutional norm announced in an individual case will bind those involved in future situations calling for a constitutional choice thus depends in large part on issues such as the degree to which the internal structure of the norm admits of value judgments contrary to the thrust of the court's opinion; the degree to which the Supreme Court views differing interpretations by other courts and branches as a threat to its judicial supremacy; whether future courts will have jurisdiction to reinforce the norm; whether the norm is properly presented in a justiciable lawsuit; and whether future courts will refrain, for equitable reasons, from imposing the norm on parties to other lawsuits.

The Supreme Court has considered the effect of judgments of unconstitutionality chiefly in the context of determining the retroactive reach of its decisions of constitutional law in both the civil and criminal procedure contexts. In some sense, virtually all governmental acts have retroactive effect, because "a substantial portion of all statutes, regulations, and court decisions—even those that are nominally prospective—alter the value of prior investments simply because the future value of such investments depends upon what rules are then in force."[2] However, some governmental actions—typically, judicial decisions—purport to have binding retroactive effect in the sense that they directly govern claims arising from facts antedating the governmental action.

Retroactivity doctrine is a reflection of the applicable theory of lawmaking. If an unconstitutional statute or practice effectively never existed as a lawful justification for state action, individuals convicted under the statute or in trials which tolerated the practice were convicted unlawfully even if their trials took place before the declaration of unconstitutionality, such a declaration should have a fully retroactive effect, and previously convicted individuals should be able to win their freedom through the writ of habeas corpus. Alternatively, if a judgment of unconstitutionality governs only the case at hand, the legality of the convictions of individuals previously tried is not affected.

Traditionally, "both the common law and the Court's own decisions recognized a general rule of retrospective effect for the constitutional decisions of the Court subject to certain limited exceptions."[3] This rule derived from the belief "that the duty of the court was not to pronounce a new law, but to maintain and expound the old one."[4] In the words of Justice Holmes, "a rule of retrospective operation has governed judicial decisions for near a thousand years."[5] In contrast, statutes enacted by Congress are ordinarily construed as not having retroactive effect.

THE POLITICAL QUESTION DOCTRINE

Another justiciability doctrine instructs Article III courts to avoid deciding political questions.[6] The governing standard in this area continues to be that articulated by Justice Brennan's purportedly definitive statement of the political question doctrine in *Baker v. Carr*:[7] "Prominent on the surface of any case held to involve a political question is found either: (1) a textually demonstrable constitutional commitment to a coordinate political department; or (2) a lack of judicially discoverable and manageable standards for resolving it; or (3) the impossibility of deciding without an initial policy determination of a kind clearly for non-judicial discretion; or (4) the impossibility of a court's undertaking independent resolution without expressing lack of the respect due coordinate branches of government; or (5) an unusual need for unquestioning adherence to a political decision already made; or (6) the potentiality of embarrassment from multifarious pronouncements by various departments on one question."

Even this definitive statement contains strands of at least three different theories of the role of the Court with regard to the other branches of government. A classical view would take the court's role as announced in *Marbury v. Madison* quite rigidly, and would impose on the court the requirement of deciding all cases and issues before it unless the court finds, purely as a matter of constitutional interpretation, that the Constitution itself has committed the determination of the issue to the autonomous decision of another branch or agency of government. A prudential view of the court's role would treat the political question doctrine as a means to avoid passing on the merits of a question when reaching the merits would force the court to compromise an important principle or would undermine the court's authority. Unlike the classical or prudential views, a functional approach to the role of the court would have it consider such factors as the difficulties in gaining judicial access to relevant information, the need for uniformity of decision, and the wider responsibilities of the other branches of government, when determining whether or not to decide a certain issue or case.

One conventional view of the doctrine grounds it in the assumption that there are certain constitutional questions which are inherently non-justiciable. These political questions concern matters as to which departments of government other than the courts, or perhaps the electorate as a whole, must have the final say. With respect to these matters, the judiciary does not define constitutional limits.[8] But Louis Henkin, among others, has forcefully criticized the idea that there are parts of the Constitution to which the judiciary must be blind.[9] The political question cases, Professor Henkin argues, do not support such a proposition. In these cases, the Supreme Court concluded or could properly have concluded that a particular legislative or executive action fell within a constitutional grant of authority and without the scope of any constitutional limitation, and thus that the action at issue, because constitutionally proper, was open only to political challenge. Alternatively, Henkin argues, the court ruled or could properly have ruled that a particular constitutional restriction was unenforceable because it did not confer standing to sue upon the parties who sought to invoke it or because it required for its enforcement remedies which were judicially unmanageable or equitably unwise.

Professor Henkin is clearly right that one should not accept lightly the proposition that there are provisions of the Constitution which the courts may not independently interpret, since any such proposition is plainly inconsistent with *Marbury v. Madison's* basic assumption that the Constitution as a whole is judicially declarable law.[10] In order to account for the political question doctrine, however, it is not necessary to postulate that there are parts of the Constitution to which the judiciary is blind. The Supreme Court does not surrender its power of judicial review by holding that, while a particular provision may grant Congress or the executive authority to act, it is not susceptible of an interpretation that would yield judicially enforceable rights, rights whose enforcement would either constrain congressional or executive action or alternatively provide the basis for an exercise of judicial power parallel to the actions of the political branches. Such a holding does not deprive the Court of all power to interpret a given constitutional provision: the Court retains the power to determine whether a particular congressional or executive action comes within the terms of the constitutional grant of authority, and whether it transgresses a cross-cutting constitutional limitation. Moreover, such a holding is not simply a ruling on standing or on the propriety of equitable remedies. In rendering such a holding, the Supreme Court is not concerned with the character of a litigant's inquiry or the shape of potential remedies as such, but rather with the possibility of depriving rights from the provision or provisions of the Constitution at issue. It is possible to test putative rights by imagining the sorts of inquiry their asserted infringement would bring about or by considering the sorts of remedies the enforcement would require, but the ultimate issue is whether it is possible and appropriate to translate the principles underlying the constitutional provision at issue into restrictions on government, or affirmative definitions of individual liberty, which courts can articulate and apply.

The political question cases themselves suggest that it is this inquiry—the inquiry into whether particular constitutional provisions yield judicially enforceable rights—which has concerned the Supreme Court. Because this inquiry ultimately focuses on the limits of judicial competency, the political question doctrine is plainly a part of justiciability doctrine as a whole.

The central line of political question cases runs from *Luther v.* to *Borden Baker v. Carr. Luther* arose out of Dorr's Rebellion: an ultimately unsuccessful attempt by Rhode Island citizens who were disenfranchised under the original colonial charter to force the adoption of a new and more democratic constitution despite the opposition of the government established under the charter. The specific issue *Luther* raised was whether soldiers of the charter government committed a trespass by breaking into plaintiff's home at a point in the rebellion when the rebels had prematurely proclaimed the adoption of a new constitution notwithstanding the charter government's continued insistence on the governing power of the charter. In resolving this issue, the Supreme Court had to consider two questions: whether a federal court could independently determine which of two competing governments was the true government of Rhode Island; and, even if the charter government was in power, whether that government, by proclaiming martial law, had acted unlawfully by departing from principles of republican government in contravention of the Guaranty Clause of Article IV, paragraph 4.[11]

The court concluded that a federal court could not independently decide which state government was legitimately in power. The question was not one which fell within judicial competence: the evidentiary problems alone would be staggering. Congress, moreover, did possess such a power under the Guaranty Clause, which in this case it had delegated to the president, who had exercised it. The fact that Congress possessed the power confirmed that the power was lacking in the judiciary: this was not the sort of question which would admit of conflicting answers, a possibility if more than one branch of government could pass on it. With respect to the question of whether, if it were the lawful government, the charter government had acted unlawfully in adopting martial law, the court took a more activist approach: it assumed that a federal court could decide whether a state government had violated the Guaranty Clause, but held that in this case, since the period of martial law was of only brief duration, Rhode Island had not acted unconstitutionally.

A number of nineteenth-century cases in which litigants invoked the protection of the Guaranty Clause follow the pattern of *Luther v. Borden*: the Supreme Court did not doubt that the Guaranty Clause could be applied to protect individual rights but held that, on the facts of the particular case, the challenged state action did not constitute a departure from principles of republican government.[12] In *Pacific States Telephone & Telegraph Co. v. Oregon*, however, the Supreme Court held that the question whether a state government is republican, like the question of which of two competing "governments" in fact governs, is one which federal courts are not competent to answer; thus, the Guaranty Clause is not a source of judicially enforceable private rights. Chief Justice White colorfully assumed that, if one feature of a state government—there Oregon's initiative mechanism—caused the structure of state government to depart from republican principles, then a federal court would have to treat the state government as a nullity, practically award a decree absolving from all obligation to contribute to the support or obey the laws of the outlaw government, and build by judicial action upon the ruins of the previously established government a new one. Needless to say, such action would be different in kind from the steps a federal court would ordinarily take in protecting individual rights, since ordinarily an individual challenges specific government action and not the government itself. Accordingly, the Court concluded, to recognize federal judicial power under the Guaranty Clause would be to recognize a judicial power so great as to obliterate the division between judicial authority and legislative power.

Chief Justice White's decisive assumption was dubious: if a court found that a particular feature of state government rendered the government unrepublican, why could not the court simply declare the feature invalid? White's basic approach, however, is characteristic of political question jurisprudence. An issue is political not because it is one of particular concern to the political branches of government but because the constitutional provisions which litigants would invoke as guides to resolution of the issue do not lend themselves to judicial application. A plurality of the Supreme Court departed from this approach in *Colegrove v. Green*. Voters challenged the constitutionality of a state's malapportioned congressional districts. Justice Frankfurter, joined by three other Justices, wrote the principal opinion, holding that the appellants ask of this court what is beyond its competence to grant: due regard for the effective working of our government reveals this issue to be of a peculiarly political nature and therefore not meet for judicial determination. Justice Frankfurter noted his view that a court was without remedial power to reapportion voting districts by itself, and further observed that the Constitution plainly granted authority to Congress to deal with the problem. He never identified, however, the various provisions of the United States Constitution which the voters invoked, and accordingly did not ground his analysis in any conclusion that the particular provisions which the litigants would have the court enforce did not suggest criteria which courts could apply to protect individual rights. Instead, the Justice treated the issue itself as beyond judicial competence: "Courts ought not to enter this political thicket."[13]

The Supreme Court, however, decisively repudiated Justice Frankfurter's analysis in *Baker v. Carr*. This was another apportionment case, involving a constitutional challenge to a state's districting of its state legislature. Justice Brenna's majority opinion unequivocally rejected the *Colegrove* formulation of the political question doctrine: "the doctrine of which we treat is one of political questions not one of political cases. The courts cannot reject as no lawsuit a bona fide controversy as to whether some action denominated 'political' exceeds political authority."[14] Instead, Justice Brennan asked whether the constitutional provision which the litigants invoked could be successfully translated into judicially enforceable rights. Plaintiffs had argued that, because the populations of the various legislative districts differed, the votes of residents of the more populous districts were debased relative to the votes of residents of less populous districts. This inequality of treatment, plaintiffs claimed, violated the Fourteenth Amendment Equal Protection Clause. The court had little difficulty in finding the Equal Protection Clause to be judicially enforceable.

The theme of these central cases—that the political question doctrine involves an inquiry into the ability of courts to derive enforceable rights from the constitutional provisions which the litigants invoke—echoes in the Supreme Court's other political question decisions. In *Coleman v. Miller*,[15] three Justices of the Supreme Court, in announcing the Court's decision, held that the questions of whether a state could ratify a proposed constitutional amendment it had once rejected, and whether a proposed amendment lapses into oblivion if not ratified within a reasonable period of time, were political questions. With respect to the first issue, the plurality found no basis in either Constitution or statute for judicial action. As to the second, the plurality asked: "Where are to be found the criteria for such a judicial determination?" Indeed, four justices were prepared to adopt the radical view of the political question doctrine criticized by Professor Henkin: "Congress has sole and complete control over the amending process, subject to no judicial review." After *Baker v. Carr*, it seems doubtful that *Coleman* can be read as an absolute bar to any judicial review of the amendment process, and commentators on the subject tend to disagree mainly on the scope of the undoubtedly limited judicial review that is appropriate in governing the process by which amendments proposed by Congress are ratified by the states.[16] The need for a substantial judicial role in supervising the process of calling and conducting a new constitutional convention, on the application of two-thirds of the states pursuant to Article V, seems considerably clearer. The constitutional appropriateness of the substance of proposed amendments, however, is almost certainly committed to judicially unreviewable resolution by the political branches of government.

In *Chicago & S. Air Lines v. Waterman S.S. Corp.*,[17] the court held that federal courts could not apply ordinary procedures for judicial review of administrative action in dealing with presidential orders concerning international air routes: "The very nature of executive decisions as to foreign policy is political and judicial. Such decisions are delicate, complex and involve large elements of prophecy. . . They are decisions of a kind for which the Judiciary has neither aptitude, facilities nor responsibility." Again, despite emphasis on judicially manageable standards, *Waterman* is something of a deviant case. Perhaps because the application of no constitutional provision was at issue, the Court emphasized the political nature of the question as much as the absence of judicially manageable standards. In this context, though, because the judicial rule at stake was one governing review of fact-finding, the two inquiries amounted to much the same thing.

CASE LAW SINCE *BAKER V. CARR*

The Supreme Court's decisions since *Baker v. Carr* more clearly reflect the approach to the political question doctrine which *Baker* exemplifies. In *United States v. Nixon,*[18] for instance, the Supreme Court held that the intra-executive nature of the dispute between President Nixon and Special Prosecutor Jaworski did not give rise to a political question. Because the president had himself restricted his discretion to deal with Jaworski, the president, until he repealed the regulations limiting his discretion, could refuse Jaworski's demands only by asserting a valid claim of privilege; the issue of privilege, of course, was of a type which is traditionally justiciable. Similarly in *Powell v. MaCormack*, the Supreme Court concluded that the political question doctrine did not bar its review of the House of Representatives' exercise of Article I, paragraph 5 power to judge the qualifications of its members. Article I, paragraph 5 did not grant the House unreviewable discretion, the court concluded, but rather authorized the House to exclude only those members who did not meet the three standing qualifications of Article 1, paragraph 2, or several other qualifications not there relevant. Thus, the court held that judicial review was possible at least to determine whether the House had in fact acted on the basis of the Article 1, paragraph 2 criteria, which the defendants conceded that Congressman Powell met.

In *Davis v. Bandemer,*[19] the court, in an opinion written by Justice White, applied *Baker* to find a legislative restricting case justiciable in a context substantially more problematic than that involved in the *Baker* case. *Davis* reviewed the constitutionality of political gerrymandering conducted by Republican state legislators in Indiana, who redrew state legislative districts subsequent to the 1980 census to hamper the electoral prospects of Democratic candidates. Evaluating the Democrats' claim that, despite the equivalence of population in each district, the redistricting plan impermissibly diluted the strength of the Democratic votes as a group, the court discounted the absence of readily defensible standards for adjudicating such claims, reading *Baker* as holding generally that legislative line-drawing in this districting context is susceptible of adjudication under the applicable constitutional criteria. Given its past acceptance of racial gerrymandering claims, the court viewed such claims by political groups as entitled in principle to similar treatment. Three justices, through Justice O'Connor's opinion, decried this abstract analysis and the lack of any judicially manageable standards to resolve the claims of the multitude of societal groups thereby invited to fight heatedly partisan redistricting battles in federal court, and could perceive no basis for a group right of equal political power underlying the Fourteenth Amendment. These justices also reasoned that, unlike deviations from the one person-one vote principle, political gerrymanders have a built-in tendency to be self-limiting, inasmuch as their deployment requires a political party to sacrifice safe seats in a strategic bid for more seats. For this reason, the need to relax justiciability constraints seems weaker in this context than in that of *Baker*. Adopting the somewhat implausible posture that political considerations should not count in applying the political question doctrine, Justice White's opinion saw no need to address Justice O'Connor shrewd analysis on its merits.

Gilligan v. Morgan[20] is one of only two cases since *Baker v. Carr* in which the Supreme Court has invoked the political question doctrine to hold an issue non-justiciable. Plaintiffs had asked the federal courts to evaluate the training of the Ohio National Guard under the Fourteenth Amendment Due Process

Clause: if that training was found constitutionally deficient, they sought appropriate injunctive relief. The Supreme Court's decision that the issue was not justiciable turned on a number of factors. Chief among them were the facts that Article I, paragraph 8 authorized Congress to engage in just such supervision, and that judicial review in this area would be essentially standardless: it is difficult to conceive of an area of governmental activity in which the courts have less competence. The complex, subtle, and professional decisions as to the composition, training equipping, and control of a military force are essentially professional military judgments, subject always to civilian control of the legislative and executive branches."[21]

Four Justices sought to invoke political question again in *Goldwater v. Carter,*[22] which vacated a court of appeals decision that the president had power—having withdrawn diplomatic recognition from the government of China with which the treaty had been made and having substituted diplomatic recognition of the People's Republic of China—to terminate a treaty with Taiwan without the approval of the Senate. The plurality took the view that the president's power to abrogate a treaty was a question that was political and therefore non-justiciable and accordingly should be left for resolution by the president and Congress. Likening the case to *Coleman v. Miller,* the plurality argued that only political standards could resolve the matter—that the Constitution specifies the process by which treaties are to be created but says nothing about how, or by whom, they be ended, just as it details procedures for the adoption but not the rejection of constitutional amendments. Justice Powell concurred in the judgment on the ground that the suit, brought by a few individual members of Congress, was not ripe because neither the Senate nor the House had created a constitutional impasse through direct challenge on the issue. Justice Brennan persuasively argued for affirmance of the lower court's decision on the merits, reasoning that, although the political question doctrine bars review of foreign policy judgments entrusted to another branch of government, it does not pertain when a court is faced with the antecedent question whether a particular branch has been constitutionally designated as the repository of political decision-making power. If, as all appeared to concede, the president acted within his constitutionally delegated sphere in derecognizing the former government of Taiwan and of mainland China, then he presumably had authority to terminate, as an agreement with a no longer existing government, any treaty between the United States and that former government, where nothing in the treaty itself purports to tie the president's hands on the matter, and where the Constitution says nothing that precludes such unilateral presidential action in United.

In *United States v. Munoz-Flores,*[23] the court held that a dispute under the Origination Clause, Article I, paragraph 7, cl. 1, which mandates that all bills for raising revenue originate in the House of Representatives, does not present a justiciable political question. The case turned on an argument by the solicitor general that a court would express lack of respect for the House of Representatives by invalidating a law on Origination Clause grounds, because the House itself occasionally polices compliance with the clause by sending legislation back to the Senate when, in the opinion of the House, the legislation is a revenue-raising bill that should have originated in the House of Representatives. To strike down a law that the House passed and did not send back to the Senate would, according to the government, impermissibly second-guess the House's judgment.

The court rejected that argument, reasoning that whatever was meant in *Baker v. Carr* by an expression of a "lack of respect," the government's interpretation was not the correct one. If it were, every judicial resolution of a constitutional challenge to a congressional enactment would be impermissible. For example, Congress often explicitly considers the constitutionality of pending bills, and its enactment of any law reflects at least its implicit judgment that the measure on its face comports with the Constitution. Yet such congressional consideration of constitutional questions does not foreclose subsequent judicial scrutiny of the law's constitutionality.

The government attempted to distinguish the Origination Clause from other constitutional provisions by arguing that the purpose of the clause is not to protect the rights of individual citizens, but only to safeguard the institutional prerogatives of the House vis-à-vis the Senate. If, in a given case, the House has decided that a particular bill poses no Origination Clause difficulty, judicial invalidation would be an insulting form of paternalism. The court parried these contentions as well, noting that that fact that one institution of government has mechanisms available to guard against incursions into its power by other governmental institutions does not require that the judiciary remove itself from the controversy by labelling the issue a political question. Furthermore, the court continued, the Origination Clause serves more than structural concerns; by vesting initial control over revenue-raising bills in the more representative Chamber, the clause protects individual rights as well.

Justice Scalia, concurring in the judgment, advanced a provocative theory. He maintained that, under *Field v. Clark*,[24] federal courts should not undertake an independent investigation into the origination of the statute at issue, although he conceded that courts could determine what sorts of bills constitute bills for raising revenue, Article I, paragraph 7, cl. 1. The attraction of Justice Scalia's approach is that the question of where a bill in fact originated may look little a factual issue, so that perhaps a court could not review Congress' judgment on this subject without impugning the honesty of those who designated the bill as having in fact originated in the House rather than Senate. What qualifies as a revenue bill, on the other hand, is a legal question better suited to judicial than congressional resolution.

The majority answered Justice Scalia by limiting *Field* to situations not involving a constitutional constraint on the power of Congress enact legislation. The limits to this approach are as yet unexplored, but it appears that a host of internal congressional procedures could be characterized as "constitutional requirements binding Congress" whose violation might present justiciable controversies under *Munoz-Flores*. These include Article I, paragraph 5, clause 2, which provides that a majority of each House is necessary to constitute a quorum to conduct "Business"; Article I, paragraph 5, clause 4, which prohibits either House, without the consent of the other, from adjourning for more than three days, nor to any other place than that in which the two Houses shall be sitting; paragraph 7, which specifies that Congress cannot override a presidential veto unless the votes of all voting members are publicly recorded in the journal of proceedings; and the Twentieth Amendment, which prescribes that the Houses of Congress must assemble at noon on the third day of January each year, unless by law another day is selected. The court had already held that the political question doctrine does not bar a court from reviewing the House of Representatives' exercise of power to judge the qualifications of its members. At some point, the court will have to draw a line defining a class of procedural rules that do not play a significant role in safeguarding liberty and are solely the concern of Congress.

The court started down such a road in *Nixon v. United States*, holding that a challenge by Walter L. Nixon, former Chief Justice of the U.S. District Court for the Southern District of Mississippi, to the Senate's use of a committee to hear testimony and gather other evidence in his impeachment trial amounted to a non-justiciable political question. The court focused on Article I, paragraph 3, clause 6, which provides that the Senate shall have the sole power to try all impeachments. When sitting for that purpose, they shall be on oath or affirmation. When the president of the United States is tried, the Chief Justice shall preside: and no person shall be convicted without the concurrence of two-thirds of the members present.

The court rejected the argument that the word "try" in the first sentence of Article I, paragraph 3, clause 6 precludes the Senate from delegating to a select committee that "the word try lacks sufficient precision to afford any judicially manageable standard of review." This conclusion was fortified by the presence of three very specific requirements that the Constitution does not impose on the Senate when trying impeachments. The members must be under oath, a two-thirds vote is required to convict, and the Chief Justice presides when the president is tried. Moreover, the court stressed the importance of the Senate's sole power to try impeachments: notably, in only one other place in the Constitution is there an explicit grant of sole authority to any branch on any issue. Further, there is no reference in either the Framers' or ratifiers' debates to the possibility of judicial review of Senate impeachment decisions. Indeed, such review would generate severe practical difficulties. For example, the nation must languish in a dangerous limbo if a former president, although punitively removed from office, challenged the lawfulness of the Senate impeachment trial used to convict him—a judicial process (together with an appeal) that might drag out over several years.

In the case of judicial impeachments, permitting Supreme Court review would have a potentially delegitimizing effect: it would place final reviewing authority with respect to impeachments in the hands of the same body that the impeachment process is meant to regulate.[25] Hence, the Court concluded, the Constitution makes a textually demonstrable commitment to the Senate of the conduct of impeachment trials.

Writing separately, Justice White and Justice Souter each expressed a quite different view of the political question doctrine, each raising the spectre of Senatorial abuses of power. Justice Souter agreed that the *Nixon* case presented a political question, but he contended that the political question doctrine derives in large part from prudential concerns about the respect we owe the political departments. Justice Souter urged that the issue be addressed on a case-by-case basis, depending on the facts of the particular situation at hand. He concluded that deference to the Senate was appropriate in Judge Nixon's case because the clause contemplates that the Senate may determine, within broad boundaries, such subsidiary issues as the procedures for receipt and consideration of evidence necessary to satisfy its duty to try impeachments. He also noted other significant considerations, such as the pragmatic concern that judicial review of an impeachment trial would under the best of circumstances entail significant disruption of government. However, Justice Souter warned that, if the Senate were to act in a manner seriously threatening the integrity of its results, convicting, say, upon a coin toss, or upon a summary determination that an officer of the United States was simply a bad guy, judicial interference might well be appropriate.

Justice White, joined by Justice Blackmun, maintained that the Impeachment Trial Clause does not present non-justiciable political questions, and in fact imposes on the Senate a number of procedural requirements that are judicially enforceable. "Were the Senate, for example, to adopt the practice of automatically entering a judgment of conviction whenever articles of impeachment were delivered from the House, it is quite clear that the Senate will have failed to try impeachments."[26] In the end, however, Justice White agreed that the requirements of the clause were satisfied in Judge Nixon's case.

The court also reaffirmed the vitality of *Baker v. Carr* in a pair of political question decisions involving two challenges to the apportionment of representatives among the several states based on the 1990 census. In *U.S. Department of Commerce v. Montana*, the court reversed the judgment of a three-judge court that had held unconstitutional a 1941 statute prescribing the method of equal proportions as the method to be used for determining the number of representatives to which each state is entitled. The United States argued that Congress' selection of any particular apportionment formula to implement the constitutional provision that Representatives shall be apportioned among the several States . . . according to their respective Numbers"[27] was not subject to judicial review, but the court disagreed. Noting the government's concession that Congress has a judicially enforceable obligation to select an apportionment plan that is related to population, the court determined that the "gravamen of the Government's argument is that the District Court erred in concluding that the Constitution imposes the more rigorous requirement of greatest possible equality in the size of congressional districts . . . The Government takes issue not with the existence of a judicially enforceable right, but with the definition of such right."[28] The court concluded that the case before it was political only insofar as it raised an issue of great importance to the political branches. The court quite rightly rejected the suggestion that the involvement of Congress, a coordinate branch of government, rendered the matter a political question, and the court determined that the same reasons that supported the justiciability of challenges to state legislative districts, as in *Baker v. Carr* itself, applied with equal force to the issues presented by the congressional apportionment of House seats among the states. The court followed the same rationale in *Franklin v. Massachusetts* in holding that a challenge to the method in the 1990 census for counting federal employees serving overseas (which resulted in a reapportionment in which Massachusetts lost a House seat) did not present a political question. And in *Department of Commerce v. United States House of Representatives*, the court entertained a challenge to the Census Bureau's plan to use statistical sampling for the year 2000 decennial census, with no suggestion that it posed a political question the court struck down the census plan, with respect to apportionment data as the inconsistent with the Census Act.

The political question doctrine also featured prominently in two lower federal court decisions regarding the War Powers Clause of the Constitution and the War Powers Resolution.[29] U.S. District Judge Royce Lamberth ruled that a suit by a National Guard sergeant challenging his deployment to the Persian Gulf presented a non-justiciable political question because the power to commit U.S. forces belonged not to one branch alone but rather to the executive and legislature to together: Article I, Paragraph 8, clause 11 states that Congress shall have power to declare war, but Article II, paragraph 2, clause 1 names the president commander-in-chief of the Army and Navy. The powers granted to the politically accountable branches, Judge Lamberth maintained, enabled them to resolve the dispute themselves. For example, if Congress considers the president's current deployment of forces in the Persian Gulf to violate the Constitution, or if Congress considers the country on the verge of being unconstitutionally brought to war, or if Congress concludes at any time that the president's actions in the gulf have usurped Congress's constitutional role, Congress has many options to check the president. Congress can itself declare war, exercise its appropriation power to prevent further offensive and/or defensive military action in the Persian Gulf, or even impeach the president. Judge Lamberth added that the Judicial Branch is poorly equipped to intrude into the realm of foreign affairs where the Constitution grants operational powers only to the two political branches and where decisions are made based on political and policy considerations.

The notion that judicial authority evaporates when an ambiguity arises in the Constitution's allocation of a given power is profoundly counterintuitive, however. The political question doctrine is usually invoked in precisely the opposite situation, where there is a textually demonstrable constitutional commitment of the issue to a coordinate political department. Where the Constitution is in need of interpretation, it is emphatically the province and duty of the judicial department to say what the law is.[30]

As Justice Brennan has explained, properly understood, the political question doctrine restrains courts from reviewing an exercise of foreign policy judgment by the coordinate political branch to which authority to make that judgment has been constitutionally committed. But the doctrine does not pertain when a court is faced with the antecedent question whether a particular branch has been constitutionally designated as the repository of political decision-making power.[31] And the argument that, when it comes to the war power, Congress and the president have the weapons to settle the dispute by themselves, could be made in any separation of powers case.

For these reasons, U.S. District Judge Harold Greene seemed to reach the right result when he found justiciable rather than political the legal question posed in the suit by 54 members of Congress seeking to enjoin the president from initiating an attack against Iraq without first obtaining congressional approval. Judge Greene persuasively rejected the objection that whether an offensive military operation constitutes a war requiring congressional approval, or simply an attack undertaken by the president in his capacity as commander-in-chief, is not a question of objective fact, but a matter involving judgment based upon considerations of foreign affairs and national security that a court could not understand. To be sure, defining war may be difficult and Judge Greene indicated that in a case that is factually close or fraught with intricate military and diplomatic baggage, some degree of deference to the executive might be appropriate. But courts have historically decided cases having a substantial impact on foreign and defense policy,[32] and courts have determined whether the country was at war for many purposes—the construction of treaties, statutes, and so on and so forth. It is therefore apparent that the judiciary has both the constitutional duty and the competence to decide an otherwise justiciable case involving the power of the president to commit the nation to war without congressional authorization.

JUDICIAL FEDERALISM: THE POLICIES OF PRESERVING THE INTEGRITY OF STATE LAW AND RESPECTING THE INSTITUTIONAL AUTONOMY OF STATE JUDICIAL SYSTEMS

The Supreme Court in recent years has continued its emphasis on judicial federalism—that is, the idea that federal courts must exercise their power with a keen appreciation of the essential role played by the states and their judicial systems in the constitutional structure.[33] This emphasis has often led the court to see order in chaotic variety and to detect the principle of state sovereignty in cases involving a wide range of topics, including statutory limitations on federal jurisdiction, retroactivity, standing, and the power to make federal common law. Thus, Justice O'Connor began a 1991 opinion concerning the procedural rules to be used by federal courts in reviewing the claims of state prisoners on federal habeas corpus with the comment, "This is a case about federalism."[34] In *United States v. Lopez*, the court opined that it has participated in maintaining the federal balance through judicial exposition of doctrines such as abstention, the rules for determining the primacy of state law, the whole jurisprudence of preemption, and many of the rules governing the habeas corpus jurisprudence.

In *Arizonans for Official English v. Arizona*,[35] which dismissed on mootness grounds a challenge to a state constitutional provision making English the official state language, the court saw the mootness doctrine, too, as an important means of protecting the integrity of state law: "Warnings against premature adjudication of constitutional questions bear heightened attention when a federal court is asked to invalidate a State's law, for the federal tribunal risks friction-generating error when it endeavors to construe a novel State Act not yet reviewed by the State's highest court."

ABSTENTION DOCTRINES

The rhetoric and results of judicial federalism are perhaps best exemplified by the rather amorphous abstention doctrines, defining exceptions to the virtually unflagging obligation of federal courts to exercise the jurisdiction vested in them[36] by requiring them to abstain in certain cases where necessary to promote the integrity of state law and respect the autonomy of state judicial bodies. The abstention doctrines derive from the discretion historically employed by courts of equity and reflect principles of federalism and comity. Thus, the court has explained, "our longstanding application of these abstention doctrines reflects the common law background against which the statutes conferring jurisdiction were enacted."[37] This tradition informs our understanding of the jurisdiction Congress has conferred upon the federal courts, and explains the development of the abstention doctrines. In *Quackenbush v. Allstate Ins. Co.* the court held that federal courts have the power to dismiss or remand cases based on abstention principles only where the relief sought is equitable or otherwise discretionary. In cases for money damages, federal courts may stay the actions based on abstention principles, but the court opined that those principles do not support the outright dismissal or remand of damages actions.

The Supreme Court has developed, without express congressional approval, three distinct forms of abstention, which bear the names of early cases in each arena. The first two abstention doctrines evince a desire to limit federal-court interpretation of ambiguous state law where special concerns are present. In brief, under *Pullman*[38] abstention, federal courts should abstain from decision when difficult and unsettled questions of state law must be resolved before a substantial federal constitutional question can be decided; such abstention avoids both unnecessary adjudication of federal questions and needless friction with state policies from possibly erroneous state law interpretation. Animated by a similar concern is the requirement that litigants generally exhaust state administrative remedies prior to seeking federal court review. A second, somewhat related abstention doctrine—*Colorado River* abstention—only vaguely developed and of far less practical significance, does not require the presence of a federal constitutional question but rather counsels federal courts to abstain in cases where decision of state law issues would intrude greatly on especially important state interests considered particularly well-suited to state court consideration.

The abstention doctrine that most directly promotes judicial federalism and has the broadest potential scope is *Younger* abstention, designed to help preserve the institutional autonomy of state judicial processes by limiting attempts by litigants to obtain federal declaratory or injunctive relief on constitutional grounds where such relief may interfere with certain types of ongoing state proceedings in which they are involved, and which provide an adequate opportunity to raise the constitutional claims. Such interference is doubly offensive: it not only hinders state efforts to maintain a smoothly running judicial system but also denies the principle of comity—the fundamental premise of judicial federalism which holds that, since both federal and state courts have a duty to enforce the Constitution, there is no constitutional basis, in the absence of some demonstrable infirmity in the state judicial process itself, for preferring federal courts to state courts as adjudicators of federal constitutional claims.

There are important interrelationships among the various abstention doctrines; as one critic has noted. "The division of the abstention cases into concrete doctrines may be more imaginary than real. The abstention doctrines defy strict categorization, so it is not surprising that courts and commentators define the categories in different terms, and that the categories change over time. But the court has rightly warned, it is impermissible to concoct an abstention doctrine out of white cloth, even where such a doctrine would in fact be consistent with the established practices of the federal courts.

CRITICS OF ABSTENTION DOCTRINES

Some commentators have criticized the judge-made abstention doctrines on separation of powers grounds because the doctrines permit federal courts to decline jurisdiction vested in them by Congress;[39] by definition, abstention doctrines come into play only when a federal court has jurisdiction over the case and parties. The court has sometimes fueled this criticism by observing that federal courts lack the authority to abstain from the exercise of jurisdiction that has been conferred.

But it is possible to argue persuasively, in response to the separation of powers critique, that Congress has delegated to federal courts the power to decline jurisdiction in particular cases: that Congress did not mean to confer on federal courts jurisdiction that would gratuitously disrupt the operation of state-court systems; that the exercise of ungranted jurisdiction—surely forbidden to federal courts—is not the same as a decision not to exercise what is granted; that abstention is consistent with the judicial power established in Article III, which charges federal courts with the task of adjudicating individual cases and controversies according to law and equity; that abstention doctrines reflect a complex of considerations designed to soften the tensions inherent in a system that contemplates parallel judicial processes; and that Congress retains ultimate primacy over federal court jurisdiction because it is able by statute to nullify abstention doctrines if it so chooses. Thus, the Court has simultaneously recognized the undisputed constitutional principle that Congress, and not the judiciary, defines the scope of federal jurisdiction within the constitutionally permissible bounds, but maintained that this principle does not eliminate, and the categorical assertions upon it do not call into question, the federal courts' discretion in determining whether to grant certain types of relief—a discretion that was part of the common law background against which the statutes conferring jurisdiction were enacted.[40] Whatever the merits of the separation of powers critique, the court has remained singularly unmoved. It is probable, however, that the court will continue to insist that the areas in which abstention is permitted be carefully defined and that abstention remain the exception and not the rule.

These considerations are relevant not only in the context of federal district court injunctive or declaratory relief against allegedly unconstitutional state action, but also in the context of Supreme Court review of state court decisions. Like the federal district courts, the Supreme Court can mistakenly construe ambiguous state law and, by hearing a case that has not yet finished its progress through the state judicial system, can disrupt the processes of that system and violate the premises of comity. At least in theory, however, the statutory requirement of a final judgment which conditions the Supreme Court's jurisdiction to review state court decisions, as well as the court's own discretionary powers, protect the court from itself sinning against federalism values. Accordingly, the court's chief doctrinal concern will properly continue to focus on controlling the lower federal courts.

NOTES

1. See Wechsler, supra. The United States government in particular is not bound by the doctrine of non-mutual offensive collateral estoppel, see *United States v. Mendoza*, 464 U.S. 154 (1984). The government may therefore selectively litigate statutory or constitutional issues in a succession of cases involving different parties—e.g., when it is attempting to generate a circuit conflict or otherwise to create a suitable test to take to the Supreme Court.

2. Louis Kaplow, "An Economic Analysis of Legal Transitions," 99 *Harvard Law Review* 509, 515 (1986).

3. *Robinson v. Neil*, 409 U.S. 505, 507 (1973).

4. *Linkletter v. Walker*, 381 U.S. 618, 622–23 (1965), citing Blackstone, *Commentaries* 69 (15th ed. 1809).

5. *Kuhn v. Fairmont Coal Co.* 215 U.S. 349, 372 (1910) (J. Holms, dissenting).

6. See Michael Tigar, The Political Question Doctrine and Foreign Relations, 17 *UCLA Law Review* 1135 (1970).

7. 369 U.S. 186, 217 (1962).

8. On this, the classical, political and functional theories see Wechsler, "Toward Neutral Principles of Constitutional Law" 73 *Harvard Law Review* 7–9 (1959).

9. Louis Henkin, "Is there a Political Question Doctrine" 85 *Yale Law Journal* 597 (1976).

10. But, see Iacovos Kareklas, ΦΙΛΟΣΟΦΙΑ ΤΟΥ ΔΙΚΑΙΟΥ (Athens: NOMIKI BIBLIOTHIKI, 2012), for a complete analysis of the constitutional doctrine of ministerial accountability in the common law tradition, particularly in the United Kingdom, where it is stressed with powerful constitutional law and theory arguments that there are certain issues of political practice deriving from constitutional custom that are beyond the province of judicial jurisdiction.

11. The Guaranty Clause, sometimes called the Republican Form of Government Clause, provides: "The United States shall guarantee to every State in this Union a Republican Form of Government, and shall protect each of them against invasion; and on Application of the Legislature, or of the Executive (when the Legislature cannot be convened) against domestic violence."

12. See *Forsyth v. Hammond*, 166 U.S. 506, 519 (1897).

13. 328 US at 556.

14. 369 U.S. at 217.

15. 307 U.S. 433 (1939).

16. Professor (and former Acting Solicitor General) Walter Dellinger has argued that the plurality opinion in *Coleman* is profoundly misguided, and that an active judicial role in governing the constitutional amendment process is essential to ensuring that its legitimacy is supported by agreement on basic rules which operate with reasonable certainty ("The Legitimacy of Constitutional Change: Rethinking the Amendment Process" 97 *Harvard Law Review* 386 [1983]).

17. 333 U.S. 103 (1948).

18. 418 U.S. 683 (1974).

19. 478 U.S. 109 (1986).

20. 413 U.S. 1 (1973).

21. 413 U.S. at 10.

22. 444 U.S. 996 (1979).

23. 495 U.S., 385 (1990).

24. 143 U.S. 649, 671 (1892).

25. *Baker v. Carr*, 369 U.S. 186, 217 (1962).

26. 506 U.S. at 246 (White J. joined by Blackmun, J., concurring in the judgment).

27. Article I, paragraph 2, cl 3.

28. 503 U.S. at 457.

29. *Dellums v. Bush* 752 F.Supp. 1141 (D.D.C. 1990); Ange v. Bush, 752 F.Supp 509 (D.D.C. 1990).

30. *Marbury v. Madison*, 5 U.S. (1 Cranch) 137, 177 (1803).

31. *Goldwater v. Carter*, 444 U.S. 996, 1006–1007 (1979) (statement of Brennan J.).

32. For example *Dames v. Regan*, 453 U.S. 654 (1981), upholding presidential orders relegating private parties with claims against Iran to U.S.-Iran claims tribunal.

33. For a commentary, Louise Weinberg, "The New Judicial Federalism" 29 Stanford Law Review 1191 (1977).

34. *Coleman v. Thompson*, 501 U.S. 722, 726 (1991).

35. 520 U.S. 43 (1997).

36. *Deakins v. Monaghan*, 484 U.S. 193, 203 (1988).

37. *Quackenbush v. Allstate Ins. Co.*, 517 U.S. 706, 726 (1996).

38. *Railroad Comm'n of Texas v. Pullman Co.*, 312 U.S. 496 (1941).

39. George D. Brown, "When Federalism and Separation of Powers Collide: Rethinking Younger Abstention," *George Washington Law Review* 114, 116 (1990).

40. *New Orleans Public Service, Inc. v. Council of City of New Orleans*, 491 U.S. 350, 359 (1989).

Chapter 15

Federal Executive Power

THE PRESIDENT AS CHIEF EXECUTIVE: POWERS OF APPOINTMENT

One of the president's chief powers as head of the executive establishment is that of appointing federal officers. Article II, paragraph 2, clause 2 provides in pertinent part: "The President shall nominate, and by and with the Advice and Consent of the Senate, shall appoint . . . all other Officers of the United States, whose Appointments are not herein otherwise provided for, and which shall be established by Law; but the Congress may by Law vest the Appointment of such inferior Officers, as they think proper, in the President alone, in the Courts of Law, or in the Heads of Departments."

It is typical of the Constitution's scheme for separating legislative and executive authority that the offices in question are to be chosen by the president subject to the Senate's confirmation. In *Springer v. Government of the Philippine Islands* the Supreme Court indicated that Congress may not control law enforcement process by retaining power to appoint the individual who will execute its laws. Much as the Bill of Attainder Clause of Article I, paragraph 9 prevents Congress from circumventing the checks of the executive and judicial branches by identifying the individuals who are to be burdened by federal statutes, so the Appointments Clause, rather than merely dealing with etiquette or protocol, seeks to preserve an executive check upon legislative authority in the interest of avoiding an undue concentration of power in Congress.

The 1974 amendments to the Federal Election Campaign Act of 1971, for example, established an eight-member Federal Election Commission and vested in it primary responsibility for administering and enforcing the Act by bringing civil actions against violators, making rules for carrying out the act's provisions, temporarily disqualifying federal candidates for failing to file required reports, and authorizing convention expenditures in excess of the act's specified limits. Because such powers of enforcement, rule making, and adjudication could not be regarded as merely in aid of the legislative function of Congress, they could be exercised only by persons who are officers of the United States. But four of the six voting members of the commission were appointed by the president *pro tempore* of the Senate and by the Speaker of the House although the Appointments Clause requires all Officers of the United States to be appointed by the president, the head of an executive department, or the courts of law. Thus the court held in *Buckley v. Valeo* that the Federal Election Commission was unconstitutionally composed, stressing that Congress could not, merely because it concluded that such a measure was necessary and proper to the discharge of its substantive and legislative authority vest in itself, or in its officers, the authority to appoint officers of the United States any more than it could pass a bill of attainder or *ex post facto* law contrary to the prohibitions contained in paragraph 9 of Article I.

The clear impermissibility of Congress' efforts to bestow the appointment power on itself should be distinguished from the more complex issue whether Congress should be allowed to delegate substantive power to itself; the difference illuminates the animating principle of the Appointments Clause. A conclusion that legislative self-reference is unconstitutional seems to underlie the court's analysis of the legislative veto in *INS v. Chadha*. Although the Chadha majority never voiced the premise that Congress may delegate authority to others but not to itself, the decision's pivotal rationale seems indeed to be found in this assumption. In a somewhat cryptic footnote, the court admitted that agencies and executive officers commonly wield quasi-legislative power without the safeguards of presentment and bi-camerality. The court distinguished these exercises of power by noting that those who wield it are executive officers appointed by the president or his subordinates and subject in significant degree to judicial control.

Thus the objection in *Chadha* to the exercise of statutorily delegated power by all or part of Congress—as opposed to such exercised by an agent or agency external to Congress—may be restated as the proposition that entrusting members of Congress with such power confers upon federal lawmakers the mantle of officers of the United States government, in violation of the Appointments Clause and of the Incompatibility Clause.

The core concern of these two clauses—concern tied closely to the Framers' rejection of parliamentary government—is to ensure that federal executive power remain structurally independent of Congress and of the congressional power base. The executive power is not to be dispersed among a series of ministries selected from or subordinate to the national legislature, each headed by a member of Congress or similar officer representing a discrete state or local constituency within Congress' ambit. Therefore, the Constitution requires certain specially mentioned officers—primarily ambassadors and Supreme Court justices—to be nominated by the president and confirmed by the Senate, and all inferior officers to be appointed not by Congress but through congressionally fixed procedures, by the president alone, the courts of law or the heads of departments. This arrangement leaves Congress free to designate its own agents to exercise powers essentially of an investigative and informative nature but as a practical matter assures that, with the exception of judicially appointed inferior officers, who will usually be clerks and other court officials, any appointee exercising significant authority pursuant to the laws of the United States will be selected by the president or by a department head answerable to the president. It is through subordinates, and only through them, that the president can take that the laws be faithfully executed.

THE PRESIDENT AS CHIEF EXECUTIVE: POWERS OF REMOVAL AND CONTROL

The Constitution nowhere explicitly indicates whether Congress or the president or both possess the power to remove appointed officers other than federal judges[1] and subordinate employees. However, the Supreme Court has attempted to fill this constitutional void by linking the power of removal to the power of appointment explicitly defined in Article II, paragraph 2.

Congressional assertion of the power to limit presidential removal of executive officers dates from the Tenure of Office Act of 1867, which forbade presidential removal of designated cabinet members without the consent of the Senate. The Tenure of Office Act (even though repealed in 1887) and subsequent related legislation were declared unconstitutional by the Supreme Court in 1926 in *Myers v. United States*.[2] The court there struck down a congressional provision that certain postmasters, appointed by the president with the approval of the Senate, could not be removed by the president without the Senate's consent. Chief Justice Taft's majority opinion in *Myers*, delivered over the dissents of Justices Holmes, Brandeis, and McReynolds, is the primary source of the modern theory of removal. Taft concluded that the power of removal of executive officers is incident to the power of appointment, and therefore that the president has the exclusive power of removing executive officers of the United States whom he has appointed by and with the advice and consent of the Senate. He found further support of his conclusion that removal was then peculiar province of the president in the chief executive's charge to ensure that the laws be faithfully executed.

The court's exegesis in *Myers* went so far beyond what was necessary to dispose of the case before it that it was susceptible of two fundamentally distinct readings. Myers could be understood to mean that Congress may not place any limits on the president's power to remove executive officers; or it could be read as embodying the proposition that, whatever the limits of presidential removal power, Congress could not cede to itself any role in removing government officials. The former reading was repudiated in Humphrey's *Executor v. United States*,[3] where the court drastically narrowed the application of the *Myers* rule. Specifically, the court ruled that the president could not, at his pleasure, remove from office, before the expiration of his statutory term, a Federal Trade Commissioner where Congress had sought to deny such discretion to the president. The court reasoned that the Necessary and Proper Clause endowed Congress with the power to create federal offices independent of the president in order to implement congressional statutes and to safeguard that independence by insulating the holders of such officers from dismissal at the caprice of the chief executive: the authority of Congress, in creating quasi-legislative or quasi-judicial agencies, to require them to act in discharge of their duties independently of executive control, cannot well be doubted; and that authority includes, as an appropriate incident, power to fix the period during which they shall continue in office, and to forbid their removal except for cause in the meantime. The *Myers* proposition was explicitly limited: it was held to apply only to the removal of purely executive officers.

The difference in emphasis of the *Myers* and the *Humphrey's Executor* cases is striking. In *Myers,* the court assumed that the exclusive locus of the removal power was identical to that of the appointment power. Although the court's premise that the president alone possesses the power of appointment is dubious—he may nominate officers by himself, but he can appoint them only by and with the advice and consent of the Senate—it is clear that a major moving force in *Myers* was the allure of constitutional symmetry. In *Humphrey's Executor* the court pursued a more functional approach: the character of the office rather than the locus of its appointment determined whether the president was to enjoy unrestricted removal power.

The Supreme Court subsequently underscored the distinction between these two cases. In *Wiener v. United States*, the court posited that the difference in outcomes of *Myers* and *Humphrey's Executor* derived from the difference in functions between those who are part of the executive establishment and those whose tasks require absolute freedom from executive interference. In other words, those whose decisions the executive cannot alter, the Executive cannot remove on his own authority. The court therefore held that since the War Claims Act precluded the president from influencing the commission in passing on a particular claim, the president could not remove, on his Article II authority, War Claims Commissioner Wiener.

The functional test, as articulated in *Humphrey's Executor* and elucidated in *Wiener*, is hardly free from ambiguity. Such a case could turn on statutory construction, but it will not always be clear whether Congress intended that a particular office operate independent of the president, especially if Congress neither prescribes nor proscribes a procedure of removal.

The predicament is even more troubling when a given officer charged with some quasi-judicial or quasi-legislative tasks and some purely executive obligations. Nor has this ambiguity escaped notice by the court. In *Humphrey's Executor* the justices admonished: "to the extent that, between the decision in the *Myers* case, which sustains the unrestrictable power of the President to remove purely executive officers, and our present decision that such power does not extend to an office such as here involved, there shall remain a field of doubt, we leave such cases as may fall within the it for future consideration and determination as they may arise."[4]

THE PRESIDENT AS CHIEF EXECUTIVE: POWER TO INTERPRET THE LAW

The Constitution does not mention the power to interpret federal law and to decide whether a statute is unconstitutional, nor does the Constitution expressly assign that power to any of the three branches of government. The federal judiciary assumed the power to say what the law is in *Marbury v. Madison* not because of any special constitutional assignment of that authority or any special constitutional competence superior to that of the other two branches, but, supposedly, because law-interpreting power is ancillary to the federal courts' enumerated authority to decide cases and controversies under Article III: those who apply the rule to particular cases must of necessity expound and interpret the rule. The president too has a constitutionally assigned role in applying the law in particular cases—he is vested with the executive power of the United States and charged to take care that the laws be faithfully executed. Could the power to interpret the law be incidental to this power to execute the law, just as it is incidental to the power to apply the law in adjudications?

There is general agreement that the president has the power, and perhaps the duty, to take constitutional rules, principles, and values into account when considering whether to veto a bill before it becomes law. In the early days of the Republic, the veto was exercised exclusively on constitutional grounds. President Andrew Jackson provided the classic justification for this power in explaining his veto of a bill reauthorizing a national bank, which he believed to be unconstitutional even though the Supreme Court had held otherwise in *Osborne v. Bank of the United States*:[5]

The Congress, the executive, and the court must each for itself be guided by its own opinion of the Constitution. Each public officer who takes an oath to support the Constitution swears that he will support it as he understands it, and not as it is understood by others. It is as much the duty of the House of Representatives, of the Senate, and of the president to decide upon the constitutionality of any bill or resolution which may be presented to them for passage or approval as it is of the supreme judges when it may be brought to them for judicial decision. The opinion of the judges has no more authority over Congress than the opinion of Congress has over the judges, and on that point the president is independent of both. The authority of the Supreme Court must not, therefore, be permitted to control Congress or the executive when acting in their legislative capacities, but to have only such influence as the force of their reasoning may deserve.[6]

Similarly, thepPresident may pardon a defendant convicted under a statute that the president believes is unconstitutional. The Sedition Act of 1798, for instance, which criminalized criticism of the government, was enacted by a Federalist Congress and applied by Federalist judges against political opponents under President John Adams, under whom Thomas Jefferson—who deemed the act unconstitutional—served as vice president. President Jefferson, upon taking office after the election of 1800, directed the attorney-general and all United States attorneys to cease prosecutions under the act. Jefferson pardoned all those who had been convicted under the act. President Jefferson defended the prerogative of the executive, as a fully equal coordinate branch of government, to decide for itself, within its own sphere, what is and what is not unconstitutional:

You seem to think it devolved on the judges to decide on the validity of the sedition law. But nothing in the Constitution has given them a right to decide for the Executive, more than to the Executive to decide for them. Both magistracies are equally independent in the sphere of action assigned to them. The judges, believing the law constitutional, had a right to pass a sentence of fine and imprisonment; because the power was placed in their hands by the Constitution. But the executive, believing the law to be unconstitutional, were bound to remit the execution of it; because that power had been confided to them by the Constitution. That instrument meant that its co-ordinate branches should be checks on each other. But, the opinion which gives to the judges the right to decide what laws are constitutional, and what not, not only for themselves in their own sphere of action, but for the legislature and the executive also, in their spheres, would make the judiciary a despotic branch.[7]

Indeed, in practice the executive's power to interpret the law may in some respects actually exceed that of the judicial branch. This is a function of the breadth of objects to which the executive power extends—to practically every matter of national governance, not just litigation; to the constitutional powers of the executive that may be used to implement and enforce adherence to its interpretation of the laws, including the pardon, veto, appointment, and commander-in-chief powers; and to the unique, strategic position of the executive as often the first and typically also the last branch to act on any given issue of legal controversy. Contrary to the conventional wisdom that assigns the judiciary the last word on questions of legal interpretation, in actual practice the executive often enjoys that power, by virtue of its role in deciding whether and how to execute judicial decrees. Hamilton defended the Constitution against the Anti-Federalist charge that it established judicial supremacy by pointing out that the judiciary, unlike the other branches, lacked such powers as the sword or the purse, and therefore was the repository only of judgment, not force or will, and must ultimately depend on the aid of the executive arm even for the efficacy of its judgments. As President Andrew Jackson is supposed to have said after the Supreme Court's decision in *Worcester v. Georgia*,[8] "John Marshall has made a decision, now let him enforce it."

But may the president act contrary to statutory law on the ground that, in his or her view, it departs from the Constitution? Such a power might be considered the executive equivalent of the judicial practice of severing unconstitutional provisions from statutes already enacted. A strong argument can be made that the president, as part of his constitutional duty to take care that the laws be faithfully executed, must ensure that the Constitution, the highest law, is faithfully observed. According to this argument, in any case where the president perceives a conflict between the Constitution and a statute that he or she is asked to execute, the president should honor the former and ignore the latter. After all, the Supreme Court has said on more than one occasion that an unconstitutional statute is "no law at all."[9]

This theory may sound more radical than it really is. The notion that the executive branch must enforce the law according to the executive's view of what the Constitution requires is in fact a widely accepted one, so long as the executive does not usurp the role of the Article III judiciary as the ultimate expositor of the Constitution in actual cases and controversies. The court has recognized that, "in the performance of assigned constitutional duties each branch of government must initially interpret the Constitution."[10] For example, prosecutors every day make decisions not to bring criminal charges against defendants solely on the ground that, in their view, critical evidence against those defendants has been unconstitutionally obtained and that, as a result, there is not sufficient admissible evidence to go to trial. Similarly, if the court invalidates a law on constitutional grounds, the executive branch acts entirely properly by speeding compliance with the newly announced norm and refusing to enforce other laws that share the same constitutional flaw. And few would insist that the president must enforce an obviously unconstitutional statute (perhaps enacted over the president's veto), such as a bill of attainder ordering the immediate summary execution of a named person and purporting to foreclose any possibility of judicial review by the victim. Even private citizens have the power and the legal authority to engage in constitutional interpretation in the sense that they may disobey a statute they believe to be unconstitutional and escape punishment under it if their views are subsequently confirmed by a reviewing court.[11] It is thus rather unremarkable to posit an analogous power on the part of the president to take his or her own views of the Constitution into account when executing the law.

But the authority to interpret the Constitution in the absence of a binding judicial construction does not imply that the executive branch may simply disregard or nullify a judicial interpretation of the Constitution with which the executive disagrees except an interpretation announced in a since-discredited decision whose overturning is widely assumed to be imminent. *Marbury v. Madison* establishes the federal judiciary, at the apex of which the Supreme Court sits, as the ultimate interpreter of the Constitution. Thus, the Attorney-General Meese's statement in April 1985 that the executive branch would refuse to enforce the competition in Contracting Act of 1984—regardless of whether lower federal courts upheld its constitutionality—was indefensible and was rightly condemned by a Ninth Circuit Panel in *Lear Siegler, Inc. v. Lehman*. The notion that only a decision of the Supreme Court—and not that of an inferior federal court—is binding on Congress and the president in disputes between those two branches seems entirely unprincipled. There is no indication in the Constitution that the judicial power of a congressionally created lower federal court over matters in which it properly has jurisdiction is less extensive than that of the Supreme Court. The status of the U.S. District Courts and Courts of Appeals as inferior courts under Article III surely does not imply any constitutional basis for asserting that the president need obey only those judicial orders that issue from the Supreme Court.

NOTES

1. The Constitution does explicitly circumscribe the power of all branches of government to remove federal judges from office. Article III, paragraph 1 provides: "The Judges, both of the supreme and inferior Courts, shall hold their Offices during good Behaviour." Federal judges appointed to Article III courts cannot, therefore be removed as the president's will even though such judges are appointed by the president. Of course, these judges, like other officers of the United States, can be removed through the impeachment mechanism.

2. 272 U.S. 52 (1926).

3. 295 U.S. 602 (1935).

4. *Humphrey's Executor*, 295 U.S. at 632.

5. 22 U.S. (9 Wheat.) 738 (1824).

6. A Compilation of the Messages and Papers of the President 1789–1897, at 582 (James D. Richardson ed., 1897).

7. The Writings of Thomas Jefferson 49, 50–51 (Albert Bragh ed., 1905): letter to Mr. John Adams, 11 September 1804. Note that this letter was written after the decision in *Marbury v. Madison.*

8. 31 U.S. (6 Pet) 515 (1832).

9. *Norton v. Shelby County*, 118 U.S. 425, 442 (1886).

10. *United States v. Nixon*, 418 U.S. 683, 703 (1974).

11. *Cox v. Louisiana*, 379 U.S. 536, 558 (1965).

Chapter 16

Federal Legislative Power

CONGRESSIONAL AUTHORITY AND THE IMPLICATIONS OF STATE SOVEREIGNTY: THE SCOPE AND LIMITS OF CONGRESSIONAL POWER

It is noteworthy that Article I, paragraph 1 endows Congress not with all legislative power, but only with the legislative powers herein granted. In theory, Congress is thus a legislative body possessing only limited powers, those granted to it by the Constitution.

History demonstrates that Congress and the two bodies that comprise it have various powers under the Constitution, some textually explicit and others only implicit. Among the explicit powers other than the most important, which is the power to legislate, are the powers of the House to impeach and of the Senate to convict or to acquit someone whom the House has impeached. The power of the House to initiate appropriations measures; the power of the Senate to give or withhold its consent to various appointments under Article II; the power by a two-thirds vote to override a presidential veto; the power to create lower federal courts and to regulate the jurisdiction of the courts, including the appellate jurisdiction of the Supreme Court; the power of the Senate to give or withhold its consent to treaties; the power to declare war; the power to give or withhold consent to states with respect to imposts or duties on imports or exports, duties of tonnage, the keeping by states of troops or ships of war in time of peace, agreements or compacts among states or between states and foreign powers, or states engaging in war absent actual invasion or imminent danger; the power to organize, arm, and discipline the militia and to provide for calling forth the militia to execute federal law, suppress insurrections, and repel invasions; the power to prescribe the manner in which state acts, records, and judicial proceedings are to be given full faith and credit; the power to admit new states to the Union; the power to send constitutional amendments out to the nation on a vote of two-thirds of both houses, or to call a convention for proposing amendments on the application of two-thirds of the state legislatures; and the power to guarantee every state a republican form of government.

It is important to note an implicit or ancillary power belonging to Congress that is at times every bit as important as the power to which it is supposedly appurtenant. That is the power of investigation, typically and most dramatically exemplified by hearings, some of them in executive session but most of them in the glare of the lights and with the nation watching. Such investigations have served an important role in ventilating issues of profound national concern. The modern function of hearings is often simply to focus the national attention and place a pressing issue on the nation's agenda. Some might say that, in certain legislative sessions, such consciousness-raising ranks among Congress' most constructive accomplishments. Even if no particular legislation is in view or results, there is a constitutional matter nothing inherently objectionable about such cases of exposure for exposure's sake it might constitute a kind of legislative punishment, even if not quite trial by legislature and a bill of attainder.

Although congressional authority to conduct investigations, and in the process to compel testimony, is not explicitly recognized by the Constitution, this power is necessary in connection with Congress' quasi-judicial powers of impeachment and self-regulation. But the Supreme Court has quite properly held the investigatory power to be broader, as an essential and appropriate auxiliary to the legislative function, thus making it implicit in Article I, paragraph 1 grant of legislative Powers to Congress.[1] The power of inquiry is as penetrating and far-reaching as the potential power to enact laws and appropriate funds under the Constitution. Investigations in aid of legislation encompass inquiries concerning the administration of existing laws as well as proposed or possibly needed statutes.[2] Congress undeniably has legitimate concerns in ensuring, on behalf of a watching nation, that appropriations are well spent and that creatures of legislative creation are adequately supervised through oversight hearings, and in performing a variety of other investigatory functions which have only a tenuous link to any future legislation. The Necessary and Proper Clause, Article I, paragraph 8, clause 18, amply justifies holding hearings public or otherwise, since it's never hard to explain why any given inquiry might turn up information useful in some way to one or more of the myriad tasks entrusted to Congress by the Constitution. Congress may of course issue and enforce subpoenas to effectuate its investigatory power.

The congressional power of investigation is, however, limited by the separation of powers. Congress may not usurp the functions of the courts. This certainly does not mean that Congress may not investigate matters relevant to past or future legislation that are also pertinent to litigation under way in federal or state courts. Although the Supreme Court held in *Kilbourn v. Thompson* that Congress could not investigate a matter concurrently within the jurisdiction of a federal court,[3] the Court in a subsequent decision effectively and properly confined *Kilbourn* to the proposition that congressional investigation may proceed only pursuant to a valid congressional power, holding in *Sinclair v. United States* that the authority of Congress "to require pertinent disclosures in aid of its own constitutional power is not abridged because the information sought to be elicited may also be of use in pending suits."[4]

Although not loosely restricting the substantive scope of congressional investigations, the Supreme Court has required Congress to adopt important procedural safeguards in the conduct of its investigations. Because the Bill of Rights limits the lawmaking process as well as the content of resulting legislation, congressional investigators must respect the Fifth Amendment prohibition of unreasonable searches and seizures, and the requirement of due process that, if government actors promulgate rules limiting their own conduct, they must comply with such rules.[5] More significantly, the court has held that due process and the formally limited character of congressional investigatory power (1) require Congress, in delegating its investigatory authority to particular committees, to state clearly the scope of a given committee's authority and (2) require an investigating committee, if the materiality of its inquiry is challenged by a witness, and if the subject matter of the investigation has not previously been made to appear with indisputable clarity, to state for the record the subject under inquiry and the manner in which the propounded questions are pertinent thereto.[6]

For most of the latter half of the twentieth century, the Supreme Court has focused its attention on developing external limits on congressional power—limits which derive from particular aspects of the separation of powers, or from specific constraints on congressional power, such as those contained in Article I, paragraph 9 and in the Bill of Rights. In recent years, however, the court has revived the application of internal and structural limits, each of which had been thought dead at various points in the past half century. Clearly, Congress is bound by its oath to look to the Constitution in the course of legislating, and is free to formulate its own conclusions as to what the Constitution requires. Even if the Supreme Court ultimately fails to impose significant limits on the scope of the Constitution's grants of power to Congress, the political processes through which Congress reaches its conclusions as well as custom and tradition, may fix limits on congressional power no less real simply because they cannot be found on the pages of the United States reports.

THE TAXING POWER

Article I, paragraph 8 declares that Congress shall have power to lay and collect taxes, duties, imposts, and excises. This power to tax is an independent source of federal authority. Congress may tax subjects that it may not be authorized to regulate directly under any of its enumerated regulatory powers. An extended discussion of limitations on the use of federal taxes to raise revenue is beyond the scope of this work. The specific focus here is on the use of taxes as an indirect regulatory device. Nevertheless, it is useful to note the limitations of congressional taxing power incorporated in the body of the Constitution.

The very sentence that confers the taxing power upon Congress contains one of its most central limitations: that all duties, imposts, and excises shall be uniform throughout the United States. This requirement is of geographic uniformity only; so long as the tax structure does not discriminate among the states, it does not matter that a tax may not be uniform as it applies to particular individuals.[7] The uniformity requirement applies to all indirect taxes—those that (1) tax the privilege of doing business or of performing some act, and (2) are ordinarily imposed on persons other than the ultimate consumers.

Two other limitations on the taxing power appear in Article I, paragraph 9. Unlike the cross-cutting limitations in the Bill of Rights, which can apply to the exercise of any congressional power, these limitations are specific to the exercise of Congress' taxing power; they are analogous to the uniformity requirement that appears in the same sentence as the taxing power. Their specificity means that, despite their appearance in other clauses, they are probably better understood as integral and inseparable components of the taxing power (and therefore as internal limits), rather than as independent, external limits on congressional power.

The more important of these limits in Article I, paragraph 9 is that imposed by the Export Clause, which provides that "No Tax or Duty shall be laid on Articles exported from any State." The Supreme Court has interpreted this provision as prohibiting the imposition of taxes on goods in export transit, even if those taxes do not discriminate against exports.[8] Moreover, the court has treated the clause as applying not only to taxes on exports themselves but also to taxes on services and activities closely related to the export process.[9]

Article I, paragraph 9, also states that no capitation, or other direct, tax shall be laid, unless in Proportion to the Census. Article I, paragraph 2 provides that direct taxes shall be apportioned among the several states which may be included within this Union, according to their respective numbers. A direct tax is one imposed upon property as such, rather than on the performance of an act. Because of the impractical apportionment requirement attaching to direct taxes, the fate of federal income taxation in the nineteenth century turned on the content the Supreme Court gave to the distinction between direct and indirect taxes. In *Springer v. United States*, the court held a Civil War income tax to be an indirect excise tax. But in *Pollock v. Farmers' Loan & Trust Co.* a majority of the justices ruled that, insofar as the source of income is property, in income tax is a direct tax, and is therefore invalid unless apportioned. By 1911, however, the Supreme Court had again reversed direction, holding in *Flint v. Stone Tracy Co.*[10] that a tax on corporations measured by income was not a direct tax but an excise tax on the privilege of doing business in the corporate form. The confusion was put to an end in 1913 with the ratification of the Sixteenth Amendment, which provides: "Congress shall have power to lay and to collect taxes on incomes, from whatever source derived, without apportionment among the several States, and without regard to any census or emuneration."

Turning next from what may be taxed to whether taxes be used to shape behavior, we begin by noting that almost any tax will achieve an ancillary regulatory effect by increasing the costs of the taxed activities for individuals or corporations. If Congress has authority independent of its taxing power to regulate the taxed subject, this regulatory effect is not constitutionally troublesome. In such cases, even if the tax is plainly regulatory in purpose and effect, it may be upheld under the Necessary and Proper Clause as a means of regulating an activity properly the subject of congressional regulation. Thus, in *Veazie Bank v. Fenno*[11] for example, the Supreme Court upheld a federal tax on banknotes issued by state banks, even though the effect of the tax was to drive such notes out of circulation, since Congress had the power under Article I, paragraph 8 to regulate currency through taxation as well as by other means.

However, if no independent source of federal regulatory authority justifies a congressional tax, classification of the tax as a regulatory rather than a revenue measure may be determinative of its constitutionality. The principle of classification on which the Supreme Court has traditionally relied can be briefly summarized: (1) A tax is a valid revenue measure if it achieves its regulatory effect through its rate structure or if its regulatory provisions bear a reasonable relation to its enforcement as a tax measure. (2) A tax is a regulatory tax—and hence invalid if not otherwise authorized—if its very application presupposes taxpayer violation of a series of specified conditions promulgated along with tax.

The 1937 decision in *Sonzinsky v. United States*[12] upholding a license tax on firearms dealers, marked the beginning of a quiescent period for the prohibition on regulatory. Indeed since that time, the court has not invalidated an exaction as a regulatory tax unmoored to an independent source of congressional authority. That this period began in 1937 is no coincidence. The key factor was not doubt the court's expansive interpretation of the Commerce Clause. The breadth of the commerce power, as construed by the court starting in 1937, rendered moot any consideration of whether a tax was regulatory; because there always seemed to be an independent source of federal regulatory authority (usually the Commerce Clause or the Commerce Clause augmented by the Necessary and Proper Clause), nothing would turn on the revenue/regulation distinction. Accordingly, if *United States v. Lopez*[13] marks the beginning of a new era in which the court cabins Congress' commerce power, it may also render salient, for the first time in more than half a century. The distinction between regulatory and revenue taxes for purposes of Congress' powers. It may be prophetic in the sense that Lopez, like *Sonzinski*, involved Congress' power with respect to firearms—although, to be sure, only federal power to outlaw possession of a gun was rejected in *Lopez* while dealing in guns was the subject of the federal tax upheld in *Sonzinski.*

Article I is not the only provision of the Constitution that grants lawmaking power to Congress. Between 1865 and 1870, the Constitution was amended three times, as Congress repeatedly acted to safeguard individual rights inadequately protected prior to the Civil War. The Thirteenth Amendment outlawed slavery and involuntary servitude, except as duly administered punishment for crime. The Fourteenth Amendment guaranteed all persons the privileges of immunities of United States citizenship, due process of law, and the equal protection of the laws, and made every United States citizen, by operation of law, a citizen of whichever state he or she chooses as a place in which to reside. And the Fifteenth Amendment denied both the federal government and the states power to deprive United States citizens of the right to vote on account of race, color, or previous condition of servitude.

Each of these amendments authorized Congress to enforce by appropriate legislation the rights the amendment recognized. In doing so, each responded to the inadequacies of the prior state law regime for the protection of civil rights by self-consciously and fundamentally altering the balance of power in favor of the federal government in general and its legislative branch in particular. As the Supreme Court has acknowledges, the Civil War Amendments "were specifically designed as an expansion of federal power and an intrusion on state sovereignty."[14]

Immediately after each amendment's ratification (except the Nineteenth), Congress adopted enforcing legislation. Initially, in *Ex parte Virginia*,[15] the Supreme Court appeared willing to interpret Congress' power to enact appropriate legislation broadly, in line with *McCulloch v. Maryland*,[16] at least as regards the selection of means to accomplish a given end, concluding that whatever legislation is adapted to carry out the objects the amendments have in view, whatever tends to enforce submission to the prohibitions they contain, and to secure to all persons the enjoyment of perfect equality of civil rights and the equal protection of the laws against state denial or invasion, if not prohibited, is brought within the domain of congressional power. However, the Court proceeded in the 1883 Civil Rights Cases, to construe restrictively much of Congress' post-Civil War enforcement legislation by adopting an extremely narrow view of the legitimate objects of the amendments,[17] thus preserving in law the autonomy that the states had largely lost politically in the wake of the Civil War. Following its initial flurry of legislation, Congress, reflecting the changed political climate of the post-Reconstruction era, ceased for three quarters of a century its efforts to enforce the Civil War Amendments. This lengthy legislative inaction, the judicial silence, and the expanding recognition of Congress' commerce power after 1937 that appeared to indicate that virtually any legislation could be supported on that ground without reference to the amendments, combined to suggest that Congress' powers under the Civil War Amendments were destined to be merely of historical interest.

Two subsequent developments have, however, focused renewed attention on Congress' Civil War Amendment powers. First, in the 1960s, there was a resurgence of congressional interest in protecting individual rights. Congress initially side-stepped potential controversies over the scope of its Civil War Amendment powers by framing its major anti-discrimination legislation as a regulation of interstate commerce. But subsequent legislation, particularly in the voting rights area, required the Supreme Court to confront squarely' authority to enforce, and, simultaneously, to interpret, the Civil War Amendments. More recently, congressional mandates for race-based affirmative action; legislation purporting to enforce or interpret the substantive rights in the Bill of Rights that the court has held incorporated against the states by the Due Process Clause of the Fourteenth Amendment; and the legislation regulating activities that bear no direct relation to state action, broadened the issue further.

Meanwhile, Congress' Civil War Amendments authority has assumed further significance as the Supreme Court has revitalized the constraints of federalism on Congress' Article I powers. Because the Civil War Amendments self-consciously rejected the original model of federalism within their zone of operation, the court's modern decisions in Article I cases invoking the Tenth and Eleventh Amendments and related rules are not fully applicable to legislation enforcing the Civil War Amendments. Congress' ability, unhindered by the political costs of having to satisfy clear statement requirements and unobstructed by the structural limitations of the Tenth and Eleventh Amendments, to achieve results under the Civil War Amendments that it could not achieve under Article I places new importance on the internal limitations of the Civil War Amendments' enforcement powers, and on the external limitations imposed on those powers by the Bill of Rights.

Increasingly since the 1960s, the court has had to consider how much deference is due to Congress in its choice of means to enforce the Civil War Amendments; what, if any, latitude Congress should be given to define the ends sought by those amendments—the rights to be protected—and the extent to which judicially established limitations on the substantive scope of the amendments when they appear in self-executing form—particularly the state action requirement under the Fourteenth and Fifteenth Amendments—limit Congress' power when it acts to enforce or implement those amendments.

In the 1960s, the Court chose *Ex parte Virginia's* deferential approach over the restrictive doctrines of the *Civil Rights cases* and, as in its Commerce Clause jurisprudence, implied that the power of Congress to enforce the Thirteenth, Fourteenth, and Fifteenth Amendments was without internal or structural limits, other than the minimal rationality standard of *McCulloch v. Maryland*, which the court took to be the measure of Congress' power to fit means to ends under each of the Civil War Amendments as well as under Article I. But a 1970s decision, holding that Congress exceeded its Fourteenth Amendment power in legislating a lowered voting age for state elections,[18] signaled that congressional power to enforce the Civil War Amendments may not be entirely free of significant internal constraints—an implication confirmed by the court's announcement in 1997 of the proportionality requirement for congressional enactments pursuant to paragraph 5 of the Fourteenth Amendment.[19]

CONGRESSIONAL POWER TO ENFORCE THE THIRTEENTH AMENDMENT

The Thirteenth Amendment provides in paragraph 1 that "neither slavery nor involuntary servitude, except as a punishment for a crime whereof the party shall have been duly convicted, shall exist within the United States, or any place subject to their jurisdiction." Section 2 provides that "Congress shall have power to enforce this article by appropriate legislation." Although this power, like Congress' other Civil War Amendment enforcement powers, has been employed primarily to remedy past and present racial discrimination—and although many federal statutes can therefore be grounded either on paragraph 2 of the Thirteenth Amendment, or on paragraph 5 of the Fourteenth, the Thirteenth Amendment differs from the Fourteenth and Fifteenth in that, even absent implementing legislation, it is not subject to a state action requirement. In the *Civil Rights Cases*, the Court concluded that the Thirteenth Amendment was self-executing, and that it authorized Congress to regulate not only state action, but private conduct as well. Insofar as state action may be required under the Fourteenth and Fifteenth Amendments, therefore, the Thirteenth Amendment retains a most distinctive importance.

Initially, the Supreme Court read paragraph 2 as a narrow grant of power. The court held in the *Civil Rights cases* that legislation thereunder could concern itself only with slavery and its incidents. "The long existence of African slavery in this country," the court concluded, "gave us very distinct notions of what it was, and what were its necessary incidents." In "abolishing all badges and all incidents of slavery," Congress could not "adjust what may be called the social rights of men and races in the community; but only . . . declare and vindicate those fundamental rights which appertain to the essence of citizenship, and the enjoyment or deprivation of which constitutes the essential distinction between freedom and slavery."[20] It would be running the slavery argument into the ground to make it apply to every act of discrimination which a person may see fit to make as to the guests he will entertain, or as to the people he will take into his coach or cab or car, or admit to his concert or theatre, or deal with in other matters of intercourse or business. Subsequent decisions further restricted congressional power. In *Hodges v. United States*[21] the Supreme Court held that Congress, acting to enforce the Thirteenth Amendment, could proscribe only those private acts which created a state of entire subjection of one person to the will of another. No mere personal assault or trespass or appropriation operates to reduce the individual to a condition of slavery. Moreover, in *Corrigan v. Buckley*[22] and *Hurd v. Hodge*[23] the court decided that the Thirteenth Amendment did not grant Congress power to prohibit agreements among whites to refuse to deal with blacks (e.g., racially restrictive covenants).

In *Jones v. Alfred H. Mayer Co.*,[24] however, the Supreme Court dramatically redefined the scope of congressional power under the Thirteenth Amendment. Overruling *Hodges v. United States,*[25] the court rejected the notion that any judicially defined concept of slavery and its entailments significantly limits the scope of congressional power: "Congress has the power under the Thirteenth Amendment rationally to determine what are the badges and incidents of slavery, and the authority to translate the determination into effective legislation."

Jones' rejection of *Hodges* seems compelling. Given that, as the court had held in the *Civil Rights Cases*, the Thirteenth Amendment's prohibition is self-executing, it is unclear what role paragraph 2 would give to Congress over and above paragraph 1 if, as the *Hodges* majority held, the content of the prohibition is fixed and immune from congressional elaboration. Nevertheless, the broad language of the *Jones* opinion is also not without difficulties. If it is read literally, Congress possesses an almost unlimited power to protect individual rights under the Thirteenth Amendment.

Seemingly, Congress is free to recognize whatever rights it wishes, define the infringement of those rights as a form of domination and subordination and thus an aspect of slavery, and proscribe such infringement as a violation of the Thirteenth Amendment. On this view, Congress would possess nearly plenary authority under the Thirteenth Amendment to protect all but the most trivial individual rights from both governmental and private invasion. This dilemma—how to accommodate the congressional discretion implicit in the power to enforce rights by appropriate legislation while at the same time limiting Congress to its enumerated powers and preserving the practice of judicial review—pervades the jurisprudence of Congress' Civil War Amendment powers.

Cases later appearing have not required the Supreme Court to consider what internal limitations on Congress' power *Jones* omitted to mention. Since the immediate post–Civil War era, Congress has enacted little legislation which relies upon the Thirteenth Amendment for constitutional authorization. The court has been largely confined to responding to efforts to resurrect long-ignored post–Civil War statutes. These statutes typically raise problems of construction, given the inherent difficulties of reconciling ambiguous century-old legislative text, structure and history with contemporary conceptions of rights. The case of *United States v. Kozminski*[26] is illustrative. There, the court considered the scope of two 1909 criminal statutes, one prohibiting conspiracies to interfere with rights secured by the Constitution, including the right not to be subjected to involuntary servitude, the other prohibiting the knowing and willfully holding of another person in involuntary servitude. The court deemed Congress' power to enact the statutes clear and undisputed, but split as to the scope of involuntary servitude. Writing for a five-justice majority, Justice O'Connor found as a matter of statutory construction that the legislation intended to adopt without elaboration or qualification the judicial definition of involuntary servitude under paragraph 1 of the Thirteenth Amendment, and that, while the Thirteenth Amendment generally prohibits the compulsion of labor by means of threatened physical or legal coercion, it does not encompass coercion of other means. Justices Brennan and Stevens concurred in the judgment, arguing that the means of coercion are not determinative in light of the Thirteenth Amendment's broad aim not merely to end slavery but to maintain a system of completely free and voluntary labor throughout the United States. Even the majority, however, appeared to leave open the possibility that Congress could legislate more broadly to enforce the amendment: Justice O'Connor qualified her definition of involuntary servitude as the definition applicable absent change by Congress, and called the task of defining the term "inherently legislative."

Other recent statutory Supreme Court decisions do pointedly avoid assuming that Congress' Thirteenth Amendment power is plenary. The court has not repudiated those of its early decisions, plainly grounded in the language of the Thirteenth Amendment, which declare that persons of all races and nationalities, and not African Americans alone, may claim the benefits of the Thirteenth Amendment's proscription of slavery and its incidents. Indeed, the court has held that whites victimized by racial discrimination are entitled to the protections of civil rights statute enacted by Congress shortly after the Civil War in the exercise of its Thirteenth Amendment powers.[27] The Supreme Court has, however, indicated in dictum its considerable doubt that the Thirteenth Amendment can be read to grant Congress general authority to protect all individual rights against all invidiously discriminatory treatment—not to mention open-ended authority to protect anyone it perceives as in danger of victimization from whatever kind of oppression Congress deems in need of correction by federal law. In *Norwood v. Harrison*, in discussing the Thirteenth Amendment, the court was willing to say no more than that "some private discrimination is subject to special remedial legislation in certain circumstances under paragraph 2 of the Thirteenth Amendment."[28] More significantly, in *Griffin v. Breckenridge* Justice Steward spoke for the court about the constitutional shoals that would be lie in the path of interpreting [42 U.S.C.] paragraph 1985 (3) as a general federal tort law[29] and further observed that "we need not find the language of paragraph (1985) 3 now before us constitutional in all its possible applications.[30]

The court again addressed paragraph 1985 (3) in *Bray v. Alexandria Wome's Health Clinic.*[31] Justice Scalia, writing for a 5–4 majority, held that this 1871 legislation, which renders actionable private conspiracies to deprive individuals of, or to hinder state officials from securing, the equal protection of the laws or the privileges or immunities guaranteed by the Fourteenth Amendment, applies only in the conspiracy discriminatory animus toward a group designated as a suspect class by the court's equal protection jurisprudence, and at least generally applies only if the conspiracy is aimed at constitutional rights judicially recognized as protected against purely private interference. The majority thus interpreted ambiguous statutory language narrowly to reflect the state action and intent requirements generally applicable to judicial enforcement of the Equal Protection Clause. But it did not hold that the Constitution mandated that result, and conceded that Congress may provide remedies for discriminatory effects without the evidence of discriminatory intent that a judicial remedy would require.

ENFORCING THE FIFTEENTH AMENDMENT

The Fifteenth Amendment's guarantee of a racially unconditioned right to vote, like the various guarantees of the Fourteenth Amendment, is self-executing.

On a number of occasions, litigants have persuaded the Supreme Court that states have violated the limitation of the Fifteenth Amendment imposes upon them even in the absence of implementing federal legislation. Until the 1960s, apart from several early statutes, Congress confined its legislation enforcing the Fifteenth Amendment largely to procedural measures designed to facilitate judicial enforcement of the constitutional guarantee.[32] The Supreme Court had little difficulty upholding such measures as appropriate legislation. By 1965, however, Congress has concluded that judicial remedies were too time-consuming and could be circumvented too readily to provide effective enforcement for Fifteenth Amendment rights. Accordingly Congress enacted the Voting Rights Act of 1965, probably the most radical piece of civil rights legislation since Reconstruction. The Voting Rights Act had two principal features of relevance to Fifteenth Amendment jurisprudence. First, the act authorized the attorney general to suspend voting tests and to send federal voting examiners into any state whose voter registration pattern met certain criteria. Although the attorney general's determinations were subject to a narrow form of judicial review, this first provision substituted administrative remedies for judicial relief as the principal means of enforcing the Fifteenth Amendment. Second, the Voting Rights Act did not require the attorney general to make the detailed determination a court would make before acting, but rather authorized enforcement procedures wherever the use of certain tests or devices in registering voters coincided with the circumstance that less than 50 percent of voting age residents were in fact registered. The states could seek a judicial finding of no racial discrimination in order to block enforcement of the Voting Rights Act, but administrative rules of thumb essentially replaced the fact-finding criteria that courts had previously developed in the course of constitutional adjudication.

The constitutionality of these provisions was settled in *South Carolina v. Katzenbach*, where the court rejected the argument that Congress may do no more than to forbid violations of the Fifteenth Amendment in general terms—that the task of fashioning specific remedies or applying them to particular localities must necessarily be left entirely to the courts; "Congress is not circumscribed by any such artificial rules under paragraph 2 of the Fifteenth Amendment."[33] Instead, the Fifteenth Amendment left Congress chiefly responsible for implementing the rights created. To this end, congressional power must be measured by the generous standard fixed by Chief Justice Marshall in *McCulloch v. Maryland*: "Let the end be legitimate, let it be within the scope of the constitution, and all means which are appropriate, which are plainly adapted to the end, which are not prohibited, but consistent with the letter and spirit of the constitution, are constitutional."[34] The Supreme Court readily found that the remedial and fact-finding provisions of the Voting Rights Act met the traditional rationality test. The court has recognized that the Voting Rights Act, by its nature, intrudes on state sovereignty, but has reasoned that the act was passed pursuant to Congress' authority under the Fifteenth Amendment and the Reconstruction Amendments by their nature contemplate some intrusion into the areas traditionally reserved to the states. The court has therefore rejected attempts to read the Voting Rights Act narrowly in order to avoid treading on rights constitutionally reserved to the states.

The contrast between the jurisprudence of outright Fourteenth and Fifteenth Amendment violations and the power of Congress to enforce those amendments is highlighted by a comparison of *City of Mobile v. Bolden*[35] and *City of Rome v. United States*,[36] decided the same day in 1980. In *Mobile*, a black resident challenged the constitutionality of a state legislative apportionment plan which utilized at-large elections of multiple representatives from a single district, effectively blocking the election of black candidates by the sizable black minority of Mobile, Alabama. Justice Steward's plurality opinion held that the Mobile election scheme was adopted or maintained with intent to discriminate. Mobile's electoral scheme was not challenged under the Voting Rights Act—which applies only to changes in voting procedures made since 1965—because it had been in place since 1911.

The *Rome* litigation challenged the city's annexation of sixty outlying areas and a change to a system of electing members of the city commission at large; both changes had transpired since 1965. Although this was virtually the same kind of system which the court upheld in Mobile, and even though the district court explicitly found that none of the *Rome* electoral changes was made for a discriminatory purpose, the changes were disallowed under the Voting Rights Act. The district court had concluded that the Voting Rights Act required the court to invalidate the changes if they had either the purpose or the effect of diluting black voting strength. In a 6–3 decision, the Supreme Court agreed, and found that Congress had the power under paragraph 2 of the Fifteenth Amendment to prohibit these electoral changes and annexations even though they were not intentionally discriminatory.

Justice Marshall's opinion for the court held that Congress could conclude that because electoral changes by jurisdictions with a demonstrable history of intentional racial discrimination in voting create the risk of purposeful discrimination, it was proper for Congress to prohibit changes that have a discriminatory impact. Thus the court held that Congress may establish a prophylactic rule—almost a rule of evidence—by deciding that certain types of changes in electoral law which have the effect of burdening minorities should be forbidden because many of them may have been discriminatorily motivated.

Then Justice Rehnquist (as he then was) charged in dissent that this holding amounted to granting Congress an independent privilege to interpret the substance of the Fifteenth Amendment itself. His reading, however, overstated the majority's position in *Rome*. Because district courts may take years to examine all the evidence relevant to the issue of discriminatory purpose in a voting rights case, and because the local government may too easily disguise the real reason for its actions, the court held that Congress may choose to circumvent the problems of proof. To do so, Congress created a general rule based on its own finding that certain practices are so likely to have been adopted for discriminatory reasons that they should be prohibited altogether. Justice Rehnquist argued that, while Congress did have the power to establish a presumption that certain kinds of electoral changes were undertaken for discriminatory reasons, Congress may not establish an irrebuttable, which he believed the court applied in *Rome*. Such a presumption, he argued, amounted to a substantive change in the Fifteenth Amendment, one the court has not viewed as a proper construction of that amendment. The problems of proof are too difficult, too complex for a case by case adjudication. Since electoral changes and annexations have been used in the past for purposes of discrimination, Congress can outlaw them all.

In addition, a ban on particular election practices that are themselves constitutionally inoffensive could be justified instrumentally. Thus while Rome asserts a broad congressional power to enforce the Fifteenth Amendment, it need not be read an independent assertion of congressional power to interpret it.

After the decisions in *Mobile* and *Rome*, Congress amended the Voting Rights Act to make challenges easier and to move the courts toward a result rather than an intent test. At the time of *Mobile*, paragraph 2 of the act stated that no voting qualification or prerequisite to voting or standard, practice or procedure shall be imposed or applied by any state or political subdivision to deny or abridge the right of any citizen of the United States to vote on account of race or color. *Mobile* interpreted paragraph 2 as intended to have an effect no different from that of the Fifteenth Amendment itself. Congress disagreed with that interpretation of its legislation, and found that such a regime would be inadequate to address the effects of past discrimination. In 1982, Congress substituted the words "in a manner which results in a denial or abridgment of" for the words "to deny or abridge." The Voting Rights Act Amendments of 1982 added: "The extent to which members of a protected class have been elected to office in the State or political subdivision is one circumstance which may be considered: Provided, that nothing in this section establishes a right to have members of a protected class elected in numbers equal to their proportion in the population."

The Supreme Court has not yet settled whether, with this change, Congress exceeded its power to enforce the Fifteenth Amendment in light of the court's own employment of an intent test to adjudicate claims under paragraph 1 of the amendment. However, in holding that states have a compelling interest in complying with them, a majority of the court has strongly implied that the 1982 amendments are constitutional.[37] As Justice O'Connor has suggested, a decade and a half of enforcement of the amendments by the Supreme Court, albeit without confronting a direct constitutional challenge, and unanimous lower court support for their constitutionality, strongly reinforce that conclusion.

Moreover, as a matter of principle, the approach taken in Rome, relying on Congress' fact-finding capacities as justification for its prophylactic approach in extending liability beyond cases of proven discriminatory intent, seems to justify that conclusion.

CONGRESSIONAL POWERS IN FOREIGN AFFAIRS: WAR

This section turns to an area where state sovereignty is not really a factor not because the powers in question were designed to limit or override state sovereignty, but because those powers all deal with the nations external affairs and thus address matters on which the nation must speak with but a single voice.

Fully eleven of the powers that Article I, paragraph 8 grants Congress deal in some way with foreign affairs. This section does not attempt to survey all these grants of authority. Instead, it focuses on the constitutional limits of one form of congressional action: domestic legislation enacted under Congress' war powers. With respect to this subject, the object of the inquiry is to describe the extent to which the peculiarly national character of the power granted Congress limits judicial review of legislation seemingly inconsistent with the usual restraints on congressional power.

Article I, paragraph 8 gives Congress the powers to declare war, raise and support armies, through appropriations lasting no longer than two years, provide and maintain a Navy, make rules for the government and regulation of the land and naval forces and provide for organizing, arming and disciplining, the militia, and for governing such part of them as may be employed in the service of the United States. The Supreme Court has held that these war powers, in conjunction with the Necessary and Proper Clause, grant Congress authority to take numerous actions in wartime which would be unconstitutional in peacetime. Such congressional action may both assume responsibilities ordinarily left to the states and restrict the scope of private rights.

In World War I, for example, Congress enacted, and the Supreme Court subsequently upheld, a national prohibition law—justified as a wartime efficiency measure—prior to the ratification of the Eighteenth Amendment. And in World War II, the Supreme Court affirmed the power of Congress to authorize federal control of prices and rents, as well as other allocation regulations, even though the congressional action severely restricted access to procedural channels for testing the validity of government's actions: "In total war it is necessary that a civilian make sacrifices of his property and profits with at least the same fortitude as that with which a drafted soldier makes his traditional sacrifices of comfort, security and life itself."[38] In both World Wars congressional domestic regulation undertaken as part of the war effort was notable for its duration: wartime laws persisted in force after hostilities terminated, and after both wars the Supreme Court upheld that persistence as falling within the direction of Congress in the exercise of its war powers.[39]

Congressional action in World War I and World War II also illustrates the sorts of direct wartime restrictions of private rights the Supreme Court has understood the Constitution to permit. In World War I, Congress passed laws punishing seditious utterances: the Supreme Court upheld their enforcement, noting the exigencies of war as part of the basis for its rulings.[40] Justice Holmes noted in *Schenck v. United States*—a case remembered more for its rhetorical protection of free speech than for its result—that when a nation is at war many things that might be said in time of peace are such a hindrance to its effort that their utterance will not be endured so long as men fight and no court would regard them as protected by any constitutional right. In World War II, Congress authorized the detention and relocation of Japanese residents in the western United States, including persons of Japanese ancestry who were native-born American citizens. Although the congressional action involved the use of an ordinarily forbidden racial criterion, the Supreme Court refused to intervene: "when under conditions of modern warfare our shores are threatened by hostile forces, the power to protect must be commensurate with the threatened danger."[41]

In retrospect, the Supreme Court's tolerance of the wartime excess of Congress and of the executive seems wrong, but in retrospect it is also clear that the Court saw no reasonable alternative to deference. This is the paradox of the war powers: because they are exercised in emergency, they are the constitutional grants of authority that the Supreme Court is least likely to limit—out of deference to superior legislative fact-finding or executive expertise, out of prudent awareness of the limits of judicial power, and out of simple unfamiliarity with the issues raised. The difficulty inherent in judicial limitation of the war powers, especially during war itself, is ultimately one of the strongest arguments for strict judicial enforcement of individual rights in peacetime. If the judiciary does not remind Congress of its constitutional obligations when such reminder is possible, it is less than likely that Congress will remember to restrain itself when the courts see no practical alternative to silence.

The facts that the Supreme Court has generally deferred to the political branches in time of war and that any other judicial course of action might raise insuperable difficulties do not mean that blanket deference is appropriate. There are a number of bases upon which the court could, and arguably should, distinguish between proper and improper deference. Perhaps the most obvious basis flows from the text and structure of the Constitution itself. That document explicitly provides for certain enhancements of governmental power in time of war. Thus, the Third Amendment prohibits the quartering of a soldier in any house without the consent of the owner in time of peace, but in time of war such quartering is permitted if in a manner prescribed by law. Similarly the Fifth Amendment provides that "No person shall be held to answer for a capital, or otherwise infamous crime, unless on a presentment or indictment of a Grant Jury, except in cases arising in the land or naval forces, or in the Militia, when in actual service in time of War or public danger." These specific exceptions to the rules obtaining in peacetime arguably counsel against the court engrafting other exceptions of its own.

NOTES

1. *McGrain v. Daugherty*, 273 U.S. 135, 174 (1937).
2. *Watkins v. United States*, 354 U.S. 178, 187 (1957).
3. 103 U.S. (13 Otto) 168, 193–196 (1881).
4. 279 U.S. 263, 295 (1929).
5. *Yellin v. United States*, 384 U.S. 702 (1966).
6. Watkins, 354 U.S. at 214–215.
7. *Knowlton v. Moore*, 178 U.S. 41 (1900).
8. *United States v. IBM*, 517 U.S. 843 (1996).
9. *Thames v. Mersey Marine Ins. Co. v. United States*, 237 U.S. 19 (1915).
10. 220 U.S. 107 (1911).
11. 75 U.S. (8 Wall.) 533 (1869).
12. 300 U.S. 506 (1937).
13. 514 U.S. 549 (1995).
14. *City of Rome v. United States*, 446 U.S. 156, 179 (1980).
15. 100 U.S. (10 Otto) 339 (1879).
16. 17 U.S. (4 Wheat.) 316 (1819).
17. *Hodges v. United States*, 203 U.S. 1 (1906) (Civil Rights Act of 1866); *James v. Bowman*, 190 U.S. 127 (1903) (Enforcement Act); *Civil Rights Cases*, 109 U.S. 3 (1883) (Civil Rights Act of 1875).
18. *Oregon v. Mitchell*, 400 U.S. 112 (1970).
19. *City of Boerne v. Flores*, 521 U.S. 507 (1997).
20. *Civil Rights Cases, ante*, 22.
21. 203.U.S. 1, 17 (1906).

22. 271 U.S. 323, 330–331 (1926).
23. 334 U.S. 24, 31 (1948).
24. 392 U.S. 409 (1968).
25. 203 U.S. 1 (1906).
26. 487 U.S. 931 (1988).
27. *McDonald v. Santa Fe Trail Tranp. Co.* 427 U.S. 273, 285–96 (1976).
28. 413 U.S. 455, 470 (1973).
29. 403 U.S. 88, 102 (1971).
30. *Supra*, at 104.
31. 506 U.S. 263 (1993)
32. The Civil Rights Act 1957, 71 Stat. 634, authorized the attorney general to seek injunctions against interference with the right to vote on racial grounds.
33. 383 U.S. 301, 327 (1966).
34. 17 U.S. (4 Wheat.) 316, 421 (1819).
35. 446 U.S. 55 (1980).
36. 446 U.S. 156 (1980).
37. *Bush v. Vera*, 517 U.S. at 990–992.
38. *Lichter v. United States*, 334 U.S. 742, 754 (1948).
39. *Woods v. Cloyd W. Miller Co.*, 333 U.S. 138, 144 (1948).
40. *Schenck v. United States*, 249 U.S. 47, 52 (1919); *Debs v. United States*, 249 U.S. 211, 215 (1919).
41. Korematsu v. United States, 323 U.S. 214, 220 (1944).

PART V

United States Federation: A Model for Cyprus

Chapter 17

Union-Preserving Aspects of Federalism

STATE ACTION UNCONSTITUTIONAL UNTIL CONGRESSIONALLY AUTHORIZED

Just as restrictions on actions by the national government considered to threaten the separate existence and vitality of state and local governments play a prominent role in the Constitution's architecture, there exist a variety of Union-reinforcing restrictions on state and local power that are crucial in preserving the overall constitutional structure.

First, such restrictions may take the form of textually explicit prohibitions of certain kinds of state action, such as the ban on state treaties and state coining of money, or the Supremacy Clause ban on any state action that conflicts with valid federal law. These explicit prohibitions and requirements, although directed in the first instance against the states, also bind the national government; federal legislation purportedly authorizing a state to make a treaty or coin money would of course be unconstitutional, as would federal legislation purporting to make the law of California, for example, trump any act of Congress whenever a conflict might arise. Similarly, Congress could presumably not waive the Article IV guarantee of privileges and immunities to the citizens of each state.

Second, there are explicit restrictions that the text makes waivable by Congress, such as the Interstate Compact, the Import-Export, and the duty of Tonnage Clauses.

Third, there are Union-reinforcing restrictions that derive from the constitutional structure as a whole, understood in conjunction with certain grants of power to Congress—an understanding in which it is accepted that Congress may exercise its power to authorize state actions that would otherwise be ruled out by the Constitution's structure, including the giving of power to Congress. These include the dormant Interstate, Foreign and Indian Commerce Clauses, the essence of which is a judicially elaborated set of principles defining those state actions that, because of their discrimination against or burden on interstate or foreign or Indian commerce, are unconstitutional unless and until authorized by congressional legislation pursuant to the Commerce Clause.

Fourth, there are Union-reinforcing restrictions that flow from the Constitution's structure alone, without any reliance upon giving of power to Congress, and that are clearly as binding on Congress as on the states. Such restrictions include the ban on state secession, the rules that flow from the core principle that in the Union of states citizens choose states rather than states choosing citizens, and the principle that neither the states nor Congress may reshape the relationships specified in the Constitution between citizens of the nation and their federal representatives.

A perennial question for the judiciary has been how to define both its own authority and that of Congress in the joint task of adjusting the balance of power among the people, the states, and the nation, especially in delineating the structurally inferred limitations upon state action. Although significant aspects of that balance are at times left judicially unsupervised,[1] even many of the judges and commentators who are ordinarily quite hesitant about federal judicial intervention into legislative choice are inclined to support a relatively active role for the federal judiciary when the isolating or hostile forces of localism are manifested in state legislation, or when such legislation manifests the even more threatening and aggressive tendency to project state or local power beyond the state's borders. This is particularly true when state or local law is challenged under the Supremacy Clause or the Commerce Clause or some combination of the two, since in such cases federal judges are called upon to make what they deem a proper allocation of power in a manner that is merely tentative and subject to reallocation by Congress. It has been widely assumed[2] that, if such intervention had been limited to the judicial invalidation of state and local action that conflicts with existing federal legislation, we would surely experience frictions.

Unlike those constitutional provisions that establish the relationship of the citizen to government in general, the Commerce Clause of Article I and the privileges and immunities and full faith and Credit Clauses of Article IV certainly delineate both the relationship of the states to one another and the treatment that one state must accord the citizens of another. And the Supremacy Clause, of course, defines the hierarchy of federalism. Without these provisions, the Union as we know it could not exist.[3] For the very reason that these clauses are constitutionally indispensable, judicial review of state and local actions alleged to violate them is necessarily robust. As Ernest Brown observed in what remains one of the most considerate analyses in this area,[4] the mechanisms of our government give to Congress no opportunity or duty of reviewing, to test for compatibility with the federal system, state statutes even in their skeletal form as enacted, much less as fleshed by application, interpretation, and administration. Nor has Congress been so idle that such matters could be assured a place on its agenda without competition from other business which might often be deemed more pressing; in Justice Jackson's phrase, the inertia of government would be heavily on the side of the centrifugal forces of localism."[5]

The thrust of the Supreme Court's work in federal-state relations has been to locate the inertia of government on the other side—on the side of the centralizing impulses of nationhood and union. But that thrust has been at times deflected, in part perhaps for lack of clear judicial vision, but in larger part because of intersecting forces and considerations that it would have been folly for judges to ignore. International comparisons illustrate that the U.S. approach to these issues of federalism is not the only possible way to accommodate the conflicting interests at stake.[6]

Finally, it is evident that there is much more than a formal link between the federalism-based idea of shielding persons from the parochial tendencies of localism and the broader notion of protecting individuals against unfair and oppressive action by the state.[7]

NOTES

1. *Garcia v. San Antonio Metro. Transit Auth.*, 469 U.S. 528 (1985).
2. *The License Cases*, 46 U.S. (5 How.) 504, 573 (1847).
3. Although it is theoretically conceivable that Congress, acting under the Commerce Clause, could by statute have mandated the kinds of interstate comity that are constitutionally compelled by the privileges and immunities and full faith and Credit Clauses of art. IV, resting so vast a superstructure of interstate relations on so relatively limited a base seems highly implausible in a world not already powerfully shaped by art. IV's unifying force.
4. Ernest Brown, "The Open Economy: Mr. Frankfurter and the Position of the Judiciary," 67 *Yale Law Journal* 219, 220 (1957).
5. Brown, citing Justice Jackson's concurring opinion in *Duckworth v. Arkansas*, 314 U.S., 390, 400 (1941).
6. For example, paragraph 121 of the Canadian Constitution Act, 1867, provides that all Articles of the growth, produce, or manufacture of any one of the provinces shall, from and after the Union, be admitted free into each of the other provinces. The section applies only to explicit interprovincial tariffs, not tariff barriers, applies only to goods and not to capital, services or labor, and appears to bind only the provinces and not the federal government.
7. Michael Lawrence, "Toward a more Coherent Dormant Commerce Clause: A Proposed Unitary Framework," 21 *Harvard Journal of Law and Public Policy* 395 (1998).

PART VI

The Cyprus Problem and International Security

Chapter 18

The Security Aspect of the Cyprus Problem

INTERNATIONAL LAW RAMIFICATIONS

The present chapter analyzes the security policy that should be pursued in settling the international problem of Cyprus. Initially, it proves that the international community through the United Nations has not been successful in providing security for Cyprus over the last decades; it proves that the system of Guarantor States does not comply with rules of international political morality. Then, it explores ways in which security can be achieved in cooperation with the United Kingdom government and the British Sovereign Base Areas. Further it extensively examines how NATO, and, in particular, the United States, Greece, and Israel could fruitfully contribute to security arrangements on the island. Furthermore, gas politics is pointed out as being a factor which could ensure security in the Mediterranean region in the context of the current negotiations for a solution of the Cyprus issue.

The aspect of security is perhaps the most important one of the international Cyprus problem. In the course of negotiations it becomes imperative for all interested states to reach a settlement envisaging for measures which will safeguard their strategic interests and policies. The current effort for solution of the problem of Cyprus has so far proved that the issue of Guarantor Powers, that is, of states undertaking to guarantee the security and independence, and integrity of the Republic of Cyprus is more complex than one would imagine. Whatever the eventual settlement of the Cyprus problem may be, that is, whatever constitutional form the state shall take at the conclusion of any agreement, be that a federation (under discussion over the last decades) or a reestablishment of an independent Cyprus State along the lines of the Zurich and London Accords of 1959, the following security policies should, in my view, be taken seriously into consideration.

First, it must be stressed that the United Nations political organs' role has proved to be disappointing in the case of Cyprus, and not much can be expected of them in securing the integrity and security of the present and future Cyprus State. Although in terms of peacekeeping an evaluation of their contribution could indicate that their performance has been satisfactory,[1] the same cannot be said of their role in peace enforcement action, in spite of the various UN resolutions calling for termination of foreign occupation in Cyprus after the military intervention of Turkey in 1974.[2] The question remains: Why cannot the United Nations take enforcement action especially in such sensitive cases and issues as the one of Cyprus is? The answer may be found in the composition of the United Nations. The United Nations is not a world government nor a super-state. It is an association of sovereign states. Although the decisions taken under Chapter VII of the UN Charter must be enforced and complied with, the practical measures are rather different, mainly because of political expediencies involved.[3] The veto provision, either used or threatened as a deterrent against a resolution addressed to one of the Security Council members, despite its fruitful effect on certain occasions, surely has prevented the implementation or enforcement of certain important resolutions. It is in part because of this factor that it is sometimes argued that there is no such thing as an *International Community*, but rather there only exists an *international society*.

Secondly, and more importantly, the existing Cyprus Republic Treaty of Guarantee, on which Turkey has relied so as to justify its military intervention of Cyprus,[4] cannot (any more) provide a trustworthy political and legal basis for security of the Cyprus State.[5] It was accepted in academic theories, before the passing of the UN Charter, that armed intervention is legal when is done on the basis of a right provided for by treaty. The legality of such an intervention finds support in the majority of academic writings of that era. Phillimore, writing in the nineteenth century, one of the advocates of such a view, considers intervention legal, in case this is guaranteed by treaty right.[6] The preceding view is also shared by Oppenheim,[7] Lawrence[8] and Westlake.[9]

Professor Brownlie wrote that states may lawfully confer by treaty a right to intervene by the use of armed force within the territorial or other legally permitted limits of their jurisdiction. They may also give *ad hoc* consent to the entry of foreign forces on their territory, to the passage of foreign forces and to operations by foreign forces on their territory.[10] Brownlie gives some examples indicating that a right to intervene by force on the territory of another state could properly be conferred by treaty. Article 3 of the Treaty of 22 May 1903, between Cuba and the United States provided: "*The government of Cuba consents that the United States may exercise the right to intervene for the preservation of Cuban independence, the maintenance of a government adequate for the protection of life, property, and individual liberty.*"[11] Another example is the General Treaty of Friendship and Co-Operation signed by the United States and Panama on 2 March 1936. Article 10 provided: *"In case of an international conflagration or the existence of any threat of aggression which would endanger the security of the Republic of Panama or the security of the Panama Canal, the Governments of the United States of America and the Republic of Panama will take such measures of prevention and defense as they may consider necessary for the protection of their common interests*." An identical provision in Article 7 of the Treaty of 1903 was the basis for the United States armed intervention in Panama in 1904 for the purpose of restoring order.[12]

In spite of the above, the principles of sovereignty and self-determination, and equality of states, as stipulated in the U.N. Charter, have put into doubt the right of military intervention conferred by treaty. Very many jurists and political scientists have denied that such a treaty may be valid. A valid treaty presupposes lawful provisions. It is true that states have the capacity, by virtue of sovereignty, to conclude treaties on any matter whatever. It is equally true, however, that in the international legal order there exist legal rules, which states—parties to a treaty—cannot, and should not, ignore. The rationale underlying this axiom is that the international community, like every well-ordered society, should see to the moral coexistence of its members. As Lauterpacht very well put it, "*the parties conclude a treaty not in a legal vacuum, but against a background of existing rules of international law*."[13] According to these *general principles of law*, a treaty comprising unlawful provisions is void. Unquestionably, *general principles of law* are in force under international law. The question which naturally follows is *which* are those international law principles violation of which renders a treaty void? Answer: the *peremptory norms of international law* otherwise known as *jus cogens*. The basis of these principles may be found in natural law. Article 53 of the Vienna Convention on the Law of Treaties, signed at Vienna in 1969, provides as follows: "A treaty is void if, at the time of its conclusion conflicts with a peremptory norm of international law. For the purposes of the present Convention, a peremptory norm of general international law is a norm accepted and recognized by the international community of States as a whole as a norm from which no derogation is permitted and which can be modified only by a subsequent norm of general international law having the same character."[14] The definition of a peremptory norm is more skillful than appears at first sight. A rule cannot become a peremptory norm unless it is "accepted and recognized (as such) by the international community of States as a whole," a requirement which is too logical to be challenged. At present very few rules pass this threshold. There is considerable agreement on the *prohibition of the use of force*, of genocide, slavery, of gross violations of the right of peoples to self-determination, and of racial discrimination. The International Law Commission, in its commentary on the draft of the Vienna

Convention, identified the Charter's prohibition of the use of inter-State force as a "conspicuous example" of *jus cogens.*[15] In view of the above, it could be argued that the rule of general international law prohibiting the unilateral use of force, especially as laid down by Article 2(4) of the U.N. Charter, constitutes *jus cogens*. Article 103 of the U.N. Charter may be cited as evidence of the existence of a peremptory norm of international law going against the conclusion of treaties providing for unilateral military intervention.[16] From the above discussion it may be inferred that article IV (2) of the Cyprus Treaty of Guarantee conflicts with *jus cogens* and is invalid.

Thirdly, the status of the British Sovereign Base Areas (SBA), I submit, should remain utterly unaffected by any security policy arrangements regarding the Republic of Cyprus. The bases, could, in my opinion, play a very constructive and useful role in the preservation of security of the island in virtually protecting the independence, territorial integrity, and constitutional order of the Republic from external dangers in the wider region of the Middle East as well as internal threats. Periodical demonstrations by a tiny minority of citizens against the remaining of the British Bases on the island should be viewed as a rather negligible and isolated incident. Nevertheless, it should be made clear to the British government that these demonstrations could acquire greater dimensions if the UK, on a given occasion, acts in a manner prejudicial to the national interests and security of the Republic.

Fourth, the role of NATO and the United States of America in any security settlement has to be taken into account quite seriously. The security of the island could be placed under the aegis of NATO. Such an arrangement would definitely serve the strategic interests of both Greece and Turkey, themselves NATO allies, as well as the United States of America. Toward attaining this purpose, part of the British bases either in Deceleia or Episcope could be conveniently turned into a NATO Base.[17] But if any future government of the Republic feels that a strategic plan of this kind could find the people of the island encircled by Turkish forces running the risk of ethnic extermination in a given conflict situation, it may be better abandoned. Instead, NATO could be accorded a military base in the peninsula of Karpasia, along the lines of the Dean Acheson Plan.

The Acheson Plan, in its amended form, could have provided the framework for a viable settlement to the Cyprus issue. It took into account the national aspirations of the Greeks of Cyprus, provided for the protection of the Turkish community, and satisfied the strategic needs of both Greece and Turkey. It provided, in its final draft, inter alia, for immediate union of Cyprus with Greece. This would be accompanied with recognition of sovereignty of the Greek Crown, the Greek central government, and the Greek Parliament (the Republic of Greece) over Cyprus; a military base on a fifty-year lease to be granted to Turkey, the area of which is not more than 4.5 percent of the territory of Cyprus; a common security body between Greece and Turkey to be established with an American representative taking part in this body.[18] Although the Greek government had accepted the terms of the plan, the proposals were rejected by the then president of the Republic of Cyprus as well as Turkey.[19] It ought to be said, though, that the Cypriot president was opposed to an acceptance of the plan driven not by purely political but rather personal motives also. Quite plainly, in order to retain his position as president of the Cyprus Republic and toward this direction secure the continuous support of the Cyprus Communist Party, he yielded to the pressures exerted by the latter to reject the plan.

Fifthly, if the above mentioned proposal of according a military base to NATO in the peninsula of Karpasia would be unwanted on part of interested governments, and for that matter the people of the island as such, the United States alone should be welcome to have an important role in maintaining peace and security on the island. The military base of the United States in Lefkonico, currently in the occupied part of the territory of Cyprus, could continue to operate without interruption. Alternatively, part of a British base could be turned into a U.S. one this time. This would facilitate air and land surveillance and campaigns on part of the United States in the Middle East. What is more, the United States may use the base for actual military operations—especially aircrafts raids—against states in the region which are considered as constituting threat to the U.S. national or international security by holding or producing nuclear weapons. It has to be emphasized, however, that these propositions and military concessions cannot be made in a vacuum. The United States must use their political influence to persuade all interested governments that the above measures are best for the security and expediencies for all concerned. The United Kingdom (which has already undertaken, by virtue of the existing Cyprus Republic Treaty of Guarantee, to safeguard the independence and territorial integrity of the island), should take decisive steps toward the same direction. Treating the Turkish State as their most important strategic ally in the region and looking down upon Cyprus (and Greece) is perhaps not the best path to pursue, let me say. In an attempt to achieve a policy of containment of the former Soviet Union (a Cold War goal, which, it seems, goes on), and thereby promoting good relations with Turkey at the expense of peace and security in Cyprus, they eventually may lead things to the opposite result from the one wished for. Such a line of policy may stir up the possibility of a Greco-Turkish conflict, which, if ignited, would almost certainly bring about involvement of Russia and eruption of warlike situations in the Middle East region and the adjacent Aegean Sea.

Sixth, the military cooperation between Cyprus and Greece and the corresponding doctrine of the Common Defense Area constitutes no doubt one of the most important options from the political and strategic point of view.

The doctrine was laid down in Athens by the premiers of the two states in 1993. The purpose of the doctrine is to suggest the adoption of a preventive strategy on part of Athens and Nicosia, with the sole aim of effectively facing a Turkish threat. According to the doctrine, any attempt on part of Turkey to launch an armed attack against the State of Cyprus or move its troops beyond the current buffer zone (which divides the occupied part of the island from the area controlled by the Cyprus government), shall constitute *casus belli* and shall be militarily resisted to. The result of a conflict in Cyprus is unpredictable of course. In order that a well-organized military strategy is laid down, the ministers of the respective defense ministries and the chief commanders of the army headquarters meet regularly in both Cyprus and Greece. A proposition in this article is that this doctrine should be retained and strengthened in any circumstances, even after a settlement on the security issue of Cyprus is reached. A conclusion of this brief recourse to this doctrine is that Cyprus, without the consistent and strong support of Greece, both in the military and diplomatic field, is vulnerable to a Turkish threat, imminent as it is in view of the thousands of Turkish troops illegally stationed on the island currently. Thus, the view that Greece is too far away to protect Cyprus and contribute to the security of the Greek Cypriots, is from the strategic standpoint, utterly wrong.

Seventh, cooperation between Cyprus and Israel need be strengthened. Two issues must be briefly examined; these should be elaborated in the context of the military cooperation (or military axis as it is often termed) between Israel and Turkey. One the one hand, Cyprus and Greece have to do their best, so that the peace process may progress in the Middle East. On the other, and more fundamentally, the relations between the Greek world at large and Israel, which admittedly have not always been the best ones, should develop. Cyprus traditionally maintains friendly relations with Israel. At a final analysis, survival of the State of Israel and Israeli interests generally depend not on any kind of relation or cooperation with Islamic countries, but on strong relations with the West, particularly with the United States, not to a significantly lesser extent with Greece, herself a pioneer of Western political culture and an ally of the United States. These relations inevitably go through stability in the eastern Mediterranean. Any control of the Middle East by countries not particularly friendly to the interests of Israel is not compatible with the notion of survival of the State of Israel. In this region, Cyprus as well as Greece could play a significant role, so that peace and stability can be achieved and retained. Military cooperation between Cyprus and Israel toward this direction, in terms of naval exercises in particular, would surely be a gradual step forward. Evidently, it has to be expressly stated that this coordination ought necessarily to be conducted on a genuine basis. It may take place before and after any security arrangement of the Cyprus issue.

Also, Cyprus can play a vital, if not decisive, role in fulfilling Israel's aspiration to join the European Union in the long run. As a full member of the EU and having close relations with Greece and other member states, Cyprus perhaps holds the key to Israel's future accession to the European Community, given of course that the European integration process progresses steadily and EU member states are willing to expand the frontiers of the Union. This becomes even more difficult in the absence of a consistent common foreign and security policy in the regional organization. Brexit has recently shown that Euro-skepticism has been very intense, not accidentally so in the United Kingdom that cannot accept diminution of its sovereignty (quite justifiably) by having to comply with directives of the European Union and policies therein by large. Conversely, a security arrangement of the Cyprus issue goes through Israel, in that Israel could play a very important role in this process, given its close ties with the United States, a key actor or protagonist in the Cyprus question. Simultaneously, by being involved in a security settlement on Cyprus, Israel may benefit the more in the sense that the Cyprus government can assure and ensure that the island will continue to be a safe place for Israelis wishing to live or work on Cyprus.

Furthermore, Cyprus and Israel could cooperate closely, as they have begun to do, in the field of oil exploitation in the eastern Mediterranean.[20] It could as well be the case that oil and gas politics could prove to be a main factor in ensuring that the Mediterranean and Middle East regions are secure over many decades to come. A strategic alliance between Israel, Cyprus, Greece, and the United States in this regard could be a powerful measure that might ensure security in the area.

Finally, any security policy on Cyprus must ensure realization and implementation of human rights in their entirety for the Cypriot people. In the first place any constitutional settlement should make sure that fundamental human rights of all communities on the island are protected, as these are stipulated in international instruments. As regards foreign and security policy, this need be conducted not in disregard of citizens' rights.[21] Sometimes the concept of security in foreign policy is seen as too narrow in being concentrated on safety against military threats.[22] A task that also need to be done is to ask the following: In planning security policy, should we not decide what we are for in the world and promote it? In accordance with this principle and the issues that have been analyzed in the course of this article, security on the Cyprus Republic could successfully be achieved, simultaneously securing that the Mediterranean region is a safe, peaceful, and ordered place.

NOTES

1. See generally Rosalyn Higgins, *United Nations Peacekeeping: Documents and Commentary* (issued under the auspices of the Royal Institute of International Affairs, Oxford: Oxford University Press, 1969), Derek Bowett, *United Nations Forces* (New York: Frederick Praeger, 1964).

2. The Resolutions of the U.N. Security Council and General Assembly indicate that the Turkish invasion was an illegal act. Mention shall be made only to some of them which characteristically stress the unlawfulness of the military intervention. See the Resolutions of the Security Council 353 (1974) of 20 July 1974, 354 (1974) of 23 July 1974, 355 (1974) of 1 August 1974, 358 (1974), 359 (1974) of 15 August 1974, 360 (1974) of 16 August 1974, 361(1974) of 30 August 1974, 364 (1974) of 16 December 1974. Security Council Resolution 353 (1974), passed on 20 of July 1974, reads as follows:

> *"1. Calls upon all States to respect the sovereignty, independence and territorial integrity of Cyprus;*
>
> *2. Calls upon all parties to the present fighting as a first step to cease all firing;*
>
> *3. Demands an immediate end to foreign military intervention in the Republic of Cyprus that is in contravention of paragraph 1 above.*"

The Security Council by Resolution 365 (1974) adopts General Assembly Resolution 3212: UN General Assembly Resolution 3212 (1974): "1. Calls upon all states to respect the sovereignty, independence, territorial integrity and non-alignment of the Republic of Cyprus and to refrain from all acts and interventions directed against it; 2. Urges the speedy withdrawal of all foreign armed forces and foreign military personnel from the Republic of Cyprus and the cessation of all foreign interference in its affairs." It is noteworthy that, although the United Nations resolutions do not expressly go against the Turkish invasion, they amply illustrate that the intervention was an illegality. Further, it should be stressed that the words "calls upon," used in the resolutions, have, according to some scholars, binding force (Leland Goodrich and Edvard Hambro, *The Charter of the United Nations,* Boston: World Peace Foundation, 1946, 545).

3. United Nations Charter (United Nations Treaty Collection) Chapter VII: Action with respect to threats to the peace, breaches of the peace, and acts of aggression: Article 41: The Security Council may decide what measures not involving the use of armed force are to be employed to give effect to its decisions, and it may call upon the Members of the United Nations to apply such measures. These may include complete or partial interruption of economic relations and of rail, sea, air, postal, telegraphic, radio, and other means of communication and the severance of diplomatic relations; Article 42: Should the Security Council consider the measures provided for in Article 41 would be inadequate, it may take such action by air, sea, or land forces as may be necessary to maintain or restore international peace and security.

4. Article IV, which constitutes the strongest basis of the Turkish argument provides the following: "in the event of a breach of the provisions of the present Treaty,

Greece, Turkey and the United Kingdom undertake to consult together with respect to the representations or measures necessary to ensure observance of those provisions. In so far as common or concerted action may not prove possible, each of the three guaranteeing Powers reserves the right to take action with the sole aim of re-establishing the state of affairs created by the present Treaty" (*Treaty of Guarantee of the Republic of Cyprus*).

5. See Kareklas, "International Law and Diplomacy on the Turkish Military Intervention of Cyprus," *Working Paper* No. 18/2011 (Athens: Hellenic Foundation for European and Foreign Policy, 2011) for an extensive analysis of the issue.

6. See R. Phillimore, *Commentaries Upon International Law* (London, 1879), vol. I, 474.

7. See Oppenheim, *International Law, War and Neutrality*, Vol. II (7th ed. Hersch Lauterpacht, London, 1952), 307.

8. See T. J. Lawrence, *The Principles of International Law* (London, 1920), 121–123. By the Treaty of London 1863, Greece was put under the guarantee of these powers as a "monarchical, independent, and constitutional State." Greece entered the great war on the side of Great Britain and her allies. The majority of the nation was enthusiastically in favor of the Entente cause, and of giving effect to a treaty with Serbia (an ally of Great Britain, France and Russia) under which Greece was bound to assist Serbia in the event of war between Serbia and a third power. On 2 October 1915, the British and French governments landed 150,000 troops at the Greek port of Salonika. They did this with the hearty approval of Minister Venizelos and of an overwhelming majority of the Greek populace for the purpose of aiding Serbia that was at war with Austria and Germany.

9. J. Westlake, *International Law* (Cambridge University Press, 1910) Vol. I, 304.

10. Ian Brownlie, *International Law and the Use of Force by States* (Oxford: Oxford University Press, 1963), 317.

11. This provision, however, did not appear in the later treaty of 29 May 1934: "Supplement: Official Documents," *American Journal of International Law* 28 (1934): 97.

12. Oppenheim, *International Law, ante*, p. 307; Ian Brownlie, *International Law and the Use of Force by States* (Oxford: Oxford University Press, 1963), 320.

13. Hersch Lauterpacht, *The Function of Law in the International Community* (Oxford: Oxford University Press, 1933), 109.

14. Text in *International Legal Materials* 8 (1969): 679; Ian Brownlie (ed.) *Basic Documents in International Law* (Oxford: Oxford University Press, 1985), 388.

15. International Law Commission, "Report of the International Law Commission, 18th Session" 172 [1966] II *Yearbook of the International Law Commission*, 248–249, 261.

16. *U.N. Charter, Article* 103: "In the event of a conflict between the obligations of the Members of the United Nations under the present Charter and their obligations under any other international agreement, their obligations under the present Charter shall prevail." The Vienna Convention on the Law of Treaties 1969 provides that the rules which it sets out regarding the rights and obligations of states parties to successive treaties relating to the same subject matter are subject to this Article.

17. However, such a proposition might meet the resistance of the British government that has always been firmly against control of Cyprus by Greece, and therefore denied Enosis (Union of Cyprus with Greece). Why the British denied Enosis? From 1951 onward the Greek government made it clear that in return for Enosis it was quite willing to grant Britain whatever bases she required either in Cyprus itself, or on the Greek mainland. This made the connection between Western defense and the necessity for continued British sovereignty problematical. One British official summed it up as follows: "If we link Cyprus with NATO and implicitly admit its value lies in its usefulness for NATO purposes we destroy the case for the retention of the sovereignty by the U.K. on strategic grounds. As NATO base Cyprus could just as well belong to Greece as to us. Our whole case depends upon our need for Cyprus as an extra-NATO base for our own purposes in the Middle East (PRO, *Foreign Office*, FO 371/117653). In defining the core NATO area in 1949 special care had been taken to exclude Cyprus, although this fact was not communicated at the time to Greece or Turkey. Such an exclusion was not affected by the entry of the latter two countries into NATO during 1952 (PRO, FO 0371/1117631). In the British mind it was because Cyprus was a crown colony and that the United Kingdom therefore possessed tenure in the island, that they were adamant as to the legitimacy and continuance of their sovereignty. The most signal proof of this came in July 1954 when British Middle East headquarters covering both land and air forces was formally transferred from Suez to Cyprus. See Public Record Office, *British Cabinet Minutes* C 54 245, 21.7.54: "In a top secret briefing in 1950, British military chiefs of staff spelled out the importance of Cyprus." See also Robert Holland, *Britain and the Revolt in Cyprus* (Oxford: Oxford University Press, 1998).

18. The definition of the plan, on behalf of Acheson, by Ball, who drafted it together with Talbot, was as follows: Cyprus was seen as a threat to the United States interests because (a) of a potential Turkish intervention and thus an unavoidable Greco-Turkish war; (b) it had weakened the ties of Greece and Turkey to the United States; (c) it had strengthened the position of the Communist Party of Cyprus and the U.S.S.R. on Cyprus; (d) it had created a serious problem to the United Nations; (e) it had undermined NATO. For these factors, and in order to remove the threats, the proposed settlement of the Cyprus issue should be achieved through Union of Cyprus and Greece with: (1) territorial compensation by Greece to Turkey; (2) a Turkish military presence on Cyprus; (3) resettlement and repatriation of Turkish Cypriots that desire to do so; and (4) pledges by Greece to apply the Lausanne Treaty minority provisions on the Turkish Cypriots; disarm all irregulars; eliminate the Communist Party's influence.

19. For details about the negotiations on the Acheson Plan see United States Department of State, *Foreign Relations of the United States 1964–1968, Volume XVI, Cyprus; Greece; Turkey Documents 78–97* (Washington: United States Government Printing Office).

20. According to the Law of the Sea Convention 1982, the Cyprus Republic government has unilaterally announced an Exclusive Economic Zone (EEZ), and may therefore proceed freely toward exploitation of gas in the sea and sea-bed of its region (for the Convention on the Law of the Sea see Ian Brownlie, *Basic Documents in*

International Law, Oxford: Oxford University Press, 1985). Agreements have already been concluded with Israel and the United States.

21. R. J. Vincent, "The Reagan Administration and America's Purpose in the World, *Yearbook of World Affairs*, vol. 37 (1983).

22. See inter alia R. J. Vincent, *Human Rights in Foreign Policy* (Cambridge: Cambridge University Press).

Appendix A

Rhodes House Library Oxford Foot Papers Mss. British Empire S. 395

FOOT PAPERS1

This is a recording made for the Oxford Colonial Records Project in Oxford on 23 April 1971. It is a recording of a conversation with Lord Caradon who held colonial governorships and then became an official representative and later a ministerial representative in the United Nations. The interviewer is W. P. Kirkman who was Africa and Commonwealth Correspondent of the Times and is now secretary of the University of Cambridge Appointments Board.

In the course of the interview, Sir Hugh Foot gives valuable information on colonial history, the role of individuals in the formulation of British foreign policy, and his relations with these diplomats, provides useful insight into the constitutional-political practice of ministerial responsibility, and thoroughly elaborates on the question of Cyprus.
pages 1–10

Q. Lord Caradon, could I start by asking you at what stage in your career in the Colonial Office did you first feel a sense of commitment to the Service which, as you say in your book "A Start in Freedom" you had really joined almost by accident?

A. Well, I would say that it was a continuous process, there was no particular morning in my life when I woke up and said I was taking a different attitude. I was at Cambridge a very long time ago and it was then the expectation that a proportion of those at Cambridge, Oxford, elsewhere, mainly Cambridge, Oxford, would be going overseas to one of the overseas services to India, to the Far East, or to the general Colonial Service including particularly Africa. This was an assumption all of us had to make when we were thinking about the possibility of careers. There was a high intake in those days—an intake of well over a hundred into the Colonial Service alone and I suppose an equivalent number for India and the Far East, and the Sudan which was a separate Service. Still, I had been a younger son, I had thought of going into the Law and had studied Law in the second part of my tripos at Cambridge, but I decided then that it would be more exciting to go overseas, talked to others about what I might do, put my name down for the Sudan which was looked upon as a place where my Cambridge people went—they used to speak about the Sudan as the blacks governed by the blues. It was particularly a rowing man's haven, I used to row for my college and I put myself down for the Sudan. I don't maintain that I had any high motive for doing so, it was that I looked to an active, vigorous—I thought useful—life and this was the opportunity. I switched to Palestine later—again with no very strong motive except that it was an immediate offer against the Sudan selection which was not complete. Then gradually and naturally one became absorbed in the work of the country where you were, I was in Palestine, and devoted increasingly to the people amongst whom you were working—that's the process.

Q. Was there any stage after you had become a member of the Colonial Service when you seriously thought of leaving it to do anything else?

A. Oh no, no. I thought of resigning once or twice but I never thought of leaving because I was attracted to anything else, no it never occurred to me.

Q. When you say you thought of resigning, you mean on some issue of principle, such as you did in fact resign as Official Representative of the British Government in the United Nations much later in your career, do you mean on that kind of issue?

A. Yes, naturally, where you're absorbed in policy and concerned in the making of policy to some extent, if you are at very serious loggerheads with your Government then you may have to consider resignation. I don't think I came very close to it when I was in the Colonial Service. I did offer to resign once when I was in Cyprus when it appeared my first initiative had failed and I told the Secretary of State for the Colonies at that time I was prepared to go. He immediately told me that I mustn't, but I offered to go at the time, because I considered that my own initiative—it was my own initiative—had come to grief.

Q. This presumably was your unorthodox letter to Grivas?

A. No, no, it was before then, before then. When I went to Cyprus first I had a clear idea of what I thought should be achieved. I came home after a month or so in Cyprus, I got full approval from the British Government for what I intended to do, and then went back to put it into effect but before I got there the Turkish Government had sabotaged what we in effect were trying to achieve and I thought it was my duty therefore as it was my policy, and my policy had failed so it appeared, to offer my resignation. But immediately I was told by my Government that far from having lost confidence in me they had full confidence in me. But I had also I suppose, way back in Palestine days, I had in the back of my mind that one might wish to resign. I remember that one of my associates—Hodgkin who was a little younger than I think, he was in the Palestine administration and he came to the conclusion that he wouldn't stay dealing at that time, as we were, with rebellion, and left. I admire him for leaving, but I thought at that time I could do better by staying and that I could exercise an influence in my position of being in charge of the Samaria Division which was the whole of central Palestine in those days, and I felt that I could do more from that position than by leaving. Indeed, I had great sympathy with the High Commissioner's policy which I supported, that of General Sir Arthur Wauchope, and I knew the difficulties he was facing and the pressures he was under and I felt I should be on his side, I felt to be his man.

Q. There is of course a basic difference isn't there between the kind resignation you offered in Cyprus where in a sense you would be resigning to clear the way for somebody else to try another policy I suppose and the kind of resignation over Rhodesia in United Nations later when in effect you were resigning because you couldn't go along with the policy which had been imposed on you. I suppose as a Colonial Official, particularly as you became more senior, there must always have been some conflict between what you saw as the ideal solution and was eventually accepted as the Governor's solution. I suppose the question is really how close this comes to a complete breach?

A. I have stated the principles as I thought they should be and was very clear in my mind that an official should not normally resign. You can't run a Government on the whims of the individuals who are your subordinates and that's the general rule and you've got to put up with it, even if it's a policy you don't like. But where things coincide, one, where it's a major matter you shouldn't resign on a secondary matter however strongly you feel, secondly it's a continuing matter, you don't resign simply because something has already been done you don't like, it's got to be a continuing matter, it's also got to be a matter in which you are personally concerned, you've got to give effect to it, you've got to carry it out, you've got to defend it—where you've got those three things together then I maintain that you've got not only a right to resign but indeed a duty. But it's very rare for an official and it's quite wrong that officials should be carrying their resignations in their pockets, you can't run a Government on that basis. The people who have got to worry about policy are the ministerial representatives who have a responsibility to Parliament. When I was a junior official in Palestine I didn't feel responsible for the policy and I would only resign if I was told to do things I just hadn't the stomach to do, the quelling of a rebellion for instance. When you're a Governor you obviously have a great responsibility even for proposing the policy and you might meet resistance. I've had many disputes of course with the Government on matters which I might regard as important—very important—but not of top importance. Take for example, I remember when Littleton was Secretary of State for the Colonies, I remember having to go and argue with him on matter in which I was in dispute with the permanent officials in the Colonial Office.

Q. This was when you were Chief Secretary in Nigeria I imagine?

A. No, that was in Jamaica. And then I remember also later when I was in United Nations going to argue with Ian Macleod on a matter in which I was in dispute with the Government Officials in the Colonial Office, on both occasions I may say, Littleton in the first place and Macleod in the second, backed me and sent me and sent me back happy. I remember Littleton in this conversation we were met in his room in the House of Commons, he was very busy with Mau Mau and this was a matter of great importance to me in the new constitution we were introducing in Jamaica, I wanted it provided in the way that I had worked it out and the Colonial Office didn't agree with me and we went to the final meting and in the end when he'd listened to us both he just merely said "Roll up the map of Jamaica, let's go for a drink." What he really meant was All Right, you take it your way. And the power, I may say, of a Colonial Governor in such maters is very considerable.

Q. Yes, I ma interested, this was one of the things I thought we ought to explore, the relative weight given to the people on the spot—the views of the people on the spot, I mean particularly the Governor of course and his senior officials and people in Whitehall, I mean there was, of course, a separate service wasn't there, you didn't normally get people serving in the Colonial Service and also the Colonial Office not as—they weren't interchangeable?

A. The Colonial Office people were usually sent out for a couple of years somewhere or other—

Q. Yes, they weren't—

A. And I went home as what they call a beachcomber—

Q. Yes—

A. Which was a Colonial Service man working temporarily in the Colonial Office, I went in the Appointments Department which was a very separate department, obviously very suitable for beachcomber because you could tell the candidates what it seemed like to be out on the field, but they were separate services, yea very definitely separate and we had a great contempt for the Clerks in Whitehall and I've no doubt they had their reservations about us!

Q Did this really mean—I suppose this was the natural kind of rivalry of people in different services, but to what extent did it reflect a real difference in approach, I mean after all in Whitehall presumably the Civil Servants are very much concerned with domestic politics and the effects of policies on domestic policies, whereas you who were in Jamaica or wherever it might be were concerned with the development of Jamaica.

A. Well, to put it quite simply we were concerned with the people with whom we were working whoever they might be, the Arabs or the Jamaicans or the Nigerians and we were interested in their needs and their aspirations and the rest, more than people who were directing things from a center, but the principal Colonial Office Official that I had to deal with in particular in Africa was Andrew Cohen and I don't think you could have asked for a better man—a man of more liberal sympathy than Andrew Cohen, he was one of the great men of his time and dominated a succession of Ministers from both parties for a period of a decade or more before he went to Uganda. But other Colonial Officials we thought were stuffy and short-sighted and anti-pathetic on the matters on which we cared most. Actually it was quite a good combination I think of the two, proved they couldn't ride rough shod over us and when as a Governor or—I was for ten years I think a Colonial Secretary or Chief Secretary—we had access to the Ministry and as I say I can remember, oh, half a dozen occasions of having major argument with London and being able to go and state your case in the end to the Minister, and as I say I remember two or three important occasions when they went to along with us rather than with their own officials.

Q. You had this access, obviously as the Governor, you had it as Chief Secretary too, did you?

A. Oh I can remember occasions. I remember the occasion of the Inugu Mining riots when twenty miners were shot by Northern in Inugu way back I suppose it was 1949 maybe, something like that, and I was Chief Secretary under Sir John Macpherson, I was sent home to deal with the Secretary of State for the Colonies, Griffiths at that time, to argue with him. I didn't succeed in my argument, but I made some impression.

Q. This must have been 1950.

A. Maybe yes.

Q. I was wondering—if I may pursue this matter a little further—you did refer in your book 'A Start in Freedom,' a passing reference to one Minister who had . . . [tape broke here] you and I think you suggested that he had done it almost deliberately by insisting that he was not concerned with the local inhabitants, he was concerned purely with British interests. I wonder if you would be indiscreet enough to say who it was and also, more importantly, was this fairly common attitude of Ministers as distinct from Officials?

A. No, I'm afraid I cannot quite remember who it was that said that, but it was very rare and it was said to me provocatively, to say that he knew my line and he wasn't going to be taken in by it and I think although I may be doing him an in justice, I think it was probably Selwyn Lloyd. Selwyn Lloyd was at Cambridge with me, we knew each other very well and I can imagine him with me coming into the room saying Look here, I'm not going to talk to your liberal nonsense—he was a Liberal of course when he was at Cambridge with me.

Q. Yes. Did you have—I mean you've served in your various capacities under of course a huge range of Colonial Secretaries—was there any marked difference in the extent of interest in London in Colonial policy before the war and after the war. I mean clearly after the war the Colonial unraveling process was starting and the amount of work in Colonial—Independence Constitution making was very much greater but was there before the war—was it fair to say for instance that really affairs locally were left to be run by local officials unless there was a crisis or was there a lot of thought given to actual long-term policy in Whitehall?

A. It's difficult to say, it depended on the personalities. I'd say that Andrew Cohen exercised for a decade, may be two decades, an influence on African policy which was greater perhaps that any other Minister as far as Africa was concerned, yes. But then you've got some Ministers who were of course outstanding and had longer spells than others. I should think the two Ministers I should remember as having the greatest influence in the thirty or forty years when I was in the Overseas Administration, were Creech Jones and Lennox Boyd.

Q. Creech Jones of course held Office for only a very short time didn't he?

A. Perhaps it was because I was in Jamaica at that time and we were talking West Indian Federation that I had—I think he had been in Office.

Q. He was I think an Under Secretary.

A. An Under Secretary? At any rate he had given his mind to Colonial questions over a long period and brought his own ideas and philosophy to it and therefore did exercise I think, although it may have been particular influence to what was happening in Jamaica, he did I think bring an influence to what was happening in Africa too at that time.

Q. You mention also Lennox Boyd who was of course Colonial Secretary at a very crucial period, when you say that he exerted an influence you meant really that he was concerned intimately with the policy rather than just a ministerial figurehead?

A. He was very personally concerned with the personalities of the time. I don't think any other Minister that I've known knew the individuals so well and intimately as he did and he had a special gift for personal persuasion and people of all kinds and all over the Colonial Empire knew him and in fact still know him, and he had an original approach. I think it was not based on any different philosophy from anyone else, but it was a very sympathetic approach. I served under him a long time and had a great regard for him and have still, he was my Secretary of State when I was in Jamaica and he indeed appointed me to Cyprus, which was a courageous act.

Q. You didn't mention in your list of people who had great influence Ian McLeod, would you—

A. He was only there for a very short time wasn't he?

Q. Well he was there for two years.

A. But then you see I was not—

Q. Well you were in the last stages of Cyprus then, weren't you, 1959, Cyprus had virtually—

A. Was he Colonial Secretary in 1959?

Q. Yes, he came in the end of '59.

A. Oh. Well I didn't have much dealing with him on that issue. We were set on our course then.

Q. Yes, quite.

A. I only had dealings with him when we were in New York and we had a fight then on this issue, on whether we should walk out of Colonial Committees or not. We have walked out now recently under the new Government, but when I was there I fought year after year that we should not walk out, that we should stay and defend and justify and I succeeded. But first I had a battle on that with McLeod when I was not head of the Mission, I was an ambassador in the Mission, and I had to go and argue with Hilton Poynton who was arguing for the Colonial Office in favor of walking out and I was not and we went to McLeod and he heard us both and decided that I could do what I liked.

Q. Yes, yes.

A. That's the occasion that I knew him. I knew of course about his attitudes to African policies and the rest but I was at that time not a Colonial Governor, I was a representative at New York.

Q. So you were more concerned obviously with the Foreign Office as it were than with the Colonial Office at that stage?

A. I was concerned with presentation of our case in New York rather than actual day to day administration.

Q, Now, if we go back before the war were there any Colonial Secretaries who stand out in the pre-war years. I was wondering particularly if

Malcolm MacDonald who held office twice of course, ’35 for a short period, then ’38, did he make a great impact at that stage?

A. Well I was very junior you see, I was bottom man when he was top man and I have a great regard for him and I think that had he been backed I think we might have been able to save the worst disasters in Palestine. He was very good to me at that time, even though I was a bottom man he used to read what I wrote from the coastal plain of Palestine on the evictions of the Warrior Arabs and the rest and he used to give me a pat on the back occasionally and I had an easy relationship with him, we were not so very different in age although he was Secretary of State and I was the bottom District Officer!

Q. You mentioned earlier several different times your respect and admiration for Cohen as someone who had really given thought in Whitehall to Colonial problems over a period of two decades, is there any other official—senior official in Whitehall-who stands out in a positive way like that?

A. Yes, there are one or two. The other name that I would put in a top category of—naturally I suppose I’ve been influenced by the people who were inclined to agree with me—but John Martin was an outstanding man and a man we knew we could go to if we were in a political jam and he could understand what we were saying to him. I could think of many other names of people and able people I’ve no doubt they are as well, but I would have thought that Andrew Cohen and John Martin were the two that come immediately to my mind as people that are forward looking and progressive and imaginative.

Q. What about Sir John Mcpherson who did of course cease to be Governor and became Permanent Secretary.

A. Oh, well, I knew him in a very different capacity. First of all when I was in Palestine, or rather when I was in Transjordan, he was Chief Secretary in Jerusalem and I had dealings with him almost as my boss at that time. I served under him as Chief Secretary when he was Governor of Nigeria, so don’t connect him with the Colonial Office, though on two occasions when he was in charge of me and I worked with him very closely in both cases and with very full understanding. On the first occasion I was not very pleased with him because he pulled me back from North Africa where I was working away in Libya and brought me back to Transjordan as it was then, and I felt it was a backwater, and it was a scandal that I should be taken out of a place which was moving so fast.

Q. This was during war?

A. Yes, and I was lent for six months to establish the administration in Cyrenaica, enormously absorbed in that task—fascinating job—at the end of six months—I never imagined, in fact when I left he said I don’t expect to see you again—at the end of six months I was called back and I remember speaking to him then with fury and anger, which he took very well and later when he came as Governor of Nigeria I had already gone ahead of him as Chief Secretary and had been for six months or so before he came—

Q. Yes.

A. So we had a very close association there.

Q. I wonder if I could now ask you, in a way your career as a Colonial Administrator at various levels covered the rule, well if I may use a cliché, from the age of paternalism to an age of independence, was this in a way a reflection of your own development or had you at an early stage thought in terms of it depends on the not too distant horizon?

A. Well I was very lucky of course, I've perhaps said this before, I say it again, because I was tremendously lucky in the time when I went in because we were then in one stage and I was able then to be in a position of some authority as a Chief Secretary for ten years and a Governor for ten years, when we reaping the result of what had been done previously, and I was able, therefore, over a period of altogether thirty years to be associated with the different stages that took place, so it seemed to us, naturally. It was difficult to say that at any point we shifted our purpose, it was a development from one to the other. Paternalism raises some questions in my mind. I think there is a sort of anti-paternalism now which is unhealthy. Speaking to a member of parliament recently and talking about the population question in the world he said you can't just tell other people what to do, I don't accept that, there are world problems and we've got a right to talk about them just because we're inhabitants of the world and we don't want to go into our own shell just because we're afraid to tackle the great problems of poverty and population for instance.

Q. . . .

A. Yes, when I was in charge of Nablus Samaria in Palestine for seven years or so I was wholly devoted to the people, I was very young, I was in my twenties when I started, but nothing else mattered and I'd go and fight in Jerusalem what they needed, water supplies and crops, and the development generally and the support of the municipalities of Jenin, Nablus, Tuckarm, yes, these were my concerns, then it led to a natural process from there to a study of their aspirations and to fight a rebellion at the time of my Nablus experience, and it made it necessary for you to think of the political aspirations of the people, which you tended to share. We had two people to set some aspirations at that time, of course, but you can share them both, but you go from that stage to saying—I often used to say I remember way, way, back that the only way to train people in responsibility is to give it to them. And if you're going to train people in responsibility you've got to accept that they make the decisions—the basic decisions—and you help them, and then before you know where you're backing an independent movement, indeed you are accelerating it.

Q. Yes, yes.

A. I don't think this is anything surprising and the use of the word "paternalism" which is used insultingly as a rule doesn't help. Everyone in public life must be paternalistic, otherwise you don't go outside your front garden.

Q. Of course I suppose it's become a sort of insulting term more recently, I mean if you'd said "paternalism" before the war it would have been benevolent term, wouldn't it?

A. Well, before the war, yes. At one time of course. I agree with that, all I'm saying is that it creates reactions and emotions which are false. We are all inhabitants of the world and got a right to be interested in it.

Q. You have obviously, at periods in your life, you must have been at some stages very much involved in day to day administration and at other periods notably in your Governorships very much involved in higher policy making. Looking back, which role were you happier in?

A. Well again, I don't think you could make any distinction. I mean both are—it's no good just talking about the desirability of development, you've got to see how best to achieve it. For instance, the creation of the development areas in Cyprus and then again in Jamaica, taking a whole valley and . . .

page 13

Q.. . . approach with your senior officials, the Deputy Governor was Sir George Sinclair wasn't he and Chief Secretary was Reddaway I think.

A. Well, I don't know about that. I think I had been very lucky before and the two people that I served with before were as I say outstanding were Reddaway and Deverell, both of whom served with me in Jamaica and went on to be Governors. It was different situation in Cyprus but in Cyprus I was at the stage then when I could make my own decisions, I didn't need to work closely with others. John Reddaway had been in Cyprus since I myself was concerned with his appointment from the days when I was in the Appointments Department—I remember we selected him as classical scholar to go to Cyprus at that time, I had been associated with him when I was in Cyprus before of course, I knew him. He was a very close friend of mine, he, his wife and family, I know very well. I don't say that we always agreed, by any means, but his knowledge of the country and the language, he spoke of course perfect Greek and good Turkish, and it was of very great benefit to me to have him there as a sort of corrective!

Q. Yes, a sort of computer.

A. Well yes, we would often have differences of opinion, but it was very valuable to have someone there who knew what he was talking about. Others of course had served under John Harding and they tended to resent the arrival of a civilian and a politician, yes, I think there was some kind of that spirit. I was accused, I remember, by Foley who ran the *Cyprus Mail*—

Q. *Times* of Cyprus—

A. *Times* of Cyprus, yes that's right, of having given way to the Harding Gang. Not at all, we worked out an understanding together and came to a very good understanding. We didn't—I can feel confident it didn't in any way alter the attitude that I felt and wanted t pursue.

Q No. Is there—this question of the relationship between a Governor and his most senior / close advisers and colleagues is obviously I suppose in a sense a delicate one and you're bound of course to get different approaches and as you say you can get a good balance, but to what extent was a Governor able, had he wished, to be sort of dictator to his own senior officials, to what extent did he have to listen to them?

A. Oh, well it was difficult if he was in his Executive Council and he was constantly at loggerheads with them, I suppose it would have eventually come out.

pages 16–17

Q. How did these situations, Jamaica and Nigeria, compare with Cyprus, I mean you were in Cyprus just before you went to Nigeria as Chief Secretary weren't you? At that stage of course I suppose, well, the main problem was the war, but was there at that stage any feeling that you ought to be putting pressure on the people to advance Constitution?

A. No, I don't think there was, it was a lull you see, there was the war. The Germans were in the Greek Islands you see, just across the way and everyone admitted that there must be a lull at that time, as indeed there was in Palestine in the war years and therefore you had got not only an excuse but a necessity to hold things where they were for the time being and there was no illusion, it wasn't time for constitutional advance at all in that exceptional situation in time.

Q. No, no. Could I turn to another matter. This is really about your whole approach to ruling. There's no doubt of course that aspects of your approach as Governor of Cyprus were unorthodox, obviously deliberately so, was this a special case in Cyprus or did you, at a much earlier stage in you career, adopt methods which were untypical of your fellow Colonial administrator?

A. I wouldn't make the distinction very much, we had some of us with great desire to go into the field of public relations and the rest and to communicate by dramatic action, or something, but that applied to us all to some extent, we knew that we had to carry the people with us and it was a question of how, but in Jamaica for instance, I was there for nearly ten years, you had to enter into the life of the people completely and be out speaking, taking part, proposing, initiating all the time, we were in complete control when I went there first and you had to run everything yourself, but you also had to put yourself over, you had to be known, you must go, even if you hadn't wanted to, if you'd wanted to do otherwise you must be in the Churches every Sunday, you must be at every Agricultural Show, you must think of phrases which will excite people and attract them, to be at that stage—in that wonderful stage to be a Colonial Governor you were dealing with a whole range of administrative problems but also dealing with the question of political leadership, you had to be a political leader, this was extremely important. We attempted to do it, not very successfully, in the early stages of Cyprus.

Q. Were you in your actual approach, I mean not in your policy as it were, but in the way in which you approached it, was this something—I was thinking now of Cyprus—was this something that you deliberately sat down and thought out or was your approach really I will be myself?

A. You had a purpose in mind that you had to—you walked into a situation when terrorism and violence had taken over and bad feeling between the Government and the people and you wanted to—obviously one's first need was to overcome that in some way to allow people to have some confidence in you, therefore you wanted to speak to them over the radio all the time, you wanted to do things which would help, you wanted to go and see the people in the detention camps on Christmas Day and light a candle for peace in the Greek Church and walk down the street talking to people as you went. It's a wonderful combination—never happen again I don't suppose—

Q. No.

A. It's a wonderful combination of administration and politics, except I think the politics for a Governor was more important than the administration—

Q. Yes.

A. But as I believe I said before, they must go together, they had to go together speaking of the past.

Q. To what extent was your approach and attitude affected by the place and the people among whom you worked. Now clearly it would be affected by the situation, I mean for instance was it of great importance that Jamaicans have English as their Mother Tongue whereas the Cypriots obviously don't?

A. Well it's a great help, actually the Cypriots do mostly speak English, the people we had dealings with, and there are many more English speaking, I've been felt, myself, completely at home, and lost maybe working more recently for the United Nations, for instance I was in Japan the other day and I like to assume that most of the places I've been the people speak English—they don't—I mean it's very annoying they don't! But in Cyprus if you broadcast everyone who mattered, heard you in English and understood you, and in Jamaica certainly so and in Nigeria too to a considerable extent. Language was not really a grave barrier in dealing with those who were politicians.

Q. But there presumably was a difference in Jamaica. It's not simply that people speak English, but if you like their Educational System, their general approach is very much an English one isn't it, whereas in Cyprus it clearly isn't and in Nigeria it isn't.

page 28

A.. . . as a rule you didn't know about them, you didn't have a chance to meet them, so you know one man at the top a little, not much and the officials below him, and the most important man who was head of the Caribbean Department or the West African Department whom you knew well. Later of course it was very different in Cyprus and I had as many dealings with the Foreign Secretary or indeed with the Prime Minister as I had with the Secretary of State for the Colonies, indeed rather more because it was the Foreign Secretary who came to Athens and Ankara, or the Prime Minister himself and therefore I had very direct dealings with them.

Q. What was your feeling then seeing them at work, seeing the machinery at work at this sort of level, what was your feeling about the machine itself?

A. Well, I've got no complaints about it. I'm talking about the Macmillan administration in the case of Cyprus. The Prime Minister himself took a great personal interest. I remember from the day when I made an early Report to him he said "Well if it's as bad as that I'd better have a go at it myself" and he did after that. He made it his own personal business to watch it and to give me support in times of great difficulty when a number of people were gunning form me and he wouldn't have it, he would stand by me in difficult times. Selwyn Lloyd I knew very well at Cambridge, we were there together and he was President of the Liberal Club just before me, so it was a very great help to me to be able to talk very plainly to him. I didn't have to worry, there was no question of seniority between us, we had been out speaking in the Liberal Land Campaign ourselves together and we knew each other well from those days, so that was a great help. And then as I say I had an affectionate regard for Lennox Boyd, so I was lucky with my Ministers.

pages 51–64

Q. Thank you very much. Now of course this is inevitably a rather artificial transition, but I would like now to jump across the world to Cyprus. When you were appointed to Cyprus as Governor, of course you had been there before, to what extent were you able to start giving thought to the problems you were going to face in Cyprus during the last months of your period in Jamaica?

A. Well, I knew of the appointment. I went home to London and saw the Prime Minister MacMillan who wanted to have a look at me before the appointment was completed! I didn't know then whether they'd appoint me, but when I came back they said "Yes" and so I had to switch my mind to deal with the problem of violence in Cyprus. When I had been in Cyprus before there had been no internal violence, and it was, however, a great advantage to me having been in Cyprus before, having known the Island in times of World War, but internal peace. I have sometimes, not in this connection—you've got to switch your mind from one subject to another completely. I remember telling you there was a story in Nigeria that there used to be a Member of our Council there who had come from everywhere and when I was there I wanted to know why they always called him in nickname Fijiwe. I took someone aside after a while and said "Why do they always call him Fijiwe?" "Oh," he said, "that's well known, because when he came here first he used to preface everything he said with the words 'In Fiji we did it in this way or that way' that they called him Fijiwe for ever afterwards," a sort of warning I think to all of us in different walks of life, especially colonial administration when you're moving to one problem from a very different problem, that you should wipe your mind clean of what you've been doing previously, although the lessons you've learnt stick at the back of your mind. You've got to start applying absolutely different tests and one of the absolute rules, certainly in our service, was you never should refer to any lesson you've learnt somewhere.

Q. When you were, as it were, between Posts you presumably had a period in London, and obviously you must have been, during this period, been briefed on the problem, how specific was your brief from the Government?

A. It wasn't very specific at all. I remember I had my own rough ideas of what might be done, I out them down in writing, I went to speak to the Ministers and they said yes, they thought that was all right and one went out, so I went really with an absolutely free hand and with no specific instructions. I had no written instructions I remember. I had talked in general with the Foreign Secretary and the Secretary of State for the Colonies, the Prime Minister, and went out in the general attempt to restore some confidence between the Greek community and the Turkish community and ourselves, that was my main first task to try and get the thing back on the rails again and move to a period to which British Authority would be maintained but with the Greeks and Turks both being given a fuller share in their own government.

Q. During this period of briefing did you have any meeting with your predecessor Lord Harding?

A. Yes, yes, I did and when I came back from time to time in the next six months or so I would always go to see him, tell him what was happening, get his comment and advice on what we were attempting to do and always had very happy relations with him. I don't think there was very much to it. At that time there were some comments on personalities and people whom one could turn to rely on, but I don't think it was particularly helpful, but it was certainly useful to be able to turn to him and get his comment before I started off and subsequently in the early stages.

Q. There was of course a lot of press comment at the time about—at the time of your appointment—about the great difference in the approach between you and Lord Harding. I seem to remember reading that one paper said you know "The iron hand is replaced by the velvet glove," this was a kind of cliché assessment. Did you see yourself as being basically very different from in your approach to the problem as distinct from—different in your approach in day to day work from Lord Harding?

A. Oh, I think so, I think we were different. He had been dealing as a Field-Marshall with a military problem and had made some progress but not been able to deal with it finally. I certainly looked on it as my purpose was to go and seek a political solution. It would be unfair to him to suggest that he was not looking for a political solution, of course he was, but uppermost in mind was that a change of Governor made it possible to have a change of purpose and clearly the appointment of a civilian

Governor to take over from a Military Governor should be emphasized by a persistent search to find a new way to go, that was the difference.

Q. We did briefly touch on one aspect of this earlier in this interview, but on your arrival—I've been looking at cuttings again—I notice the Observer suggested that one of your first tasks was to escape from the influence of your officials in Cyprus, now was this a fair comment, how much conflict was there, if you like, between the old regime and the new, I mean you represented the new approach, how convinced were your officials that your approach was realistic?

A. I don't doubt that. I think they were a bit surprised. I remember quite early on, I mean even going from the time when I'd just made my shirt speech after being sworn in, that I went with the General—General Kendrew it was at that time, and the principal officials, the Deputy Governor, Administrative Secretary and others, and told them the things I had in mind and they were in some respects cautious or uncertain or even critical, but there was no major difference of opinion, they were quite willing to see me have a go and to give me their full support in doing so, and in a number of the Commissioners in charge of the different districts I found a very sympathetic response to what I was trying to do because they were in a jam, they were in a hopeless negative situation, and any initiative was better than none. I got very good support and one of the surprising things was, perhaps, the support I got from the army, a succession of Generals, particularly General Kendrew and later General Darling and their Chiefs of Staff and the Intelligence Officers working under them. I had a very good understanding throughout and General Kendrew and I agreed throughout on what we should attempt to do and General Darling and I—I don't think I've ever worked more closely with anyone than I did with General Darling over a considerable period and it was a period in which we explained to each other what we wanted to do and were in I think practically full agreement. Naturally how wouldn't seek to lay down the law on the political initiative, nor would I seek to direct him on how he should deal with his military problem, but I did go every week to a military unit or other, bringing in all the officers and N.C.O.'s and tell them what we were trying to do and I look back on that—we had about 22,000 British troops in Cyprus at that time—naturally there were differences of opinion—but I look back on the fact that through a very difficult period when we were pursuing political purpose which was not always easy to justify, we did not have any open or indeed any serious breach between the Civil Authorities and the Army. We worked very well together.

Q. Talking about, just now, this moment, about your relations with your senior military advisers, you did say something earlier about the administrative secretary, Reddaway. What was your assessment, I don't mean in personal relations, but your assessment of the approach and work of the Deputy Governor George Sinclair?

A. Well, I worked very well throughout my time with George Sinclair, he was a very loyal supporter. I think that he may have been a bit surprised at times and would put a different point of view to me. He came from the previous era in the search for exercising maximum control on the one hand and searching for a political initiative on the other, he was more concerned with the first, but in many respects the political initiatives I took did not bring results, to that extent he was right, but that didn't mean we should stop searching for a political solution, we all knew that that as necessary. But I've just taken as an example, I remember that when I'd been there a short time I had to go to Athens to meet Selwyn Lloyd the Foreign Secretary and I wanted to meet Archbishop Makarios who was in Athens—I knew that we'd have to deal with him in the end. I took the advice of my Administrative and Military advisers and every one of them strongly advised me not to see him, the reaction amongst Turks would be too adverse—I did see him and nothing happened, but that's just an indication of difference of opinion, difference of judgement—an honest difference of judgement—it didn't make any difference to our personal relations. We worked together well with different views and you must indeed have different views, you don't always want to be of the same opinion, but in the end there's no doubt who gives final answer.

Q. Yes. I'm interested in what you say about this first meeting with Makarios which was in February '58 wasn't it? I seem to remember in your book you said you'd raised the question of a meeting with the Foreign Secretary Selwyn Lloyd and had got his agreements in Athens to have the meeting, to what extent was the recognition that ultimately and not too far ahead you would be dealing with Makarios, to what extent was the attitude to Makarios in H.M.G. changing already before your appointment? Perhaps to be specific one could put it in these terms, how much support was there even after his resignation for Lord Salisbury?

A. Oh, precious little amongst anyone that I had anything to do with! Of course, he had already been allowed to come back from the Seychelles to Athens which was an indication there was a relaxation in the approach to him. I was in favor of his coming back for a long period of course and pressing that it should be so, and then when he came back of working with him as closely as was possible. I don't recollect any strong difference of opinion in my political masters. There was of course amongst the British public a fairly strong feeling against Makarios in having been leader of terrorism and that had to be taken into account in dealing with the army and the rest, but I would say that from the moment that the Agreement was made Archbishop Makarios loyally carried out, although a lot of features of it were anathema to him, once he accepted them, I'll say it to his credit, he never for one moment attempted to undermine the agreement in the period of the year that we worked together to establish the Independence of Cyprus. He, of course as you know, only with the greatest reluctance accepted the Zurich Agreement and to the last moment he resisted, but it's a very striking fact that once he had accepted he never sought to go back on his word. I found him throughout a man of great courtesy with a complicated mind, most certainly, and very difficult to persuade, but once having been persuaded he would not let you down.

Q. One other thing quite early on when you—soon after you'd arrived in Cyprus—which you refer to to some extent in your book, was your decision to send this secret letter to Grivas and of course, in fact, it rebounded didn't it, this ting later, but you said, I remember in your book, that you sent it without consulting your advisers because, you knew they would have prevented you from sending it. Now I wonder if you could go into some detail, not why you sent it, because I think you dealt with this in your book, but how closely informed were you about the likely effects of it, and in particular could you say how you got it through to him? How was it delivered?

A. Yes, I don't know if I can say why it was delivered. I took the help of a well-known Greek Cypriot whom I knew and trusted and I knew he would be in touch with Grivas and I asked him to help me in doing what I explained I was up to, and that was not really very difficult, although it took some time to get through, I got no reply for some time, it certainly didn't become known for quite a long a time. I was anxious to break a deadlock. It had certainly been the duty of my advisers to advise against it, because I was offering a meeting unarmed in whatever place he wished to stipulate. No adviser of mine could have agreed to that, it would have been wrong to ask them. I thought he might out of his vanity and the rest think it was a good James Bond gesture to meet the Governor in a secret forest or something.

Q. This presumably, I mean the business of getting it through, I suppose here you were helped in the fact that you'd been in Cyprus in more peaceful times and knew a lot of people from happier days?

A. Yes, that was so, but people wouldn't have dealings with me at that particular time, the Greek Cypriots, it was very difficult to come, not many would come but one or two would, particularly from those whom I knew before, and the officials of course would come—it wasn't an official I used in this occasion, but the officials would have to come, they'd have to come when I asked them to come to Government House, so I was in touch with a number of Greek Cypriots who could give me advice.

Q.One of your first acts when you got to Cyprus was to make this Christmas Broadcast and obviously this was very much a personal initiative of yours. How much at this stage had H.M.G. decided that the lead was to take, as it were, positive constitutional steps rather than merely containing its erection, I mean clearly they had to go on dealing with this very difficult security situation, but was there a positive feeling that a constitutional-political initiative had to be taken?

A.No, I think they were really—when I came back from Cyprus and in the interim period I went out and in the month or two I was there, the first month, I really don't think they had any idea at all how to proceed. It was very difficulty to know, you were dealing with a rebellion, was there any escape from it? You couldn't escape by giving was to the demands of the rebellion, because otherwise you'd cause a war with Turkey. They were in a complete jam—we all were. What could you do, only ease the long-jam a bit, but by acts of personal decency and compassion and to go and call on the detainees on Christmas Day and to let out a number of them and to show yourself anxious to speak to the ordinary people and to ride through the villages was a first act of showing you—I think it was invaluable, I think it did some good over a long period, of anyway at any rate showing that we were not over-oppressive military machine.

Q.To what extent was the really serious situation in the Middle East as a whole—this was after all the time of the troubles in the Lebanon and Jordan coming up—to what extent did this overshadow the work for a Cyprus settlement? I ask this because Cyprus was of course a Middle East military base, as well as a Cyprus base?

A.I don't think it really had much effect, what was going on in the Middle East, except that Makarios certainly always looked upon the United Arab Republic, or whatever it was at that time—the Arab countries as supporters of his and he was very grateful form the support the Egyptians gave him and that was a long-range political investment he made in the Arab support. But on the other hand, to his credit, when the time came for Independence he refused to be bullied by the Arabs against allowing the Israeli representation and he said that he was friendly with everyone and he was going to have Israel represented just like anyone else. It was very much in his interests to do so, because the Israelis provided, at that time, the bulk of his tourist industry, but it is so that he has always maintained a very close friendship with Egypt and with the Arab countries generally who were on his side, so he maintained, but he at the same time insisted in maintaining relations with Israel.

Q. When you first went back to London early in '58 with your first plan was there a sort of strong division in the Cabinet on it?

A. No, I don't think so. It seemed to me at that time that they were ready to agree with anything that sounded sensible, and they hadn't heard anything sensible for some time from Cyprus, and they were glad to approve. I went to the cabinet meeting and they wished me well and it was while I was still at home that the telegram came from Ankara indicating that they were not at all prepared to move in that direction, so even before I went back to Cyprus initiative was frustrated.

Q. On that visit you mention in your book that you met the Archbishop of Canterbury. I wonder if he played—or the Church of England played the role at all in the question—the whole question of re-opening relations with Makarios?

A. Not very much, but I remember when I told the Archbishop of Canterbury that I was comforted to know that he agreed with me! On my general purpose.

Q. Turning to the internal politics of Cyprus at the time, early in '58 there opened the rift between the Left and the Right-Wing Greeks, the growth of support for AKEL the Communist side of the Greek movement, was it effective this breach between Grivas and the left?

A. Oh yes I think so. The communists of course had been strong in Cyprus for long time and they appeared to be growing in strength in many ways and they of course provided the Mayors of the principal towns and they seemed to be by the tests of the elections for Mayors the most powerful party in Cyprus. One of the most remarkable achievements of Makarios from the time when he took over authority, and even before, was that he managed to contain the communists by accepting them and encouraging them to come into his government. I remember one of the most difficult things I had to do was to convince the British Government to remove the ban on the Communist Party, and I remember very well when I eventually got the approval after a long battle with them, how pleased I was because it did open the door to Makarios being able to control the Communists instead of by their continued proscription, playing into their hands. It might have been a very different story if the Communists had been able to claim that they were proscribed and consequently opposing the regime.

Q At this early stage in 1958 you met—early in 1958 when this rift was becoming more apparent you met Andreas Ziartides and other left-wing leaders. Was this an attempt to get to know what made them tick, or was there any feeling that you might, as it were, widen the rift between them and the EOKA and divide and rule?

A. Oh no, most certainly not at all, on the contrary Ziartides was a very able young leader of the trade unions whom I had known before, but it was also important in that time preceding independence that we should get some understanding with the unions. There was a period of very considerable economic setback. The expenditure of the emergency was diminishing and employment was consequently seriously affected. Industry had not yet got going again, it has subsequently. The tourist industry had scarcely revived and there was a great deal of unemployment and demonstrations I remember. I remember going out to meet a demonstration outside Government House in the period when we were preparing for Independence, it was one of our principle anxieties, so to keep a communication open with the trade unions was important.

Q. You mentioned at several stages the personal involvement of Harold MacMillan in the Cyprus problem when it got worse, when it got really serious. Could you say really two things. Was his personal intervention beneficial—it was clearly a courageous thing for him to do—and the second question is which Ministers with whom you were dealing in Britain were closely involved in the formulation as distinct from the implementation of Cyprus policy?

A. Well I suppose it was the Foreign Secretary and the Secretary of State for the Colonies, the Minister of Defence to some extent who were the Ministers involved in making the policy, the Foreign Secretary increasingly I think. But it's certainly true that MacMillan himself took a close personal interest to my great benefit in the whole matter and as you remember the policy declared in the summer of 1958 was called the MacMillan plan, and justly so, he gave his mark on it. It was my proposal, chewed over by the Ministers and accepted by the Prime Minister.

Q. How much in the formulation or rather the formulation of the details of that plan, how much were NATO and the U.S.A. involved, I mean the announcement of the plan was delayed at the request of NATO wasn't it for a few days?

A. Yes, I remember it was. I can't remember the exact circumstances, I think they had been informed and wished to have some time to digest it before public announcement was made. I can't remember the exact circumstances though, or the reason for that delay.

Q. I wondered if in fact they were putting pressure on Greece and Turkey who were also NATO members.

A. Yes there was something of that and the hope that both sides would support or be pressed to support and the difficulty of what statements they would make in NATO, but I don't remember the exact circumstances of that.

Q. I wonder if I could turn to a completely different question which you have already touched on, the morale and attitude of the Army who were, of course, throughout this period under considerable pressure, but after the Famagusta incident towards the end of '58 there was short period wasn't there when the troops got out of control, how fearful were you and the General Kendrew and the other senior people involved, how fearful were you before the Famagusta incident that this kind of thing might happen?

A. Oh yes of course it was likely to happen all the time. The soldiers were being killed and when they heard of one of their members just being written off they're likely in the heat of the moment to be very rough. There was a case in the Paphos district where one of the regiments got very rough following a shooting in which one of their own men had been killed, and then of course when the wives in Famagusta were attacked, that set them off on a wild night. I went down with General Kendrew and saw what was happening at that time and we were very greatly concerned as to the up-shot—it was a very natural reaction I think if they'd killed one of the wives and shoot another, you don't get troops then to make distinctions between Greek Cypriots. They didn't kill anyone but they did a lot of—they beat a lot of people on the head at that time in that night. But on the whole the behavior of the troops was magnificent, no other troops in the world would have put up with what they put up with over a long period and the understanding I think, as I say, between the Civil Authority and the troops was excellent.

Q. You never had a moment when you thought that the thing really might get out of hand—permanently out of hand?

A. In that respect there were quite a lot of moments when I thought it was out of hand. When I looked out from—when we'd announced our 1958 policy and a day or two later, no a day or two before it was announced—I looked out from the Government House, Nicosia, and saw what looked like the whole of Nicosia aflame. It was the Turkish protest against the policy before they had even heard it! And it looked then as if it was out of hand.

Q. I remember to be in Cyprus for a short period in the middle of 1958 for *The Times* and I was there at the time there was a very major security sweep. You imposed a Censorship for 24 hours and there was this terrific security sweep, apparently because you were expecting something special in the way of terrorism. I wonder, how good were your Intelligence services at that stage?

A. Well we thought it was one of the weaknesses which existed in the Harding regime which he was the first to acknowledge and he took steps to strengthen the Intelligence which was all-important and I got the benefit of the steps which he had initiated and which we carried further and we thought that within about 6 months of my coming that we'd got the Intelligence Services into a top pitch of efficiency. I think they were extremely good and I think the round-up that you referred to was the worst time that I remember, when we had tried everything, we had declared our policy and the violence continued and appeared to be increasing, and there was nothing for it but to have another round-up of suspects based on the Intelligence of the previous months.

Q. Were you in fact good—I mean not your personally—but was your administration good at effectively interrogating the people whom you'd captured to get further intelligence?

A. Yes I think they were about as good as they could be. It's all a question of method isn't it?

Q. And skill.

A. Well, and skill, yes. It meant a great deal of Greek Cypriot accusations of violence and brutality in the questioning and it's very difficult of course to eliminate that sort of criticism or the cause for it, but we did go everything we conceivably could to stop it. The occasion I've reported before is that when a soldier came in to tell me that there was violence being used in interrogation in a remote village where there was a search operation going on, I called up General Darling and we got an armored car and went out together and walked straight into—without warning—walked straight into the interrogation room, we could find no evidence, though it could have been, there were people who had been interrogated below in the stable, but we could see no evidence of bad treatment, but the fact that we went that night was known throughout the Island and was probably the best assurance that people knew what we said about not tolerating it. On the whole, compared with any other rebellion I've ever heard of, I think that our record was a pretty good one. I mean it isn't comparable in any sense with Algiers.

Q. Algiers, no. At this period you've just referred to as really the worst time, and I certainly recall it as being a very grim time when I went there, I remember having an interview with you for *The Times* at which against what appeared to be all the evidence you spoke of Cyprus moving towards compromise. Now a month later in August '58 Grivas announced a truce. Did you at that stage have close good lines of communication out to Grivas, did you know he was going to do this?

A No, I don't think we can say so, I don't recall, but I never had any line to Grivas, I never had any means of communication to him, there was no two-way or one-way communication to him. At the end we thought we knew where he was, but that's another matter. He was not of a kind to establish dialogue with authority!

Q. There's another question about not only the Army's attitude, but also the obviously crucially important business of Greece and Turkey's attitude. To what extent was Barbara Castle's visit in the Famagusta incident, her criticism of the behavior of the army, to what extent did this have a major effect on the policy—on the chances of the policy succeeding?

A. No, I don't think so. She made some criticism—I've forgotten what she did say—but she made some criticism of the troops. I think it was after the Paphos incident particularly and she took an interest in this and questioned people who were concerned and made some statement afterwards which did her, politically I think, some harm in her constituency and the rest, but I don't think it really had any effect on the situation outside the Army. The Army were very angry, but the criticism in itself was justified, there had been bad treatment in this particular incident and I don't think it was an unhealthy thing that someone should say so.

Q. No, no. It was the manner of it which earned her criticism.

A. Oh I wouldn't have complained, myself, about what she did. I wouldn't have done it myself obviously because it was most important that I should keep the confidence of the troops but the fact that when there was an outburst of military rough-handling, no more, that it should be taken up and published in the English papers, I think is, on the whole, healthy. It wouldn't have happened in any other country.

Q. No, no. I'm rather rushing ahead because of the time, but in the December '58 talks with Greece and Turkey which were after all in a sense the end of the road apart from the Veto weren't they, this was getting the agreement with Greece and Turkey, after that it was only a matter of negotiating details, I think I'm right. How much were you personally involved in those December 1958 talks with Greece and Turkey, or were they purely international, were they sort of Government level by this stage?

A, No I think with the two governments they were at Government level and I would have not much to do with it except in communication with my own Government. What happened then as you know, there was a Constitutional Conference established with Greeks and Turks and they sat in Cyprus for many months—

Q. Yes—

A. And I had dealings with both sides at that time, because they were working out the details of the Zurich Agreement as to how it could be put into effect. I remember particularly my great admiration for the President of Turkey, when he was the representative of the Turks on that occasion. I made up a little rhyme I remember at the time which ended up "give me an hour with Professor Erim, I am completely devoted to him." He was a brilliant man, but he could see the advantage of a compromise—and one of the most penetrating brains, the most constructive and clear brains I've ever dealt with. When I saw that he was taking over the Presidency of his country—Presidency, Prime Ministership, I'm not sure which—he has now at any rate formed his own government in Turkey, I always have regarded him as one of the most brilliant men I've ever met.

Q. Yes. You did pay great tribute in your book—dealing with the events at this stage when really the three countries, Greece, Turkey and Britain were agreeing on the basis for the Constitutional discussions which you then had, I mean I think I'm right in putting it this way, you paid great tribute to Sir Pearson Dickson's initiative in the U.N. Now was this, so far as you know, his personal initiative or was this something which was his skill in following an instruction?

A. Well I suppose if he had a general instruction to do he'd got to get agreement—but the story I've often told—I referred it to him, he's dead now, of course—but I referred it to him before he died and gave him an opportunity of varying it, of correcting it, no he was content with the story he said he thought it gave him rather more credit than he thought was due to him, which was really a modest disclaimer, but the story is that when he had a certain victory he was not willing to take the victory but was determined to look for a success, and I don't know of any better story of indicating what we should be doing at the United Nations, constantly up to the end. It worked, indeed, I think that it was at the moment that the Agreement was made, in that moment of time when he came down to the U.N. from 99 Park Avenue and said "What we want today is not a victory, but a success." I don't know of any better example of personal initiative in parliamentary diplomacy.

Q. Could I ask one final question about Cyprus. When the Settlement was finally negotiated, one of the key elements of it was the position of the guarantor powers wasn't it, the three, Britain, Greece and Turkey. Was there any feeling that intervention by any of the three guarantor powers would be feasible in the case of communal trouble, as distinct from a threat from outside?

A. I don't know how much it was thought out, and I don't think it was thought out very carefully. I think that the assumption in people's minds was roughly what did, that with British bases on the spot, that if anyone had to go in and deal as a fire brigade in a sudden flareup it would probably be the British, and that's what it was, because they were there and they could do it without being on one side or the other, but it was also a fact that it was provided that any one country could intervene in order to ensure that the settlement was not upset. It made the likelihood of Turkish intervention, and therefore war with Greece and Turkey much greater.

Q.Thank you very much, indeed.

NOTE

1. MSS. *British Empire* s. 395. Author's editing and typeset.

Appendix B

The Constitution of the United States of America

We the People of the United States, in Order to form a more perfect Union, establish Justice, insure domestic Tranquility, provide for the common defense, promote the general Welfare, and secure the Blessings of Liberty to ourselves and our Posterity, do ordain and establish this Constitution for the United States of America.

ARTICLE I

Section 1: Congress

All legislative Powers herein granted shall be vested in a Congress of the United States, which shall consist of a Senate and House of Representatives.

Section 2: The House of Representatives

The House of Representatives shall be composed of Members chosen every second Year by the People of the several States, and the Electors in each State shall have the Qualifications requisite for Electors of the most numerous Branch of the State Legislature.

No Person shall be a Representative who shall not have attained to the Age of twenty five Years, and been seven Years a Citizen of the United States, and who shall not, when elected, be an Inhabitant of that State in which he shall be chosen.

Representatives and direct Taxes shall be apportioned among the several States which may be included within this Union, according to their respective Numbers, which shall be determined by adding to the whole Number of free

Persons, including those bound to Service for a Term of Years, and excluding Indians not taxed, three fifths of all other Persons. The actual Enumeration shall be made within three Years after the first Meeting of the Congress of the United States, and within every subsequent Term of ten Years, in such Manner as they shall by Law direct.The number of Representatives shall not exceed one for every thirty Thousand, but each State shall have at Least one Representative; and until such enumeration shall be made, the State of New Hampshire shall be entitled to chuse three, Massachusetts eight, Rhode-Island and Providence Plantations one, Connecticut five, New-York six, New Jersey four, Pennsylvania eight, Delaware one, Maryland six, Virginia ten, North Carolina five, South Carolina five, and Georgia three.

When vacancies happen in the Representation from any State, the Executive Authority thereof shall issue Writs of Election to fill such Vacancies.

The House of Representatives shall chuse their Speaker and other Officers;and shall have the sole Power of Impeachment.

Section 3: The Senate

The Senate of the United States shall be composed of two Senators from each State, chosen by the Legislature thereof, for six Years; and each Senator shall have one Vote.

Immediately after they shall be assembled in Consequence of the first Election, they shall be divided as equally as may be into three Classes. The Seats of the Senators of the first Class shall be vacated at the Expiration of the second Year, of the second Class at the Expiration of the fourth Year, and of the third Class at the Expiration of the sixth Year, so that one third may be chosen every second Year; and if Vacancies happen by Resignation, or otherwise, during the Recess of the Legislature of any State, the Executive thereof may make temporary Appointments until the next Meeting of the Legislature, which shall then fill such Vacancies.

No Person shall be a Senator who shall not have attained to the Age of thirty Years, and been nine Years a Citizen of the United States, and who shall not, when elected, be an Inhabitant of that State for which he shall be chosen.

The Vice President of the United States shall be President of the Senate, but shall have no Vote, unless they be equally divided.

The Senate shall chuse their other Officers, and also a President pro tempore, in the Absence of the Vice President, or when he shall exercise the Office of President of the United States.

The Senate shall have the sole Power to try all Impeachments. When sitting for that Purpose, they shall be on Oath or Affirmation. When the President of the United States is tried, the Chief Justice shall preside: And no Person shall be convicted without the Concurrence of two thirds of the Members present.

Judgment in Cases of Impeachment shall not extend further than to removal from Office, and disqualification to hold and enjoy any Office of honor, Trust or Profit under the United States: but the Party convicted shall nevertheless be liable and subject to Indictment, Trial, Judgment and Punishment, according to Law.

Section 4: Elections

The Times, Places and Manner of holding Elections for Senators and Representatives, shall be prescribed in each State by the Legislature thereof; but the Congress may at any time by Law make or alter such Regulations, except as to the Places of chusing Senators.

The Congress shall assemble at least once in every Year, and such Meeting shall be on the first Monday in December, unless they shall by Law appoint a different Day.

Section 5: Powers and Duties of Congress

Each House shall be the Judge of the Elections, Returns and Qualifications of its own Members,and a Majority of each shall constitute a Quorum to do Business; but a smaller Number may adjourn from day to day, and may be authorized to compel the Attendance of absent Members, in such Manner, and under such Penalties as each House may provide.

Each House may determine the Rules of its Proceedings, punish its Members for disorderly Behavior, and, with the Concurrence of two thirds, expel a Member.

Each House shall keep a Journal of its Proceedings, and from time to time publish the same, excepting such Parts as may in their Judgment require Secrecy; and the Yeas and Nays of the Members of either House on any question shall, at the Desire of one fifth of those Present, be entered on the Journal.

Neither House, during the Session of Congress, shall, without the Consent of the other, adjourn for more than three days, nor to any other Place than that in which the two Houses shall be sitting.

Section 6: Rights and Disabilities of Members

The Senators and Representatives shall receive a Compensation for their Services, to be ascertained by Law, and paid out of the Treasury of the United States. They shall in all Cases, except Treason, Felony and Breach of the Peace, be privileged from Arrest during their Attendance at the Session of their respective Houses, and in going to and returning from the same; and for any Speech or Debate in either House, they shall not be questioned in any other Place.

No Senator or Representative shall, during the Time for which he was elected, be appointed to any civil Office under the Authority of the United States, which shall have been created, or the Emoluments whereof shall have been encreased during such time; and no Person holding any Office under the United States, shall be a Member of either House during his Continuance in Office.

Section 7: Legislative Process

All Bills for raising Revenue shall originate in the House of Representatives; but the Senate may propose or concur with Amendments as on other Bills.

Every Bill which shall have passed the House of Representatives and the Senate, shall, before it become a Law, be presented to the President of the United States; If he approve he shall sign it, but if not he shall return it, with his Objections to that House in which it shall have originated, who shall enter the Objections at large on their Journal, and proceed to reconsider it. If after such Reconsideration two thirds of that House shall agree to pass the Bill, it shall be sent, together with the Objections, to the other House, by which it shall likewise be reconsidered, and if approved by two thirds of that House, it shall become a Law. But in all such Cases the Votes of both Houses shall be determined by Yeas and Nays, and the Names of the Persons voting for and against the Bill shall be entered on the Journal of each House respectively. If any Bill shall not be returned by the President within ten Days (Sundays excepted) after it shall have been presented to him, the Same shall be a Law, in like Manner as if he had signed it, unless the Congress by their Adjournment prevent its Return, in which Case it shall not be a Law.

Every Order, Resolution, or Vote to which the Concurrence of the Senate and House of Representatives may be necessary (except on a question of Adjournment) shall be presented to the President of the United States; and before the Same shall take Effect, shall be approved by him, or being disapproved by him, shall be repassed by two thirds of the Senate and House of Representatives, according to the Rules and Limitations prescribed in the Case of a Bill.

Section 8: Powers of Congress

The Congress shall have Power To lay and collect Taxes, Duties, Imposts and Excises, to pay the Debts and provide for the common defense and general Welfare of the United States; but all Duties, Imposts and Excises shall be uniform throughout the United States;

To borrow Money on the credit of the United States;

To regulate Commerce with foreign Nations, and among the several States, and with the Indian Tribes;

To establish a uniform Rule of Naturalization, and uniform Laws on the subject of Bankruptcies throughout the United States;

To coin Money, regulate the Value thereof, and of foreign Coin, and fix the Standard of Weights and Measures;

To provide for the Punishment of counterfeiting the Securities and current Coin of the United States;

To establish Post Offices and post Roads;

To promote the Progress of Science and useful Arts, by securing for limited Times to Authors and Inventors the exclusive Right to their respective Writings and Discoveries;

To constitute Tribunals inferior to the supreme Court;

To define and punish Piracies and Felonies committed on the high Seas, and Offenses against the Law of Nations;

To declare War, grant Letters of Marque and Reprisal, and make Rules concerning Captures on Land and Water;

To raise and support Armies, but no Appropriation of Money to that Use shall be for a longer Term than two Years;

To provide and maintain a Navy;

To make Rules for the Government and Regulation of the land and naval Forces;

To provide for calling forth the Militia to execute the Laws of the Union, suppress Insurrections and repel Invasions;

To provide for organizing, arming, and disciplining, the Militia, and for governing such Part of them as may be employed in the Service of the United States, reserving to the States respectively, the Appointment of the Officers, and the Authority of training the Militia according to the discipline prescribed by Congress;

To exercise exclusive Legislation in all Cases whatsoever, over such District (not exceeding ten Miles square) as may, by Cession of particular States, and the Acceptance of Congress, become the Seat of the Government of the United States, and to exercise like Authority over all Places purchased by the Consent of the Legislature of the State in which the Same shall be, for the Erection of Forts, Magazines, Arsenals, dock-Yards and other needful Buildings;—And

To make all Laws which shall be necessary and proper for carrying into Execution the foregoing Powers, and all other Powers vested by this Constitution in the Government of the United States, or in any Department or Officer thereof.

Section 9: Powers Denied Congress

The Migration or Importation of such Persons as any of the States now existing shall think proper to admit, shall not be prohibited by the Congress prior to the Year one thousand eight hundred and eight, but a Tax or duty may be imposed on such Importation, not exceeding ten dollars for each Person.

The Privilege of the Writ of Habeas Corpus shall not be suspended, unless when in Cases of Rebellion or Invasion the public Safety may require it.

No Bill of Attainder or ex post facto Law shall be passed.

No Capitation, or other direct, Tax shall be laid, unless in Proportion to the Census or Enumeration herein before directed to be taken.

No Tax or Duty shall be laid on Articles exported from any State.

No Preference shall be given by any Regulation of Commerce or Revenue to the Ports of one State over those of another: nor shall Vessels bound to, or from, one State, be obliged to enter, clear, or pay Duties in another.

No Money shall be drawn from the Treasury, but in Consequence of Appropriations made by Law; and a regular Statement and Account of the Receipts and Expenditures of all public Money shall be published from time to time.

No Title of Nobility shall be granted by the United States: And no Person holding any Office of Profit or Trust under them, shall, without the Consent of the Congress, accept of any present, Emolument, Office, or Title, of any kind whatever, from any King, Prince, or foreign State.

Section 10: Powers Denied to the States

No State shall enter into any Treaty, Alliance, or Confederation; grant Letters of Marque and Reprisal; coin Money; emit Bills of Credit; make any Thing but gold and silver Coin a Tender in Payment of Debts; pass any Bill of Attainder, ex post facto Law, or Law impairing the Obligation of Contracts, or grant any Title of Nobility.

No State shall, without the Consent of the Congress, lay any Imposts or Duties on Imports or Exports, except what may be absolutely necessary for executing it's inspection Laws: and the net Produce of all Duties and Imposts, laid by any State on Imports or Exports, shall be for the Use of the Treasury of the United States; and all such Laws shall be subject to the Revision and Controul of the Congress.

No State shall, without the Consent of Congress, lay any Duty of Tonnage, keep Troops, or Ships of War in time of Peace, enter into any Agreement or Compact with another State, or with a foreign Power, or engage in War, unless actually invaded, or in such imminent Danger as will not admit of delay.

ARTICLE II

Section 1

The executive Power shall be vested in a President of the United States of America.

He shall hold his Office during the Term of four Years, and, together with the Vice President, chosen for the same Term, be elected, as follows:

Each State shall appoint, in such Manner as the Legislature thereof may direct, a Number of Electors, equal to the whole Number of Senators and Representatives to which the State may be entitled in the Congress: but no Senator or Representative, or Person holding an Office of Trust or Profit under the United States, shall be appointed an Elector.

The Electors shall meet in their respective States, and vote by Ballot for two Persons, of whom one at least shall not be an Inhabitant of the same State with themselves. And they shall make a List of all the Persons voted for, and of the Number of Votes for each; which List they shall sign and certify, and transmit sealed to the Seat of the Government of the United States, directed to the President of the Senate. The President of the Senate shall, in the Presence of the Senate and House of Representatives, open all the Certificates, and the Votes shall then be counted. The Person having the greatest Number of Votes shall be the President, if such Number be a Majority of the whole Number of Electors appointed; and if there be more than one who have such Majority, and have an equal Number of Votes, then the House of Representatives shall immediately chuse by Ballot one of them for President; and if no Person have a Majority, then from the five highest on the List the said House shall in like Manner chuse the President. But in chusing the President, the Votes shall be taken by States, the Representation from each State having one Vote; A quorum for this Purpose shall consist of a Member or Members from two thirds of the States, and a Majority of all the States shall be necessary to a Choice. In every Case, after the Choice of the President, the Person having the greatest Number of Votes of the Electors shall be the Vice President. But if there should remain two or more who have equal Votes, the Senate shall chuse from them by Ballot the Vice President.

The Congress may determine the Time of chusing the Electors, and the Day on which they shall give their Votes; which Day shall be the same throughout the United States.

No Person except a natural born Citizen, or a Citizen of the United States, at the time of the Adoption of this Constitution, shall be eligible to the Office of President; neither shall any person be eligible to that Office who shall not have attained to the Age of thirty five Years, and been fourteen Years a Resident within the United States.

In Case of the Removal of the President from Office, or of his Death, Resignation, or Inability to discharge the Powers and Duties of the said Office, the Same shall devolve on the Vice President, and the Congress may by Law provide for the Case of Removal, Death, Resignation or Inability, both of the President and Vice President, declaring what Officer shall then act as President, and such Officer shall act accordingly, until the Disability be removed, or a President shall be elected.

The President shall, at stated Times, receive for his Services, a Compensation, which shall neither be increased nor diminished during the Period for which he shall have been elected, and he shall not receive within that Period any other Emolument from the United States, or any of them.

Before he enter on the Execution of his Office, he shall take the following Oath or Affirmation:--"I do solemnly swear (or affirm) that I will faithfully execute the Office of President of the United States, and will to the best of my Ability, preserve, protect and defend the Constitution of the United States."

Section 2

The President shall be Commander in Chief of the Army and Navy of the United States, and of the Militia of the several States, when called into the actual Service of the United States; he may require the Opinion, in writing, of the principal Officer in each of the executive Departments, upon any Subject relating to the Duties of their respective Offices, and he shall have Power to grant Reprieves and Pardons for Offenses against the United States, except in Cases of Impeachment.

He shall have Power, by and with the Advice and Consent of the Senate, to make Treaties, provided two thirds of the Senators present concur; and he shall nominate, and by and with the Advice and Consent of the Senate, shall appoint Ambassadors, other public Ministers and Consuls, Judges of the supreme Court, and all other Officers of the United States, whose Appointments are not herein otherwise provided for, and which shall be established by Law: but the Congress may by Law vest the Appointment of such inferior Officers, as they think proper, in the President alone, in the Courts of Law, or in the Heads of Departments.

The President shall have Power to fill up all Vacancies that may happen during the Recess of the Senate, by granting Commissions which shall expire at the End of their next Session.

Section 3

He shall from time to time give to the Congress Information of the State of the Union, and recommend to their Consideration such Measures as he shall judge necessary and expedient; he may, on extraordinary Occasions, convene both Houses, or either of them, and in Case of Disagreement between them, with Respect to the Time of Adjournment, he may adjourn them to such Time as he shall think proper; he shall receive Ambassadors and other public Ministers; he shall take Care that the Laws be faithfully executed, and shall Commission all the Officers of the United States.

Section 4

The President, Vice President and all civil Officers of the United States, shall be removed from Office on Impeachment for, and Conviction of, Treason, Bribery, or other high Crimes and Misdemeanors.

ARTICLE III

Section 1

The judicial Power of the United States, shall be vested in one supreme Court, and in such inferior Courts as the Congress may from time to time ordain and establish. The Judges, both of the supreme and inferior Courts, shall hold their Offices during good Behavior, and shall, at stated Times, receive for their Services, a Compensation, which shall not be diminished during their Continuance in Office.

Section 2

The judicial Power shall extend to all Cases, in Law and Equity, arising under this Constitution, the Laws of the United States, and Treaties made, or which shall be made, under their Authority;—to all Cases affecting Ambassadors, other public Ministers and Consuls;—to all Cases of admiralty and maritime Jurisdiction;—to Controversies to which the United States shall be a Party;--to Controversies between two or more States;—between a State and Citizens of another State;—between Citizens of different States;—between Citizens of the same State claiming Lands under Grants of different States, and between a State, or the Citizens thereof, and foreign States, Citizens or Subjects.

In all Cases affecting Ambassadors, other public Ministers and Consuls, and those in which a State shall be Party, the supreme Court shall have original Jurisdiction. In all the other Cases before mentioned, the supreme Court shall have appellate Jurisdiction, both as to Law and Fact, with such Exceptions, and under such Regulations as the Congress shall make.

The Trial of all Crimes, except in Cases of Impeachment; shall be by Jury; and such Trial shall be held in the State where the said Crimes shall have been committed; but when not committed within any State, the Trial shall be at such Place or Places as the Congress may by Law have directed.

Section 3

Treason against the United States, shall consist only in levying War against them, or in adhering to their Enemies, giving them Aid and Comfort. No Person shall be convicted of Treason unless on the Testimony of two Witnesses to the same overt Act, or on Confession in open Court.

The Congress shall have Power to declare the Punishment of Treason, but no Attainder of Treason shall work Corruption of Blood, or Forfeiture except during the Life of the Person attainted.

ARTICLE IV

Section 1

Full Faith and Credit shall be given in each State to the public Acts, Records, and judicial Proceedings of every other State. And the Congress may by general Laws prescribe the Manner in which such Acts, Records and Proceedings shall be proved, and the Effect thereof.

Section 2

The Citizens of each State shall be entitled to all Privileges and Immunities of Citizens in the several States.

A Person charged in any State with Treason, Felony, or other Crime, who shall flee from Justice, and be found in another State, shall on Demand of the executive Authority of the State from which he fled, be delivered up, to be removed to the State having Jurisdiction of the Crime.

No Person held to Service or Labour in one State, under the Laws thereof, escaping into another, shall, in Consequence of any Law or Regulation therein, be discharged from such Service or Labour, but shall be delivered up on Claim of the Party to whom such Service or Labour may be due.

Section 3

New States may be admitted by the Congress into this Union; but no new State shall be formed or erected within the Jurisdiction of any other State; nor any State be formed by the Junction of two or more States, or Parts of States, without the Consent of the Legislatures of the States concerned as well as of the Congress.

The Congress shall have Power to dispose of and make all needful Rules and Regulations respecting the Territory or other Property belonging to the United States; and nothing in this Constitution shall be so construed as to Prejudice any Claims of the United States, or of any particular State.

Section 4

The United States shall guarantee to every State in this Union a Republican Form of Government, and shall protect each of them against Invasion; and on Application of the Legislature, or of the Executive (when the Legislature cannot be convened) against domestic Violence.

ARTICLE V

The Congress, whenever two thirds of both Houses shall deem it necessary, shall propose Amendments to this Constitution, or, on the Application of the Legislatures of two thirds of the several States, shall call a Convention for proposing Amendments, which, in either Case, shall be valid to all Intents and Purposes, as Part of this Constitution, when ratified by the Legislatures of three fourths of the several States, or by Conventions in three fourths thereof, as the one or the other Mode of Ratification may be proposed by the Congress; Provided that no Amendment which may be made prior to the Year One thousand eight hundred and eight shall in any Manner affect the first and fourth Clauses in the Ninth Section of the first Article; and that no State, without its Consent, shall be deprived of its equal Suffrage in the Senate.

ARTICLE VI

All Debts contracted and Engagements entered into, before the Adoption of this Constitution, shall be as valid against the United States under this Constitution, as under the Confederation.

This Constitution, and the Laws of the United States which shall be made in Pursuance thereof; and all Treaties made, or which shall be made, under the Authority of the United States, shall be the supreme Law of the Land; and the Judges in every State shall be bound thereby, any Thing in the Constitution or Laws of any State to the Contrary notwithstanding.

The Senators and Representatives before mentioned, and the Members of the several State Legislatures, and all executive and judicial Officers, both of the United States and of the several States, shall be bound by Oath or Affirmation, to support this Constitution; but no religious Test shall ever be required as a Qualification to any Office or public Trust under the United States.

ARTICLE VII

The Ratification of the Conventions of nine States, shall be sufficient for the Establishment of this Constitution between the States so ratifying the Same.

FIRST AMENDMENT

Congress shall make no law respecting an establishment of religion, or prohibiting the free exercise thereof; or abridging the freedom of speech, or of the press; or the right of the people peaceably to assemble, and to petition the Government for a redress of grievances.

SECOND AMENDMENT

A well regulated Militia, being necessary to the security of a free State, the right of the people to keep and bear Arms, shall not be infringed.

THIRD AMENDMENT

No Soldier shall, in time of peace be quartered in any house, without the consent of the Owner, nor in time of war, but in a manner to be prescribed by law.

FOURTH AMENDMENT

The right of the people to be secure in their persons, houses, papers, and effects, against unreasonable searches and seizures, shall not be violated, and no Warrants shall issue, but upon probable cause, supported by Oath or affirmation, and particularly describing the place to be searched, and the persons or things to be seized.

FIFTH AMENDMENT

No person shall be held to answer for a capital, or otherwise infamous crime, unless on a presentment or indictment of a Grand Jury, except in cases arising in the land or naval forces, or in the Militia, when in actual service in time of War or public danger; nor shall any person be subject for the same offence to be twice put in jeopardy of life or limb; nor shall be compelled in any criminal case to be a witness against himself, nor be deprived of life, liberty, or property, without due process of law; nor shall private property be taken for public use, without just compensation.

SIXTH AMENDMENT

In all criminal prosecutions, the accused shall enjoy the right to a speedy and public trial, by an impartial jury of the State and district wherein the crime shall have been committed, which district shall have been previously ascertained by law, and to be informed of the nature and cause of the accusation; to be confronted with the witnesses against him; to have compulsory process for obtaining witnesses in his favor, and to have the Assistance of Counsel for his defense.

SEVENTH AMENDMENT

In Suits at common law, where the value in controversy shall exceed twenty dollars, the right of trial by jury shall be preserved, and no fact tried by a jury, shall be otherwise reexamined in any Court of the United States, than according to the rules of the common law.

EIGHTH AMENDMENT

Excessive bail shall not be required, nor excessive fines imposed, nor cruel and unusual punishments inflicted.

NINTH AMENDMENT

The enumeration in the Constitution, of certain rights, shall not be construed to deny or disparage others retained by the people.

TENTH AMENDMENT

The powers not delegated to the United States by the Constitution, nor prohibited by it to the States, are reserved to the States respectively, or to the people.

ELEVENTH AMENDMENT

The Judicial power of the United States shall not be construed to extend to any suit in law or equity, commenced or prosecuted against one of the United States by Citizens of another State, or by Citizens or Subjects of any Foreign State.

TWELFTH AMENDMENT

The Electors shall meet in their respective states and vote by ballot for President and Vice-President, one of whom, at least, shall not be an inhabitant of the same state with themselves; they shall name in their ballots the person voted for as President, and in distinct ballots the person voted for as Vice-President, and they shall make distinct lists of all persons voted for as President, and of all persons voted for as Vice-President, and of the number of votes for each, which lists they shall sign and certify, and transmit sealed to the seat of the government of the United States, directed to the President of the Senate;--The President of the Senate shall, in the presence of the Senate and House of Representatives, open all the certificates and the votes shall then be counted;--The person having the greatest number of votes for President, shall be the President, if such number be a majority of the whole number of Electors appointed; and if no person have such majority, then from the persons having the highest numbers not exceeding three on the list of those voted for as President, the House of Representatives shall choose immediately, by ballot, the President. But in choosing the President, the votes shall be taken by states, the representation from each state having one vote; a quorum for this purpose shall consist of a member or members from two-thirds of the states, and a majority of all the states shall be necessary to a choice. And if the House of Representatives shall not choose a President whenever the right of choice shall devolve upon them, before the fourth day of March next following, then the Vice-President shall act as President, as in case of the death or other constitutional disability of the President.--The person having the greatest number of votes as Vice-President, shall be the

Vice-President, if such number be a majority of the whole number of Electors appointed, and if no person have a majority, then from the two highest numbers on the list, the Senate shall choose the Vice-President; a quorum for the purpose shall consist of two-thirds of the whole number of Senators, and a majority of the whole number shall be necessary to a choice. But no person constitutionally ineligible to the office of President shall be eligible to that of Vice-President of the United States.

THIRTEENTH AMENDMENT

Section 1

Neither slavery nor involuntary servitude, except as a punishment for crime whereof the party shall have been duly convicted, shall exist within the United States, or any place subject to their jurisdiction.

Section 2

Congress shall have power to enforce this article by appropriate legislation.

FOURTEENTH AMENDMENT

Section 1

All persons born or naturalized in the United States, and subject to the jurisdiction thereof, are citizens of the United States and of the State wherein they reside. No State shall make or enforce any law which shall abridge the privileges or immunities of citizens of the United States; nor shall any State deprive any person of life, liberty, or property, without due process of law; nor deny to any person within its jurisdiction the equal protection of the laws.

Section 2

Representatives shall be apportioned among the several States according to their respective numbers, counting the whole number of persons in each State, excluding Indians not taxed. But when the right to vote at any election for the choice of electors for President and Vice-President of the United States, Representatives in Congress, the Executive and Judicial officers of a State, or the members of the Legislature thereof, is denied to any of the male inhabitants of such State, being twenty-one years of age, and citizens of the United States, or in any way abridged, except for participation in rebellion, or other crime, the basis of representation therein shall be reduced in the proportion which the number of such male citizens shall bear to the whole number of male citizens twenty-one years of age in such State.

Section 3

No person shall be a Senator or Representative in Congress, or elector of President and Vice-President, or hold any office, civil or military, under the United States, or under any State, who, having previously taken an oath, as a member of Congress, or as an officer of the United States, or as a member of any State legislature, or as an executive or judicial officer of any State, to support the Constitution of the United States, shall have engaged in insurrection or rebellion against the same, or given aid or comfort to the enemies thereof. But Congress may by a vote of two-thirds of each House, remove such disability.

Section 4

The validity of the public debt of the United States, authorized by law, including debts incurred for payment of pensions and bounties for services in suppressing insurrection or rebellion, shall not be questioned. But neither the United States nor any State shall assume or pay any debt or obligation incurred in aid of insurrection or rebellion against the United States, or any claim for the loss or emancipation of any slave; but all such debts, obligations and claims shall be held illegal and void.

Section 5

The Congress shall have the power to enforce, by appropriate legislation, the provisions of this article.

FIFTEENTH AMENDMENT

Section 1

The right of citizens of the United States to vote shall not be denied or abridged by the United States or by any State on account of race, color, or previous condition of servitude.

Section 2

The Congress shall have the power to enforce this article by appropriate legislation.

SIXTEENTH AMENDMENT

The Congress shall have power to lay and collect taxes on incomes, from whatever source derived, without apportionment among the several States, and without regard to any census or enumeration.

SEVENTEENTH AMENDMENT

The Senate of the United States shall be composed of two Senators from each State, elected by the people thereof, for six years; and each Senator shall have one vote. The electors in each State shall have the qualifications requisite for electors of the most numerous branch of the State legislatures.

When vacancies happen in the representation of any State in the Senate, the executive authority of such State shall issue writs of election to fill such vacancies: Provided, That the legislature of any State may empower the executive thereof to make temporary appointments until the people fill the vacancies by election as the legislature may direct.

This amendment shall not be so construed as to affect the election or term of any Senator chosen before it becomes valid as part of the Constitution.

EIGHTEENTH AMENDMENT

Section 1

After one year from the ratification of this article the manufacture, sale, or transportation of intoxicating liquors within, the importation thereof into, or the exportation thereof from the United States and all territory subject to the jurisdiction thereof for beverage purposes is hereby prohibited.

Section 2

The Congress and the several States shall have concurrent power to enforce this article by appropriate legislation.

Section 3

This article shall be inoperative unless it shall have been ratified as an amendment to the Constitution by the legislatures of the several States, as provided in the Constitution, within seven years from the date of the submission hereof to the States by the Congress.

NINETEENTH AMENDMENT

The right of citizens of the United States to vote shall not be denied or abridged by the United States or by any State on account of sex. Congress shall have power to enforce this article by appropriate legislation.

TWENTIETH AMENDMENT

Section 1

The terms of the President and the Vice President shall end at noon on the 20th day of January, and the terms of Senators and Representatives at noon on the 3d day of January, of the years in which such terms would have ended if this article had not been ratified; and the terms of their successors shall then begin.

Section 2

The Congress shall assemble at least once in every year, and such meeting shall begin at noon on the 3d day of January, unless they shall by law appoint a different day.

Section 3

If, at the time fixed for the beginning of the term of the President, the President elect shall have died, the Vice President elect shall become President. If a President shall not have been chosen before the time fixed for the beginning of his term, or if the President elect shall have failed to qualify, then the Vice President elect shall act as President until a President shall have qualified; and the Congress may by law provide for the case wherein neither a President elect nor a Vice President shall have qualified, declaring who shall then act as President, or the manner in which one who is to act shall be selected, and such person shall act accordingly until a President or Vice President shall have qualified.

Section 4

The Congress may by law provide for the case of the death of any of the persons from whom the House of Representatives may choose a President whenever the right of choice shall have devolved upon them, and for the case of the death of any of the persons from whom the Senate may choose a Vice President whenever the right of choice shall have devolved upon them.

Section 5

Sections 1 and 2 shall take effect on the 15th day of October following the ratification of this article.

Section 6

This article shall be inoperative unless it shall have been ratified as an amendment to the Constitution by the legislatures of three-fourths of the several States within seven years from the date of its submission.

TWENTY-FIRST AMENDMENT

Section 1

The eighteenth article of amendment to the Constitution of the United States is hereby repealed.

Section 2

The transportation or importation into any State, Territory, or Possession of the United States for delivery or use therein of intoxicating liquors, in violation of the laws thereof, is hereby prohibited.

Section 3

This article shall be inoperative unless it shall have been ratified as an amendment to the Constitution by conventions in the several States, as provided in the Constitution, within seven years from the date of the submission hereof to the States by the Congress.

TWENTY-SECOND AMENDMENT

Section 1

No person shall be elected to the office of the President more than twice, and no person who has held the office of President, or acted as President, for more than two years of a term to which some other person was elected President shall be elected to the office of President more than once. But this Article shall not apply to any person holding the office of President when this Article was proposed by Congress, and shall not prevent any person who may be holding the office of President, or acting as President, during the term within which this Article becomes operative from holding the office of President or acting as President during the remainder of such term.

Section 2

This article shall be inoperative unless it shall have been ratified as an amendment to the Constitution by the legislatures of three-fourths of the several States within seven years from the date of its submission to the States by the Congress.

TWENTY-THIRD AMENDMENT

Section 1

The District constituting the seat of Government of the United States shall appoint in such manner as Congress may direct: A number of electors of President and Vice President equal to the whole number of Senators and Representatives in Congress to which the District would be entitled if it were a State, but in no event more than the least populous State; they shall be in addition to those appointed by the States, but they shall be considered, for the purposes of the election of President and Vice President, to be electors appointed by a State; and they shall meet in the District and perform such duties as provided by the twelfth article of amendment.

Section 2

The Congress shall have power to enforce this article by appropriate legislation.

TWENTY-FOURTH AMENDMENT

Section 1

The right of citizens of the United States to vote in any primary or other election for President or Vice President, for electors for President or Vice President, or for Senator or Representative in Congress, shall not be denied or abridged by the United States or any State by reason of failure to pay poll tax or other tax.

Section 2

The Congress shall have power to enforce this article by appropriate legislation.

TWENTY-FIFTH AMENDMENT

Section 1

In case of the removal of the President from office or of his death or resignation, the Vice President shall become President.

Section 2

Whenever there is a vacancy in the office of the Vice President, the President shall nominate a Vice President who shall take office upon confirmation by a majority vote of both Houses of Congress.

Section 3

Whenever the President transmits to the President pro tempore of the Senate and the Speaker of the House of Representatives his written declaration that he is unable to discharge the powers and duties of his office, and until he transmits to them a written declaration to the contrary, such powers and duties shall be discharged by the Vice President as Acting President.

Section 4

Whenever the Vice President and a majority of either the principal officers of the executive departments or of such other body as Congress may by law provide, transmit to the President pro tempore of the Senate and the Speaker of the House of Representatives their written declaration that the President is unable to discharge the powers and duties of his office, the Vice President shall immediately assume the powers and duties of the office as Acting President.

Thereafter, when the President transmits to the President pro tempore of the Senate and the Speaker of the House of Representatives his written declaration that no inability exists, he shall resume the powers and duties of his office unless the Vice President and a majority of either the principal officers of the executive department or of such other body as Congress may by law provide, transmit within four days to the President pro tempore of the Senate and the Speaker of the House of Representatives their written declaration that the President is unable to discharge the powers and duties of his office. Thereupon Congress shall decide the issue, assembling within forty-eight hours for that purpose if not in session. If the Congress, within twenty-one days after receipt of the latter written declaration, or, if Congress is not in session, within twenty-one days after Congress is required to assemble, determines by two-thirds vote of both Houses that the President is unable to discharge the powers and duties of his office, the Vice President shall continue to discharge the same as Acting President; otherwise, the President shall resume the powers and duties of his office.

TWENTY-SIXTH AMENDMENT

Section 1

The right of citizens of the United States, who are eighteen years of age or older, to vote shall not be denied or abridged by the United States or by any State on account of age.

Section 2

The Congress shall have power to enforce this article by appropriate legislation.

TWENTY-SEVENTH AMENDMENT

No law, varying the compensation for the services of the Senators and Representatives, shall take effect, until an election of representatives shall have intervened.

Bibliography

Bassiouni, M. C. "Self-Determination" and the Palestinians, *American J.I.L.*, 61, pp. 31–35 (1971).

Binkley, Wilfred E. *The Man in the White House: His Powers and Duties* (Baltimore, 1959).

Bogdanor, Vernon. *Comparing Constitutions* (Oxford: Clarendon Press, 1995).

Borah, W. Woodrow and Cook, F. Sherburne. *The Aboriginal Population of Central Mexico on the Eve of the Spanish Conquest* (Berkeley: University of California, 1963).

Brown, George D. "When Federalism and Separation of Powers Collide: Rethinking Younger Abstention," *George Washington Law Review* 114, 116 (1990).

Brownlie, Ian. *Principles of Public International Law* (Oxford: Oxford University Press, 1999).

Calogeropoulos-Stratis, A. *The Right of Peoples to Self-Determination: Its Violation in the Case of Cyprus* (Athens, 1977).

Cassese, A. ed. *U.*N Law/Fundamental Rights: Two Topics in International Law (Springer, 1979).

Cassesse, Antonio. *Self-Determination of Peoples* (Cambridge: Cambridge University Press, 1995).

Chipman, Donald E. *de Guzman* and the Province of Panuco in New Spain 1518–1610 (Glendale, CA, 1967).

Churchill, Ward. *A Little Matter of Genocide: Holocaust and Denial in the Americans 1492 to the Present* (City Lights Books, San Francisco, 1997).

Collier, John. "The Vanishing American," *Nation,* January 11, 1928.

Command Papers, Cmnd. 42 *Constitutional Proposals for Cyprus, Report submitted to the Secretary of State for the Colonies* (Lord Radcliffe's Report).

Command Papers, Cmnd. 9594 (Miscellaneous No. 18 1955) *The Tripartite Conference on Eastern Mediterranean and Cyprus.*

Constitutional proposals for Cyprus, *Report submitted to the Secretary of State for the Colonies* Cmnd. 42.

Cook, Nobel David and W. George Lovell. *"Secret Judgments of God": Old* World Disease in Colonial Spanish America (University of Oklahoma Press, 1992).
Cortes, Hernan. *Letters* From Mexico (New York, Grossman, 1971).
Coufoudakis, Van. *Essays on the Cyprus Conflict (New York: Pella Publishing Company, 1976).*
Curtis, E. S. "Vanishing Indian Types: The Tribes of the Northwest Plains," *Scribner's*, June 1906.
The Cyprus Annexation Order in Council 1914 (1924).
Dekleris. *Κυπριακό 1972*–1974*: Η Τελευταία Ευκαιρία* (in Greek, Athens: Sideris).
Dellinger, Walter. "The Legitimacy of Constitutional Change: Rethinking the Amendment Process," 97 *Harvard Law Review* 386 (1983).
De Smith, Stanley A. *The Commonwealth and its Constitutions* (London: Stevens, 1964).
Dicey, A. V. *An Introduction to the Study of the Law of the Constitution* (London, 1889).
Dittenberger, Wilhelm. Sylloge Inscriptionum Graecarum (Lipsiae, 1883).
Draper, William. "The Last of the Red Race," *Cosmopolitan*, January 1902.
Eden, Anthony. *Memoirs* (London, 1960).
Ehrlich, Thomas. *International Crises and the Role of Law* (Oxford: Oxford University Press, 1974).
Emerson, Rupert. Self-Determination, *American J.I.L* vol. 65, p. 465 (1971).
Flower, B. O. "An Interesting Representative of a Vanishing Race," *Arena*, July 1896.
Foot, Sir Hugh. *A Start in Freedom* (London, 1964).
Freeman, Edward. *History of Federal Government in Greece and Italy*, 2nd ed. by J. B. Bury (1893).
Gordon, Philip and Henri Barkey. *Avoiding Cyprus Crisis, Policy Brief—July 2002*, www.brook.edu/comm/ policybriefs/pb102.ht.
Green, L. C. and Olive Patricia Duncan. *The Law of Nations in the New World* (University of Alberta Press, 1989).
Grotius, Hugo. *De Jure Belli ac Pacis, Book II* (Classics of International Law, ed. J. B. Scott, Publications of Carnegie Endowment, 1925)
Hall, H. L. A. *A Treatise in International Law* (Oxford University Press, 1924).
Hart, A. B. *Introduction to the Study of Federal Government* (Boston: Harvard University Publications, 1891).
Harvard Law School, Draft Convention on International Law. 29 *American J.I.L. Supplement, Part III (1935).*
Harvey, Charles M. "The Last Race Rally of Indians," *World's Work*, May 1904.
H. C. Debates. *Parliamentary Debates* (Hansard), vol. 451 col. 2159–2162 (1947–1948).
Henkin, Louis. "Is There a Political Question Doctrine," 85 *Yale Law Journal* 597 (1976).
Hill, George. *A History of Cyprus*, Vol. IV (Cambridge University Press, 1984).
Hill, J. L. *The Passing of the Indian and the Buffalo* (California, 1917).
Holland, Robert. *Britain and the Revolt in Cyprus* (Oxford: Oxford University Press, 1998).

Jennings, Francis. *The Invasion of America: Indians.* Colonialism and the Cant of Conquest (Chapel Hill: University of North Carolina Press, 1975).

Jennings, Ivor. *The Law and the Constitution* (London University Press, 1933).

Jennings, Ivor. *The Law the and the Constitution* (Cambridge: Cambridge University Press, 1959).

Kammen, Michael. *The Origins of the American Constitution: A Documentary History* (Penguin Books, 1984).

Kaplow, Louis. "An Economic Analysis of Legal Transitions," 99 *Harvard Law Review* 509, 515 (1986).

Kareklas, Iacovos. *International Law and Politics on Salamis* (Research Centre of Kykkos Monastery: Nicosia, 2007).

Kareklas, Iacovos. *Federal Constitution and Human Rights on Cyprus* (Harvard University Printing and Publications, 2005).

Kareklas, Iacovos. ΦΙΛΟΣΟΦΙΑ ΤΟΥ ΔΙΚΑΙΟΥ (Athens: NOMIKI BIBLIOTHIKI, 2012).

Katz, Steven. *The Holocaust in Historical Context, Volume I: The Holocaust and Mass Death before the Modern Age* (Oxford University Press, 1992).

Martin, James Kirby, Steven Mintz, Linda O. McMurry, and James H. J. Jones. (1993) *America and its People, Volume 1: To 1877, 2nd edition* (New York: Harper Collins College, 1993).

Kyriakides, Stanley. *Cyprus, Constitutionalism and Crisis Government* (University of Pennsylvania Press, Philadelphia, 1968).

Larsen, J. A. O. *Representative Government in Greek and Roman History* (Berkeley, California: University of California Press, 1955).

Leon-Portilla, Miguel, ed. *Broken Spears: The Aztec Account of the Conquest of Mexico* (Boston: Beacon Press, 1962).

Linardatos. *From Civil War to the Junta, 1952–1955* (Athens, 1978.

Lovell, George. *Conquest and Survival in Colonial Guatemala: A Historical Geography of the Cuchumatan Highlands, 1500–1821 (Montreal: McGill-Queen's University Press, 1985).*

Mann, Henry. *Ancient and Mediaeval Republics* (New York, 1879).

Marshall, Geoffrey. *Constitutional Theory* (Oxford: Oxford University Press, 1971).

McNair, Sir Arnold. *The* Law of Treaties (Oxford: Oxford University Press, 1961).

Morton, Samuel George. *Crania Americana, or, A Comparative View of Skulls of Various Aboriginal Nations of North and South America* (Philadelphia, 1893).

Mullerson, Rein. *International Law, Rights and Politics* (London, 1994).

Necatigil, Zaim. *The Turkish Position in International Law* (Oxford: Oxford University Press, 1993).

Nicholas, Barry. *Roman Law* (London, 1975).

O'Connell. *International Law Vol.* I (London, 1965).

O'Connell. Legal Aspects of the Peace Treaty with Japan, *British YB.I.L.*, vol. XIX, 423 (1965).

Office of the Legal Adviser, *Digest of United States Practice in International Law*.

Oppenheim-Lauterpacht. *International Law* (London, 1948).

Oppenheim, L. *International Law Vol. I,* (9th ed. (Sir Robert Jennings QC and Sir Arthur Watts QC, London: Longman, 1996).

Peasley, A. J. *The Constitutions of the Nations, Vol. III Europe Part I* (The Hague, 1968).

Phillimore, Robert. *Commentaries upon the International Law, vol. I* (London, 1879).

Plaza, Galo. *Report on Cyprus, 1965* (http://www.cyprusconflict.net/galo_plaza_report).

Pokagon, Simon. "The Future of the Red Man," *Forum* (August 1897).

Proceedings of the Second Pan-American Scientific Congress, Section I: Anthropology (Washington, D.C.: Smithsonian Institution, 1909–1910).

Richardson, Boyce. *People of Terra Nullius: Betrayal and Rebirth in Canada* (Seattle/Vancouver: University of Washington Press, 1993).

Richardson, James D. ed. *A Compilation of the Messages and Papers of the President 1789–1897* (1897).

Roberts-Wray, Kenneth. (1966*) Commonwealth and Colonial Law* (London).

Roeback, Carl. (1959) *Ionian Trade and Colonization* (College Art Association).

Schwartz, Bernard. (1955) *Constitutional Law* (Cambridge: Cambridge University Press).

Schwarzenberger, Georg. *A Manual of International Law* (6th ed., London, 1976).

Shaw, Malcolm. *Title to Territory in Africa* (Oxford: Clarendon Press, 1986).

Southerland, Howe, and Brown. (1961) *Constitutional Law, vol. I* (Boston).

Stannard, David. *The Politics of Holocaust Scholarship: Uniqueness as Denial* (Westview Press, 1996).

Starke, J. G. *An Introduction to International Law* (London, 1972).

Statutory Rules and Orders Revised, No. 1629, vol. II, pp. 577–578.

Supplementum Epigraphicum Graecum (Brill Publications).

Thucydides. *History of the Peloponnesian War*, Book III (Harvard University Press, Loeb Classical Library, 1921).

Tigar, Michael. "The Political Question Doctrine and Foreign Relations," 17 *UCLA Law Review* 1135 (1970).

Tornaritis. *The European Convention of Human Rights in the Legal Order of the Republic of Cyprus* (Nicosia, 1976).

Tornaritis, C. The Human Rights as Recognised and Protected by Law with Special Reference to the Law of the Cyprus, *Cyprus Law Tribune*, parts 4–6, p. 3 (1974).

Tornaritis, C. The Right to Freedom of Movement and Residence Specially nder the Law of the Republic of Cyprus, *Cyprus Law Tribune*, Nicosia, parts 1–3 (1974).

Tornaritis, Criton *Cyprus and its Constitutional and Other Legal Problems* (Nicosia 1977).

The Tripartite Conference on Eastern Mediterranean and Cyprus (1955) Cmd 9594 (Miscellaneous No. 18).

Ubelaker, Douglas, "Prehistoric New World Population Size: Historical Review and Current Appraisal of North American Estimates," *American Journal of Physical Anthropology*, No. 45 (1976).

U.S. Bureau of the Census, *Fifteenth Census of the United States, 1930: The Indian Population of the United States and Alaska* (Washington, D.C.: U.S Government Printing Office, 1937).

Varner, John Grier and Jeanette Johnston Varner. *Dogs of Conquest* (Norman University of Oklahoma Press, 1983).

Vema (Greek Newspaper), 26.1.1963.

Vema (Greek Newspaper), June 1974.

Wade William. *Constitutional Fundamentals* (London: Stevens, 1980).

Waldock. Report on the Law of Treaties, *Yearbook of the International Law Commission* (1963).

Weinberg, Louise. "The New Judicial Federalism," 29 Stanford Law Review 1191 (1977).

Wheare, *Federal Government, 4th ed.* (London, 1963).

Williams Jr., Robert A. *The American Indian in Western Legal Thought: The Discourses of Conquest* (Oxford University Press, 1990).

Borah, Woodrow W. and Sherburne F. Cook. "Conquest and Population: A Demographic Approach to Mexican History," *Proceedings of the American Philosophical Society*, No. 113 (1968).

Xydis, Stephen G. *Conflict and Conciliation, 1954–1958* (The Ohio State University Press, 1967).

Xydis, Stephen G. *Cyprus, Reluctant Republic* (The Hague, 1973).

Zotiades. The Treaty of Guarantee and the Principle of Non-Intervention, *Cyprus Today* vol. III pp. 5–8 (1965).

Zulueta, Francis de. ed. *Institutes of Gaius, II, Commentary* (Oxford: Oxford University Press, 1953).

Index

About the Author

Iacovos Kareklas was born in Nicosia on 18 October 1976. He graduated (with Apolyterion Excellent) first in his class, receiving ten academic awards from the Classics Department of the Kykkos Lyceum.

He got his BA and MA degrees in law from Cambridge University, *Magdalene College*. At the University of Cambridge, where he studied on a Cambridge Commonwealth Trust Scholarship jointly with a British Foreign Office Bursary, he won first prize in the de Smith Mooting Competition of the Cambridge University Law Society, of which he is a life member. He was particularly keen on Constitutional law and theory, which he studied in depth having as tutor Sir Derek Oulton Q.C. (drafter of the Kenya Constitution).

He holds a PhD in international law from London University (*London School of Economics and Political Science*). He specialized in all aspects of public international law and every aspect of the Cyprus problem. He conducted sustained and in depth research in the Foreign Office Archives with regard to the critical phases of the Cyprus Question. During his doctoral program, he was a teaching assistant in subjects of his specialization.

In the academic year 2003–2004 he was a postdoctoral fellow at the Department of Government, Harvard University. He did postdoctoral studies in international relations theory with special reference to the use of military force and emphasis on classical antiquity under the worldwide distinguished political scientist, Professor Stanley Hoffmann. At Harvard, he also taught the course *Classical Theories of International Relations*. In the year 2004–2005 Dr. Kareklas was appointed postdoctoral fellow at Harvard's Center for Middle Eastern studies. He became a member of the Harvard Faculty Club. In 2006 and 2007 he was elected fellow of the faculty of law (Honour School of Jurisprudence) in the University of Oxford, where he specialized in philosophy of law.

In 2008 Dr. Kareklas was elected lecturer at the European University Cyprus and was appointed coordinator of the law program. As of 2013 he is an associate professor, a rank at which he was unanimously elected. He teaches international law, philosophy of law, Constitutional law, and international politics. He further took part in many appointment and promotion committees.

He spent a year as researcher in the *Institute of Commonwealth Studies* (ICS) of London (2001–2002), the *British Institute of International and Comparative Law* (2003), and *the Oxford Centre for Criminology* (2006). He wrote his BA dissertation in the *Cambridge Institute of Criminology*, and has been a member of the *Royal Institute of International Affairs*. He has given lectures in English and American universities as well as various political organizations. Dr. Kareklas is the author of a number of books and articles in the fields of his specialization. In 2014 he launched an original series (of which he is the editor), namely *Studies in International Law and International Politics* (in Greek) published by the preeminent law publisher Sakkoulas in Athens.

www.ingramcontent.com/pod-product-compliance
Ingram Content Group UK Ltd.
Pitfield, Milton Keynes, MK11 3LW, UK
UKHW041842031026
15587UKWH00002B/953

9 781793 64273